Becoming Biliterate

A Study of Two-Way
Bilingual Immersion Education

Becoming Biliterate

A Study of Two-Way Bilingual Immersion Education

BERTHA PÉREZ
The University of Texas at San Antonio

9320

LAWRENCE ERLBAUM ASSOCIATES, PUBLISHERS
2004   Mahwah, New Jersey   London

Lawrence Erlbaum Associates, Inc., Publishers
10 Industrial Avenue
Mahwah, NJ 07430

COVER ART: *Ancestors Speak Through Her* © Rachel Thorson Véliz,
Wilmington, California

Cover design by Kathryn Houghtaling Lacey

Library of Congress Cataloging-in-Publication Data

Pérez, Bertha, 1945–
Becoming biliterate : a study of two-way bilingual immersion education /
Bertha Pérez.
p. cm.
Includes bibliographical references and index.
ISBN 0–8058–4678–6 (alk. paper)
1. Mexican American children—Education—Texas—San Antonio—
Case studies. 2. Education, Bilingual—Texas—San Antonio—Case studies.
3. Immersion method (Language teaching)—Texas—San Antonio—Case
studies. I. Title.
LC2688.S2P47 2003
370.117'09764'351—dc21   2003046230

Books published by Lawrence Erlbaum Associates are printed on acid-free paper,
and their bindings are chosen for strength and durability.

Printed in the United States of America
10 9 8 7 6 5 4 3 2

Dedicated to my mother
Maclovia G. Pérez
for raising me bilingually

Contents

Foreword

María E. Torres-Guzmán

At a national congress of educators in Chicago, shortly after Bertha gave me this book to read, a group of colleagues from Teachers College, Columbia University, gathered to discuss issues of multiple languages and of multiple multimodal literacies. At that moment most of the panelists argued that the multiplicity of languages and of literacies created spaces in between that were worthy of study. Only one of the group members argued that a flower was a flower whether hybrid or not, questioning whether the study of multiplicity in languages or in literacy had anything new to add to the knowledge of languages or of literacies. The analogy to grafting (*injertar* in Spanish) was provocative but ultimately not contradictory to what others were saying. Actually, the scientific process of grafting/ *injertar* was more illustrative of what we wanted to get at—the process of hybridization (Arteaga, 1997; García Canclini, 1995) and transculturation (Ortiz, 1947)—which takes root in the borderlands (Anzaldúa, 1999) or contact zones (Pratt, 1992).

My point at the discussion in Chicago was that we needed to trace some of the origins of this kind of thinking, all of which are perhaps problematic but pointing in the same direction. So, I will take the liberty to digress to that point. When Fernando Ortiz (1947) first published *Cuban Counterpoint,* he was challenging the term *acculturation* as it was being used in the field of anthropology. In his mind, acculturation was not an interactional exchange between two cultures but a descriptor of the power relationships between two groups, where one imposed on the other. It was the least socioeconomically powerful culture that was acculturated into the more powerful one. Transculturalism, he proposed, was not merely the acquisition of another culture, as in acculturation, nor was it a process that occurred linearly. He defined it as a process of uprooting an old culture and creating a new. In other words, it is a process "in the continual give and take of culture contact, where individuals are changed and change themselves as well as the surrounding world" (Spitta, 1995, p. 24). Transculturalism creates both discomfort and excitement. As Rosaldo (1989) concluded when he examined the dynamism of both social contexts and concepts through the changing hero in the Chicano narrative and what he calls the metamorphosis of the concept of culture in Sandra Cisneros' work:

> It took time . . . for the concept of a multiplex personal identity to move in alongside its predecessor, the "unified subject," and for the notion of culture as multiple border zones to find a place next to its predecessor, the "homogenous community." . . . The realization left me feeling at once deeply disoriented and excited at new possibilities for the social analyst as a "positioned subject." . . . New optics opened up because my attention was somehow drawn to works not usually included in the canon of interdisciplinary work for cultural studies. (p. 166)

I believe transculturalism is a viable and dynamic concept that can help us look at the process of learning and using multiple languages and multiple literacies in schools. In reading *Becoming Biliterate: A Study of Two-Way Bilingual Immersion Education,* I found Bertha Pérez's thinking to be within the context of transculturalism. In addition to her rich description of the contact zone of bilingualism in the San Antonio context at large—where code-switching between English and Spanish is an everyday scene—she takes us into what another colleague, Ofelia García, calls the struggle between diglossia and hybridity within dual language or bilingual immersion programs. Programs that through clear language policies promote diglossia—that is, the separation of languages by domain (teacher, subject, time, etc.)—are simultaneously creating spaces for hybridity to emerge in new ways, where both cultures and languages are viewed as contributors to the creation of learning environments.

Bertha Pérez starts with a concern for the education of Mexican American children: not just those who do not possess proficiency in English, but also those who do and who live in the world of hybridity, where issues of language, culture and identity are tied to and part of the belief that no matter what program comes their way (particularly programs using the native language), they will result in failure. She documents how the parents and teachers in the school undertake the task of bravely finding out, not so much what they were doing that was creating incompetence among the students, but what they could do to show the contrary. The undertaking of a 90–10 bilingual immersion program with careful attention to the research-based literature, visiting successful programs nationally, and taking an inquiry stance in the development of such a program was a foundation for the collaborative leadership that was created among administrators, teachers, and parents. How teachers and parents forged a partnership is only part of the story; there are also references to the role universities can play in this process.

The struggles of diglossia and hybridity are presented in the context of the stresses of sustainability of such a model. She candidly reveals the seemingly contradictory beliefs among the parents who want their children to have the opportunities that they did not have to learn the two languages—at the same time that they question, all the way through, the policies and practices of delaying the introduction of English literacy until second grade—as standing side by side, and as a genuine search for the opportunity to explore and to ensure a good education and social mobility for their children. As we go through the pages, we find that the same group of parents eventually came to believe in the program; and when they perceived that the program, their opportunity to explore, and their children's future was threatened from the outside, they turned to defend the program successfully.

The two programs Bertha describes were threatened three times within a five-year period. These parents and the teachers learned many political lessons through the struggles encountered. She repeatedly shows not only the care taken by the teachers, administrators, and policymakers to search for research-based models on which to build, but she also demonstrates that among other indicators of student progress, state-mandated and standardized test results show that the program is working for all children. As in many other dual language or bilingual immersion programs when well implemented, the schools become exemplary schools, defying the stereotype and the theories of social capital that promote the view that children from poverty—especially minorities who speak a language other than English—are unlikely to succeed.

The political context of the program is nicely complemented by Bertha's focus on the instructional process and the treatment of the language(s) as resources. The expanded social uses of the language in consistent diglossic ways—in new academic domains, for example—created for teachers what Bertha calls a new role of "language model" for children. Through the description of how teachers approach this role, Bertha presents a new way of looking at teaching strategies (e.g., wait time, say it in any language, think in Spanish/English, ask someone, pass and return, use of print for oral communication) and provides an expanded lens on how to make language comprehensible while focusing on higher order thinking in dual language classrooms.

The complexity of biliteracy, the balanced literacy process, and the use of biliteracy in the content areas are powerfully treated. The struggles of the traditions of literacy within each of the languages (*el método silábico,* phonological awareness, phonics instruction, orthography, words and segmentation) and the struggles of children (beginning writing, literacy transfer, writing English words in Spanish) are all examined within the cultural context of two schools and many classrooms, as well as within the cultures themselves. And while she shows that teachers maintain their diglossic stance in their modeling of language, she also shows how the children use their access to the two languages to help make sense of the content they are learning. In doing so, Bertha identifies how hybrid-learning contexts encourage children to use the knowledge of the two languages, their prior knowledge and lived experiences, and both formal and informal ways of communicating, to create voice and identity.

She ends with a reflection on the process and with a new realization about bilingual immersion programs, as labeled. The collaborators raise the political tensions of calling such a model "enrichment" in a time of economic difficulties. Why not go back to assert the rights of language minority to a good education: an education in which the native language is used and protected and in which the quality of instruction is attended to?

This book is a treasure in politics and education. Teachers, administrators, and policymakers alike will enjoy it for the interplay between what

Hornberger (1998) calls the "dynamic, nested concentric circles of interrelationships that influence each other." It is a book that presents new ways of thinking and poses new questions. And finally, it gives the possibilities of new life to the concept of transculturalism as it explores the very process of becoming biliterate through the voices of children, through the concerns of parents, through the tensions of teaching, and how they all merge in the space of politics. It illustrates what popular collectivities are capable of creating and the significance of transforming concepts such as hybridity from a negative to a positive space.

REFERENCES

Anzaldúa, G. (1999). *Borderlands/La frontera* (2nd ed.). San Francisco: Aunt Lute Books.

Arteaga, A. (1997). "Mestizaje/Difrasismo." In A. Arteuga (Ed.), *Chicano poetics: Heterotexts and hybridities* (pp. 5–19). Cambridge, UK: Cambridge University Press.

Garcia Canclini, N. (1995). *Hybrid cultures: Strategies for entering and leaving modernity.* Minneapolis: University of Minnesota Press.

Hornberger, N. H. (1998). Language policy, language education, language rights: Indigenous, immigrant, and international perspectives. *Language in Society, 27,* 439–458.

Ortiz, F. (1947). *Cuban counterpoint: Tobacco and sugar.* New York: Knopf.

Pratt, M. L. (1992). *Imperial eyes: Travel writing & transculturation.* London: Routledge.

Rosaldo, R. (1989). *Culture and truth: The remaking of social analysis.* Boston: Beacon Press.

Spitta, S. (1995). *Between two waters: Narratives of transculturation in Latin America.* Houston: Rice University Press.

Preface

The increasing number of linguistically diverse students in U.S. schools, especially Mexican and Mexican American Spanish-speaking children, continues to challenge the ways public schools are educating this population. After 30 years of controversy over bilingual education, quality education for linguistically diverse students has remained an elusive promise. Two-way bilingual immersion or dual-language education is a program with the potential of fulfilling that promise.

This book is about the education of Mexican American children and their language, literacy, and education rights. It is also about a group of educators committed to fulfilling the promise of bilingual education and providing quality, effective education for these Mexican American children. I chronicle how two-way bilingual immersion education came to be implemented in two schools and what this meant for children's language and literacy development.

Becoming Biliterate: A Study of Two-Way Bilingual Immersion Education is intended for multiple audiences. Researchers and graduate students will find the policy questions, implementation decisions, and language and literacy accounts informative. Public school administrators and teachers looking for guidance in the education of linguistically diverse students will find the book equally relevant. The focus on the details of the process of developing the two-way program will be of particular interest to those who may be considering developing two-way or dual-language programs in their own settings. Rather than a prescription or a recipe, this book offers readers an analysis of the implementation of two-way bilingual immersion education in two schools and an analytical examination of the classroom instructional practices within these schools.

The book is organized with these multiple audiences in mind. The Introduction provides the background of the study and my involvement in it. In chapter 1, readers learn about the theoretical lens I used in conducting the study and I review previous studies of two-way and dual language bilingual immersion programs. The story of the restructuring of bilingual programs in chapter 2 describes the context and the process of development of the two-way program. In chapter 3, I discuss the role, involvement, and participation of parents and the sociopolitical climate and context of the two schools.

Chapters 4 through 6 describe the classroom life as the children and teachers in the two schools learn and teach. These chapters will be of interest to preservice and in-service teachers and to language and literacy researchers. Readers will find rich examples of how the teachers place into practice the theories of first and second language and literacy acquisition. Teachers will also see what two-way bilingual immersion classrooms can look like. Chapter 4 details the language environment, instruction, and scaffolding strategies found in these classrooms. Chapter 5 focuses on examining how children developed biliteracy, especially in the early grades. In chapter 6, rich examples of how children used their biliteracy skills across academic content are provided.

Chapter 7 is an account of the pressures of testing and accountability reported by students and teachers. This chapter also reports the performance of two-way students on the state test and on assessments of language and reading. The important and instrumental roles played by the teachers in developing and sustaining the program is discussed in chapter 8. The book ends with the retelling of a new policy analysis that asked the two-way participants to reexamine and justify its continuation. Thus chapter 9 is an analysis of the continuing issues, challenges, politics, and policies facing the two-way bilingual immersion program.

This book adds to the developing body of data about how low socioeconomic, linguistically diverse, urban children learn to read, write, and problem solve. It is my hope that the reader will be challenged to examine language ideologies and to imagine a future that enables all students to develop their cultural and linguistic capital.

Acknowledgments

First and foremost, I want to express my gratitude and appreciation to the students, parents, teachers, and administrators of the two-way bilingual immersion program for their help with this book. The teachers and principals gave of their time tirelessly. Over the years, as I gained the confidences of teachers and principals, many became more than colleagues and informants of a study; I have made many friendships. The study reported in this book would not have been possible without their cooperation, support, and vigilant criticism. The teachers were especially gracious in welcoming me into their classrooms and allowing me to observe their teaching strategies and student interactions. The stress and strain of having me continuously observing, writing notes, and asking questions must have been difficult but was seldom noticeable. Although I cannot mention them by name, I hope that each will recognize and enjoy their contributions. From these teachers, as well as from the students and administrators, I have developed new perspectives not only on learning but also on living life with integrity, dignity, and grace.

I am also grateful to the University of Texas San Antonio for the professional development leave that enabled me to complete my writing of this book. The university also provided support through two graduate research assistants, Cynthia Juarez and Becky Bean, to whom I am grateful for their assistance in the transcription of field notes and through the many recursive analyses required in qualitative studies.

My colleagues Bob Milk, Belinda Flores, Mari Riojas Cortez, Ellen Clark, Josie Mendez-Negrete, Howard Smith, Rosaura Treviño-Ligon, and

Miriam Martinez have in turn encouraged, critiqued, and supported this project. They provided me many opportunities to engage in conversations and to exchange ideas about issues of biliteracy and dual-language education. These conversations and their knowledge of the two schools and the sociocultural context of San Antonio were invaluable to me and their influence is readily apparent in my work. Belinda Flores and Sharon Pardaux provided invaluable expertise and support in the analysis and interpretations of portions of the test data and in reviewing earlier drafts of portions of the manuscript. I am grateful for Belinda's insights and generous sharing of her time.

The doctoral students in the Culture, Literacy and Language Program, especially Mary Esther Huerta, Amy Nordlander, Holly Hansen-Thomas, Michael Campbell, Norma Cardenas, and Carlos Martin Veloz, helped me think through many of my hypotheses about bilingualism, dual language, hybridity, and biliteracy, as developed in this book. They also read and critiqued portions of the manuscript as I was writing it. Leo García Ornelas deserves special mention for reading and responding to early drafts and helping to clarify the organization of the book.

I am also especially grateful to María Torres-Guzmán for the many discussions that helped me clarify the multifaceted dimensions of dual-language and two-way bilingual immersion education. She afforded me the opportunity to visit, on a number of occasions, the dual-language schools in New York City—PS 83 and PS 165—which provided a broader context in which to situate my study. I am grateful for María's advice and deep concern about the education of our children.

I am very grateful to Jim Cummins and María Estela Brisk for their insightful feedback. Their comments were very helpful in focusing and improving the book. I am especially thankful for having Naomi Silverman as my editor. I have had the good fortune to have Naomi guide my two previous book projects and her insightful critiques as well as encouraging words have always been appreciated.

My family and friends have been supportive and concerned throughout this long process. I am especially appreciative of having had the opportunity to take "coke and coffee breaks" with my mother, Maclovia G. Pérez, during the writing of the manuscript. I have always admired my mother's strength and tenaciousness. During these breaks, she shared her reflections of her own education during a time when Texas had segregated schools for whites, blacks, and Mexicans and her perspectives on social justice; as I listened to those stories, my respect and admiration for her grew. I also became keenly aware of how grateful and indebted I was to her for raising me bilingually. To her I dedicate this book.

Finally, I am deeply indebted to my husband, Xavier King, not only for his support and encouragement with my involvement in the study and the writing of the manuscript, but also for his time, assistance, and patience in reading and editing numerous drafts.

Introduction

In the years between 1994 and 2001, I participated with teachers, principals, administrators, parents, and university colleagues in the ongoing task of defining, clarifying, examining, and proposing possible solutions to numerous questions about the language and literacy education of language minority children, in particular, Hispanic or Mexican American students. This book describes a longitudinal, ethnographic, and descriptive study that followed the progress of conceptualization, design, development, implementation, and continuous renewal of two-way bilingual immersion education program in two schools over a 6-year period. The two elementary schools—Bonham and Storm—are in the inner city area of San Antonio, Texas. Both are neighborhood schools that serve a majority, Mexican American school population and are only a few miles apart. Bonham is a small school situated a few blocks from the commercial and tourist center of the city and within the historic King William neighborhood. Storm is a much larger school situated close to an old agri-industrial part of the city and is surrounded by public housing.

I was part of a research group with colleagues—Bob Milk, Ellen Riojas Clark, Howard Smith, Alicia Salinas Sosa, and later, Belinda Flores and Mari Riojas Cortez—studying the restructuring and implementation of the bilingual education programs in San Antonio. Initially, the research group met on a regular basis. We discussed our research agendas, proposed study questions, planned with the school administrators and teachers, and reflected on the development of the two-way bilingual immersion program. As the years progressed and academic and professional demands forced us to focus on shorter term publishable research projects, we began to parse elements of our work between and among ourselves. We have collaboratively and individually conducted smaller studies of various aspects of student learning, instruction, teachers' and administrators' participation, parent involvement, and policy development. Some of these have been published elsewhere. This book, while building in part on this collaborative effort, reflects my concern about issues of access to bilingualism and biliteracy development of limited English and English-speaking children from Mexican American families. In writing this separate account, it is my purpose to provide information about what is happening in two-way bilingual immersion classrooms that facilitate bilingualism and biliteracy development, and to examine the roles that policymakers, administrators, teachers, and parents play in the education of Mexican American children.

Many of the parent and teacher training sessions, as well as the teachers' university classes, were partially supported through U.S. Department of Education, Title VII funded projects. Over the years, some of the teachers in the two-way bilingual immersion program were students in several of my graduate classes and in the classes of many of my colleagues. These classes were part of a Title VII school personnel program funded in 1996. Additionally, we conducted many in-service sessions with teachers and many parent information and education sessions.

Prior to 1995 and during the years that followed, I conducted numerous in-service sessions for teachers, parents, and administrators throughout the San Antonio School District. With the arrival of a new superintendent in 1994, the schools were challenged to confront academic achievement issues that had plagued the school district for many years and to identify resources—programmatic and experts—who could assist individual schools in proposing possible solutions. The superintendent also created task forces in specific instructional areas to study the problems and propose solutions. Because of my previous involvement with the district, I was asked to participate in the Bilingual Task Force and, later, the Literacy Task Force. The year-long activities of the Bilingual Task Force created a space where administrators, teachers, community members, and university professors could study, examine, and create alternatives for the education of language minority students in the district. Within this Bilingual Task

Force and the new sociopolitical context, three principals and a core group of teachers from each school began exploring the possibility of two-way bilingual immersion education for their campuses. The two-way bilingual education model was adopted at two of these schools while some elementary campuses restructured their transitional bilingual programs and others adopted a late-exit developmental bilingual education model. The middle and high schools also restructured the English as a Second Language (ESL) programs.

Because the district had a history of getting caught up in educational fads, teachers and administrators were concerned that restructuring of the programs for limited English proficient students be based or "driven" by research theory and that the process and outcomes be documented. As teachers and administrators reviewed their options they struggled with two central questions: Why, after 25 years of bilingual education in San Antonio, were limited English proficient students unsuccessful in attaining and maintaining positive long-term achievement outcomes? What could improve the opportunities and add value to the education of limited English proficient students as well as English-speaking Mexican American students? They debated the soundness of the published research on bilingual education and the limited practical applications of this research as well as its appropriateness to the local population and context. With the selection and approval by the policymakers of the two-way bilingual immersion model, the teachers and administrators turned their attention to the implementation of the program and began to ask a different set of questions. What curriculum was most appropriate? How do we recruit, inform, and gain commitments from parents? What goals and expectations were appropriate for language, literacy, and content? What would make instructional input comprehensible for English dominant children and challenging for Spanish dominant children? How do you organize the classroom environment to utilize and meet the social and cultural needs of children? What tests and what language would be used for testing? What set of skills and training did the teachers need? As the program matured, children succeeded; the political climate changed; and school personnel began to face more difficult questions. With the need to plan for the two-way bilingual immersion children's enrollment in middle school and with the program being under scrutiny because of leadership and budgetary changes, the nature or quality of the questions focused on "linguistic rights,"[1] "language loss,"[2] and "enrichment education."[3] Some of these difficult questions were: Why is two-way bilingual immersion considered enrichment education and not a basic linguistic right for not only the limited English proficient speakers but for any Mexican American child? Why had so many Mexican American children and their parents lost Spanish? Why were policymakers unwilling to support programs that guaranteed minority children the added skill of bilingualism?

These recurring questions became the guiding questions for my study. The field notes, classroom observations, student, teacher and parent interviews, and writing and reading samples were transcribed and then analyzed using the qualitative analysis techniques described by Miles and Huberman (1984) and Glesne and Peshkin (1992). These techniques were supplemented by my own insights and interpretation. I attempted to focus and identify those factors that teachers and administrators were grappling with as the program developed and evolved. The questions they were asking gave me a way of describing the progression of the issues, the lessons learned, the success and failures, and the maturation of the "ways of knowing and thinking" about language minority education. Thus, within a sociocultural theory of learning (Vygotsky, 1978), I looked to the developing theories and principles of biliteracy to inform the study, my observations and fieldwork, and especially the sense I was to make of the data collected. As I began to analyze the data and to identify the recursive patterns and themes, I checked and rechecked with teachers, parents, and administrators to test the tentative trends that were emerging. Later, the emerging themes were shared with colleagues and with other experts in

---

[1] For a discussion of the legal and educational questions concerning minority language rights and in particular Spanish language rights, see James Crawford (1992a), *Language Loyalties: A Source Book on the Official English Controversy.*

[2] In discussing the issue of language loss, Skutnabb-Kangas (2000) posed the question of whether languages disappear because of a passive natural act of loss or death due to attrition, or are in fact murdered by active or perhaps even passive state policies. She argued that many state polices with regard to education of linguistic minorities can be seen as contributing to a linguistic genocide.

[3] For a discussion of dual-language education as enrichment education, see Cloud, Genesee, and Hamayan (2000). Valdés (1997) cautioned that dual-language programs may provide enrichment education for majority students, perhaps at the expense of, and with resources targeted for, linguistic-minority students.

the fields of critical literacy, bilingual education, immigrant education, special education and biliteracy.

From the beginning of the restructuring process, and the numerous meetings and sessions, teachers were aware that my colleagues and I were studying the program. During the period that I was actively visiting the schools and school functions, after some initial self-consciousness on both my part and the part of the teachers, students, and parents, we realized that neither they nor I wanted my observing to alter the normal patterns and routines. My role was that of researcher and participant observer. During meetings and sessions in which I did not have an active role, I took notes and audiotaped if the audiotaping did not interrupt the normal conduct of the session. When I was a participant in the session, I would take notes immediately following the session.

The dilemma of influence, or the observer's paradox, was that by my presence the context of classrooms would be transformed, and that because this was not joint research between the research and the classroom teachers, questions about when and how to interact and provide feedback were in constant flux. Some teachers sought feedback, while others avoided asking about what was being observed and rarely interacted beyond those times requested by the researcher. In spite of my repeated emphasis to the teachers that my purpose was to study what was happening rather than to change their practices, my presence had an effect on the teachers' practices.

When I began visiting the classrooms to observe the classroom interactions, the children would immediately want "to show" their skills and work. Over the years, the children in the two-way bilingual immersion program had received much attention and they were used to having many visitors and videotaping by the local media. While I had initially planned to conduct some videotaping, very limited videotaping occurred because I quickly discovered that videotaping was disruptive and did not capture the everyday learning and instruction. In order to not interrupt the normal patterns and routines and to avoid the childrens' expectation of showing their work, I decided to focus on field notes and audiotaping.

In the classrooms, I began by taking notes of classroom teacher/student interactions, and would fill in context after leaving the class. However, after a few days children began asking for help, including me in the activities and, in general, involving me in the classroom learning community.

Thus, as time progressed, I found it necessary to make quick short notations and fill in field notes immediately after leaving the classroom. Students and teachers were also eager to provide me with many of the student produced artifacts. Issues of accountability were a major factor in the everyday life of these classrooms. Teachers and students voiced concern about the pressures of high-stakes testing and, at the same time, exhibited pride in the test results for their students. A discussion on student achievement on the Texas Assessment of Academic Skills (TAAS) test, Aprenda achievement test in Spanish, and the Iowa Test of Basic Skills (ITBS) is included. This achievement data is analyzed and reported as one additional source of data, and while some would like to use this as "scientific proof" of the effect of the program, I think the real effect of the program cannot be reduced to the statistical significance of test scores. To minimize bias and to strengthen the validity of the findings, I used a variety of methods. The appendix summarizes the types of methods and sources of data used in the study.

The principles that teachers, parents, and administrators have chosen to labor so tirelessly for (i.e., bilingual education and two-way bilingual immersion in particular) continue to be so politicized and controversial—even in a bilingual, bicultural city like San Antonio—that it is necessary to protect the identity of as many people as possible. Thus, I have made every effort to conceal the real names of students, parents, and teachers. The names of people in all the examples taken from observations and interviews are pseudonyms. The principals—two intelligent, powerful women—were aware of the possibility that their identity could not be concealed as easily but were committed to the need for the story of language minority children's learning to be told. As I describe the shared intellectual and everyday activities of the people in these classrooms and schools, I do so with the utmost appreciation and respect for the hard work of forging a new way of learning and becoming biliterate, and finally, with the hope that I have done justice to their collective story.

1

Language and Literacy Education of Mexican-Origin and Mexican American Children

Antonio, a bright-eyed energetic kindergartner, attempted to engage Jessica in assisting him in finding pictures of fruits in old magazines. He spoke rapidly in Spanish listing *"mazanas, naranjas, duraznos, fresas"* (apple, oranges, peaches, strawberries) as he turned the pages of a magazine while pointing to another magazine and telling Jessica, *"Tu busca en ese"* (You look in that). Jessica, a Mexican American 5-year-old who speaks mostly English, paged through the magazine. Jessica tried to keep up with Antonio as she repeated the Spanish names for the fruit, then saying softly to herself the English names, *"manzana,* apple, *naranjas,* oranges. . . ."

Antonio's parents spoke mostly Spanish with only a few words and phrases of English that they used at their work. They lived in one of the many old houses that have been converted to apartments a few blocks from school. The father worked odd jobs in the construction industry and the mother worked as a maid at one of the downtown tourist hotels.

Jessica lived with her mother and grandparents in one of the small, single-family houses in the school attendance area. Her mother worked as a sales clerk in the nearby business district and felt more comfortable speaking English. Jessica's grandparents were bilingual, but reported that at home they spoke mostly Spanish.

Both Antonio's and Jessica's parents were convinced that the only way to improve the lives of their children was by learning English, so the decision to allow their children to participate in the two-way bilingual immersion program was a very serious matter. They had attended parent awareness sessions conducted by the school. During one parent meeting, they heard how the classes were composed of equal numbers of Spanish-speaking and English-speaking children, and that approximately 90% of the classroom instruction and conversations were conducted in Spanish in kindergarten. The children in the program also had another teacher who would teach them English for the other 10% of the time. The children would also be exposed to English as they participated in school activities beyond their classroom, such as physical education, music, and others. The parents were invited to visit a kindergarten class and to speak to other parents whose children were in the two-way bilingual immersion classes. Antonio's parents took 3 weeks to make a decision. They visited the class and talked to neighbors before they agreed to give their consent for Antonio to enroll in the two-way bilingual immersion classes. For Jessica's mother, the decision was somewhat easier. Jessica's mother had finished high school and spoke English well but had experienced the need to communicate with her customers in Spanish and was often uncomfortable with the way she spoke Spanish. She said, "When customers come in speaking Spanish, I get my Spanish and English all mixed up, especially when the Mexicans (tourists) come during Christmas and Easter. They expect me to help them in Spanish; I feel embarrassed." The day after the parent awareness meeting, Jessica's mother signed the consent forms for Jessica to participate in the two-way bilingual immersion classes.

Both Antonio and Jessica made considerable progress through their primary grades. Antonio quickly learned to read although his kindergarten teacher reported that he was struggling with his writing. Jessica also learned to read Spanish by the end of kindergarten, but she persisted in translating much of the language to English, almost unconsciously, while participating in language, reading, and writing lessons.

By the spring semester of the third grade, Jessica's and Antonio's two-way bilingual immersion classes were conducted 60% of the instructional time in Spanish and 40% of the time in English. Antonio and Jessica were both making very good progress; in fact, they had just taken the Texas Assessment of Academic Skills (TAAS) required by the state and had "met minimum expectations" on all subtests. Although the Spanish TAAS was being developed and pilot tested, it was not available the year that Jessica and Antonio were in the third grade. Antonio could have been exempted from taking the TAAS because of his initial classification as limited English proficient; however, the teachers, parents, and children had decided that Antonio had made much progress and would take the test in English. By the end of the third grade, Antonio had complained to his mother that he wanted to go to the all-English classes only. Initially, the parents tried to reason with him about the advantages of knowing both languages well, but Antonio's mother reported that he was persistent in his nagging most of the summer so they decided to give in. Two years later, he successfully completed the elementary school, testing at grade level in English reading, writing, and mathematics.

Jessica adjusted to the two-way bilingual immersion classes. She made steady progress year after year and successfully completed the elementary grades. Her English oral language skills continued to develop and by the end of the fifth grade, her Spanish oral language assessment results showed her on par with her peers that had been initially identified as Spanish speakers only. Her performance on the Iowa Test of Basic Skills and Aprenda (Spanish Achievement Test) showed that she was at grade level in both languages in reading, writing, and math.

The effective and equitable education of children like Antonio and Jessica has been of concern to educators in the United States for more than 30 years. Children like Antonio, whose Spanish-speaking parents are recent immigrants, and Jessica, whose mother was educated in the United States but still uses Spanish for communication at home and in the community, are part of an increasing trend in the school-age population of Texas and the nation. This demographic trend, as well as social and political motivations, influence the development and implementation of language education policies and programs. To provide a broader background for understanding the context of the two-way bilingual immersion program described in this study, this chapter briefly presents demographic trends and discusses sociopolitical issues. This is followed by an examination of two-way or dual-language education and a discussion of research in this area. The final section lays out the sociocultural theoretical lens that I used to conduct the research reported in this book.

SCHOOLING OF LATINO SPANISH-SPEAKING CHILDREN

The Hispanic or Latino (of any race) population of Texas, according to Census 2000, was over 6 million (6,669,666) or 32% of the total Texas population. This is an increase over the 1990 census of 53% for the Hispanic population. The city of San Antonio, where this study is situated, has a Hispanic population of over seven hundred thousand (774,708) of a total population of over a million (1,144,646), or 59% of the population; and 44% report speaking Spanish at home. The increase of the city's Hispanic population from the 1990 census is 22%.[1] In Texas, over 32% of the population speak a language other than English at home. The majority of these speakers of other languages speak Spanish[2] and are Mexican Americans or of Mexican origin.

Another trend that must be considered in the education of Spanish-speaking children is the status of languages in the world. According to UNESCO World Languages Report (2001), Spanish is the third most spoken language of the world, with over 330 million speakers, exceeded by only English and Chinese. The United States is ranked among countries—after Spain, Mexico, and Argentina—with the largest number of Spanish speakers. Spanish is a major world language, spoken in more than 21 countries, which can be capitalized on, especially by Spanish speakers with knowledge of Hispanic cultures and with knowledge of English and U.S. culture.

Given these demographics and the increased globalization, what type of education is best for the growing number of Hispanic or Mexican American students? In San Antonio and Texas, this is a crucial educational as well as sociopolitical question. Although most agree that the education

---

[1] See the U.S. Census Bureau's *Census 2000 Redistricting Data* (P.L. 94-171) Summary File, Tables PL1, PL2, PL3, and PL4.

[2] Armas (2001) discusses the self-reporting of immigrant status, home language, and English language proficiency for U.S. and Texas households.

provided must be in the best interests of both Mexican American students and the larger society, few agree on the content and mode of instruction, especially with regard to language.

Sociopolitical Context of Bilingual Education

The controversy over bilingual education is not about pedagogical effectiveness but rather about whether language diversity has a place within the national culture and ideology (Crawford, 1997). According to Skutnabb-Kangas (2000), language gives individuals and groups identity and cultural expression through which group members transmit and exchange values, beliefs, practices, and aspirations. Language has the power to influence and transform the very culture of which it is a product and gives expression to. The power of language to transform society is what some find threatening and why language instruction, as in bilingual education, emerges as a controversial issue of national concern. Language choice, usage, and teaching involve complex issues of political power, cultural identity, and social status. When language is understood in this way, bilingual education is not just a useful pedagogical tool that addresses the learning needs of diverse students but also a sociopolitical tool.

The linguicism[3] of the United States of the last hundred years has had more to do with political attitudes toward the socioeconomic status of the speakers than with languages or language learning. Minority languages have been devalued when compared with English because of the community standing of the speakers of a language and the perceived usefulness in the economic markets of the language and the speakers. These attitudes create a sociopolitical context within which languages are extinguished or maintained in minority communities. For example, the insidious nativist language attitudes in the early 1900s and the subsequent negative economic and social impact convinced many generations of speakers of languages other than English that the only way to succeed in the United States was to speak English even if it meant the loss of the native language (Crawford, 1992a). These economic and social issues created the context for the implementation of bilingual education and for interpretation of bilingual education research.

---

[3]*Linguicism* is defined by Skutnabb-Kangas (2000) as the "ideologies, structures and practices, which are used to legitimate, effectuate, regulate, and reproduce an unequal division of power and resources . . . on the basis of language: (p. 30).

The sociopolitical context of education in general, but especially of bilingual education,[4] can best be understood as dynamic nested concentric circles of interrelationships that influence each other (Hornberger, 1998). Mainstream society, with the federal government as the symbolic center, forms the widest circle of context that influences policies and expectations. Crawford (1992b, 1997) aptly documented, from the first Bilingual Education Act of 1968, through the *Lau v Nichols* decision of 1974, through the Reagan era, and up to the current "English Only" debates, the background for understanding the national context of bilingual education. Regional, state, and local political contexts interact and affect federal policy and the national context. Regional economic and cultural factors create a regional context for language policies, such as in California with the passage of the Proposition 227.[5] Secada and Lightfoot (1993) argued that "the dynamic between federal and state policy is complex. And if anything, state and regional contexts are becoming increasingly important . . . states have become increasingly important as sites for debates involving language policy" (p. 38). This dynamic creates an institutional context within which community schools operate. Finally, each specific classroom has a situational context influenced not only by situational factors but also by all the other levels of context. As each circle of context defines their understanding of the need and the best interest, they bring social and political pressures to the development of an official educational policy.

However, one cannot assume that any official policy statement will be understood and interpreted as one coherent ideological position within the different levels of context (Freeman, 1998). That is to say the participants, from legislators and school board members to teachers and parents, will bring their own beliefs or political viewpoints to the interpretation of policy statements and will carry them out in rather different ways. Bilingual education, with its potential to change the societal context of minorities in the United States, especially within the economic and political systems (Bloom & Grenier, 1992) and because of its potential impact on language

---

[4]For discussions of the sociopolitical context of bilingual education in the United States, see *Language Loyalties* (Crawford, 1992b), *Hold Your Tongue* (Crawford, 1992a), and *Bilingual Education and Social Change* (Freeman, 1998).

[5]For discussion of the effect of California's Proposition 227, also known as the Unz Initiative or "English for the Children," see *Condemned Without a Trial: Bogus Arguments Against Bilingual Education* (Krashen, 1999).

planning (Skutnabb-Kangas, 2000), has often encountered resistance to implementation of hard fought official policies among and within most of these circles of context.

Although official policy sanctions a range of program options, bilingual education continues to be viewed within a context based on the primacy of English language and literacy. In spite of research (Collier, 1995; Ramírez, Yuen, Ramey, & Pasta, 1991; Thomas & Collier, 1997) that found that certain programs and practices that encourage the development of literacy and academic learning in the native language are more effective and efficacious not only in developing English but in improving overall student achievement, bilingual programs continue to be vastly different with respect to the use and the development of literacy in the native language, "ranging from total absence to benign neglect to active development" (Hornberger, 1994, p. 104). Because the sociopolitical context of bilingual education continues to be controversial, the implementation of research findings and the improvement of bilingual education are made more difficult.

For over 30 years, bilingual education in Texas, as in the rest of the United States, has been at the whim of state's sociopolitical tides. The 1906 passage of The Nationality Act, which required immigrants to speak English in order to begin the process of becoming naturalized (Leibowitz, 1982), legitimized the use of language as a mode of exclusion or discrimination. In Texas and throughout the Southwest, many Mexican American students were subjected to punishment when they used their native language to communicate in schools (Casanova & Arias, 1993). Controlling language use was a means of domination and was justified as essential to the integration and building of the state. Within the Mexican American communities, the Spanish language became an important means for self-determination and thus became the focal point in educational and political struggles.

In 1968 with the passage of the federal Bilingual Education Act, the approach to the education of non-English-speaking children, including Spanish-speaking Mexican Americans, began a new era of bilingual education.[6] According to Andersson and Boyer (1970), experimentation with bilingual education had begun a few years prior to this in San Antonio:

---

[6] At the turn of the century, a number of states recognized the use of other languages for instruction or had bilingual schools (see Andersson & Boyer, 1970). The Bilingual Education Act is known as Public Law 90-247 or Title VII of the Elementary and Secondary Education Act of 1965, as amended in 1967.

It [bilingual education] was begun in 1964, . . . Originally it was a reading-readiness program in English for Spanish-speaking children in selected schools in neighborhoods which are all Mexican American. New materials were prepared and new teaching techniques were developed. These were used for thirty minutes in the morning and thirty in the afternoon, in English in one experimental stream and in Spanish in another. By 1967 the success of the program was sufficiently recognized to permit a somewhat greater emphasis on the use of Spanish, starting in grades one and two, . . . The relatively limited emphasis on the use of Spanish—some eighty minutes a day—suggest that, . . . this program is more concerned with transfer than it is with maintenance of Spanish as such. Spanish is used essentially to build the self-concept of children and to facilitate their learning of English as the eventually exclusive medium of learning. (p. 19)

In 1969 the State of Texas approved a state law permitting bilingual education. Although the Texas law stipulated a transitional bilingual program, it also permitted the inclusion of monolingual English speakers in bilingual classes. The early policies developed by the Texas Education Agency (TEA) for the implementation of the state law also stipulated the "time and treatment" for each language and each subject area. Over the next 30 years, the amount of time allocated to the use of Spanish for instruction would fluctuate widely.[7] During many of these years, what Andersson and Boyer (1970) considered the limited use of the Spanish language for instruction in many cases remained as the high watermark.[8]

Historically, Texas schools enforced a subtractive policy that forced children to give up their native languages in favor of English. The argument made was that the maintenance of the home languages not only posed problems for the development of a national culture but also had negative effects on learning English and on academic achievement. With the passage of time and the numerous sociopolitical struggles, the official policy evolved to one of tolerating the coexistence of the languages.

Until 2001, when Texas passed a law permitting dual-language education, Texas as well as much of the country mandated transitional bilingual

---

[7]Castañeda v. Pickard (1981) and U.S. v. the State of Texas (1981), as discussed by Ovando and Collier (1985), found that the schools in south Texas were not meeting the educational needs of Mexican American students and ordered that appropriate instruction and assessment be provided in both Spanish and English.

[8]For a historical perspective of bilingual education, see González (1975).

education as the model defined and required by law. In the transitional bilingual model, children are afforded a period of time—usually 3 years —in which the child's home language can be used for learning and instruction while they learn English. The goal is to teach children English so they can participate in English-only classrooms as soon as possible. This model is based on a subtractive theory of language learning.

Additive and Subtractive Approaches to Bilingualism

For many years, bilingual programs, as a matter of public policy and often with the consent of language minority parents, used *subtractive bilingualism* (Lambert, 1984); this policy encouraged the supplanting of the first language with English. Lambert (1984) believed that this "form of bilingualism experienced by ethnolinguistic minority groups, which because of national educational policies and/or societal pressures, feel forced to put aside or subtract out their ethnic languages for a more necessary, useful, and prestigious national language" (p. 19) was devastating for children. When schools and teachers convey the message that learning English is the only way to succeed and when children perceive that learning English involves betrayal of one's cultural group, a situation is created that makes it difficult for many children to acquire high levels of English proficiency (Hakuta, 1990; Náñez, Padilla, & Máez, 1992; Scollon & Scollon, 1981; Valenzuela, 1999). The sociopolitical discourse devalues becoming bilingual and biliterate and argues that knowing languages other than English is detrimental to full participation in the American dream.

By contrast, many European countries[9] and some middle-class homes in the United States encourage *additive bilingualism,* a practice in which children are encouraged to maintain and develop not only their native language but also second and third languages (Díaz & Klingler, 1991). Social contexts that promote additive bilingualism are found in societies that

---

[9]According to Skutnabb-Kangas (2000), the Working Group on Language Options in the European Union is examining options to the language problem in a multinational and multicultural community. Although the European Union (EU), as a matter of efficiency for the internal operation of its own institutions and organizations, favors one common language, the EU encourages respect for all official languages, in spite of the high price, as the best option for a democracy. It also favors two obligatory foreign languages for everybody at school (p. 284).

value languages and perceive the acquisition of multiple languages as a positive achievement. Finland, where learning both Finnish and Swedish languages and cultures are valued (Skutnabb-Kangas, 2000), is a good example of additive bilingualism.

Effects of bilinguality on cognition or mental functioning has long been used as an argument for or against additive bilingualism. Canadian studies that examined the effects of bilinguality on cognitive ability (Lambert & Anisfeld, 1969; Peal & Lambert, 1962) found a positive influence, especially with regard to cognitive flexibility. Other research (Díaz, 1985; Landry, 1974; Lambert, Genesee, Holobow, & Chartrand, 1993) demonstrated added cognitive advantages, such as divergent thinking, pattern recognition, and problem solving, for persons with advanced levels of proficiency in second languages. Díaz & Klingler (1991) documented cognitive advantages in a study that examined bilingual preschool children's performance on classification and story-sequencing tasks but found no effect on the performance of block design tasks. They summarized their findings as well as previous research stating, "cognitive advantages have appeared for children who are simultaneous learners of both languages and for preschool and school-age children in the context of bilingual-education programs" (p. 172). This and other research conducted in the last 30 years shows, with some degree of consistency, that the early learning of a second language, either by simultaneous acquisition at home or in bilingual education programs, is associated with positive cognitive gains (Ben-Zeev, 1977; Bialystok, 1986; Cook, 1997; Díaz & Klingler, 1991; Peal & Lambert, 1962). Cook (1997) summarized the findings of this line of research this way:

> The additive effects of using a second language seem to be an increased metalinguistic awareness of phonology, syntax, and the arbitrary nature of meaning, and gains in cognitive flexibility. Even if none of these effects may be overwhelming, they certainly contradict the notion that L2 use has a detrimental effect on the user's cognitive processing in general. (p. 294)

However, findings from research conducted prior to the 1960s, using subtractive paradigms, continue to "haunt current perceptions of the effects of bilingualism and bilingual education, even among otherwise knowledgeable educators and scholars" (Casanova & Arias, 1993, p. 20). Náñez et al. (1992) attributed findings of research studies conducted prior to the 1960s to the political agenda, which "influenced psychometric researchers of the period to produce a steady flow of studies indicating that bilinguality hinders cognitive processes" (p. 45). They also examined conditions under which negative cognitive results were found and reported that these were when the second language such as English was "both the dominant and prestigious language . . . [and] the devaluation and dismantling of L1 [first language] coupled with a lack of command of L2 [second language] is seen as having subtractive (negative) effects on the individual's cognitive abilities" (p. 48).

TWO-WAY BILINGUAL IMMERSION EDUCATION

In the 1980s and 1990s, the continued attacks on bilingual education and the persistence of unfavorable educational conditions for language minority students created a sociopolitical context that required the transformation of bilingual education. Building on the research findings that maintenance bilingual models were more effective than transitional bilingual models (Ramírez et al., 1991), many educators advocated for two-way bilingual immersion as an enrichment model of language education (Cloud, Genesee, & Hamayan, 2000; Dolson & Mayer, 1992).

Two-Way Bilingual Immersion Models

Two-way bilingual immersion education is generally used to refer to approaches that promote bilingualism, biliteracy, and biculturalism for language minority and language majority students participating with and learning from each other in the same classroom. The models of two-way programs vary according to the class composition and with the percentage of time allocated to each language. Currently, more than 250 programs with the title of two-way bilingual immersion or dual language are operating in the United States (Center for Applied Linguistics, 2002).

Although the first two-way bilingual program in the United States began in 1963 with the Coral Way in Miami (Brisk, 1998), the number of programs was minimal before the 1980s. In the late 1980s, the California State Department of Education described a model of two-way bilingual programs referred to as the "90–10" model because 90% of the instruction in the beginning grades (kindergarten and first grade) was conducted in the non-English language and 10% in English. However, much variability exists in the percentage of time allocated to instruction in each language as well as to the progression of academic instruction in each language in two-way bilingual immersion programs.

Number of Two-Way Programs

According to the Center for Applied Linguistics (2002) and illustrated in Table 1.1, 16 states currently offer two-way bilingual immersion education at more than one school. Additionally, the District of Columbia, Kansas,

TABLE 1.1

Two-Way Bilingual Immersion Programs
by State, Districts, and Schools*

State	Districts	Schools
California	52	94
Texas	17	39
New York	13	20
Illinois	10	19
New Mexico	3	15
Arizona	9	14
Massachusetts	6	12
Colorado	6	7
Oregon	6	7
Virginia	2	7
Connecticut	5	6
Florida	3	5
Maryland	2	4
New Jersey	2	4
Maine	1	3
Michigan	2	2
Alaska	1	2

*Center for Applied Linguistics (2002). *Directory of Two-way Bilingual Immersion Programs in the U.S.* Retrieved April 22, 2003, from http://www.cal.org/twi/directory/tables.html. Reprinted with permission from the Center for Applied Linguistics.

TABLE 1.2
Grade Levels in Two-Way Bilingual Immersion Programs

Levels	Number
Early Elementary (only)	103
Early Elementary through Upper Elementary	99
Early Elementary through Middle School	10
Early Elementary through High School	2
Upper Elementary	14
Middle School	28
High School	4

*Center for Applied Linguistics (2002). *Directory of Two-way Bilingual Immersion Programs in the U.S.* Retrieved April 22, 2003, from http://www.cal.org/twi/ directory/tables.html. Reprinted with permission from the Center for Applied Linguistics.

Minnesota, North Carolina, Nebraska, Oklahoma, and Wisconsin offer two-way bilingual immersion in one district and one school.

Two-way bilingual immersion programs that follow the 90–10 models begin by immersing students in instruction through the non-English language. As children progress through the program, the amount of English language instruction is increased until the two languages attain parity in the delivery of instruction. That is to say, by approximately the fourth grade, half the language and academic curriculum is delivered in the non-English language and half in English. According to the Center for Applied Linguistics (2002), 244 of the two-way bilingual immersion programs use Spanish and English as the languages of instruction, 6 use French and English, 5 use Chinese and English, 4 use Korean and English, and 2 use Navajo and English. Table 1.2 shows the number of two-way bilingual immersion programs by grade level.

Composition of Two-Way Bilingual Immersion Classrooms

In two-way bilingual immersion programs, approximately half the students are native speakers of a non-English language, for example Spanish, and half are speakers of English. The primary goal of two-way bilingual immersion programs is to develop language and academic proficiency in both languages for both groups of children (Christian, Montone, Lindholm,

& Carranza, 1997; Freeman, 1998; Lindholm, 1992). Two-way bilingual immersion programs attempt to protect or elevate the status of the non-English language (Spanish in the case of this study), on the rationale that the minority language is the language with the least support for development in the wider community and culture of the United States.[10] Because of the societal context of the United States, children often choose English as their preferred or as the more socially desirable or valued language and thus will begin to communicate in English and often reject the non-English native language before they have developed academic competency in either language.

In many of the two-way bilingual immersion programs implemented in the 1980s and early 1990s, the English speakers participating were middle class, white or Anglo, and members of the majority U.S. culture. Thus the programs were "marketed" to the majority population and policymakers as *enrichment education* (Valdés, 1997). Two-way bilingual immersion programs were seen as a vehicle for mobilizing political support for bilingual education by emphasizing the advantages of an enriched education for both minority language students and majority students (Lindholm-Leary, 2001). The majority student could learn a foreign language at the elementary level and the parents would provide the political muscle that was needed to defend bilingual education during difficult times.

In reality, the speakers of the majority language, or English, participating in two-way bilingual immersion education come from diverse ethnicities. The Center for Applied Linguistics (2002) reported that the English speakers in 54% of the two-way programs surveyed had a mixture of ethnicities. The more diverse the state, the more diversity exists in the English speakers; thus, in California, 66%, and in New York, 60% of the programs reported that the English speakers did not represent one racial or ethnic majority. Texas had the highest percentage of programs, 75%, with native English speakers who are Latinos.

Given the diversity of students participating in two-way bilingual immersion education, for Hispanic and other language minority communities, it could be a way to renew and reclaim their mother tongue. Skutnabb-

---

[10]Lambert and Tucker (1972) and Lambert (1984) first made this argument with regard to immersion in English for Canadian francophones, arguing that it would "place their language and their cultural identity in jeopardy" because of the political and social relationships of the anglophone and francophone communities.

Kangas (2000) critiqued the opportunities provided to minorities in western countries when schools assess and classify children's linguistic skills:

> A poor competence in the original mother tongue (which is a result of the neglect of the mother tongue in institutions earlier on, i.e., a result of earlier oppression) is then often used to legitimate additional oppression. The child is labeled as a majority language speaker, or she is denied teaching in the original mother tongue on the grounds that she does not know it well enough or because she knows the majority language better and therefore does not 'need' mother tongue teaching. (pp. 109–110)

Texas schools and educators have argued and are working for programs where both the non-English speakers and English speakers participating in two-way bilingual immersion programs are children of Mexican or Mexican American origin. Two-way bilingual immersion programs that develop the heritage language and the ethnic culture of the students as well as the national language and culture may be a way to "create structures that would enable submerged voices to emerge" (Macedo, 1994, p. 4). In the case of the program described in this study, most of the English speakers shared an ethnic and cultural identity with the non-English speakers; that is, most of the students were Mexican or Mexican American.

BILINGUAL AND TWO-WAY BILINGUAL IMMERSION RESEARCH

Two-way bilingual immersion education in the United States has been developed on the theoretical models of the Canadian immersion programs implemented there in the 1960s and 1970s (Genesee, 1987; Lambert & Tucker, 1972; Swain & Lapkin, 1982). Studies of immersion programs in Canada (Lambert & Tucker, 1972; Swain & Lapkin, 1982) show that students from majority language groups performed at high levels of second language proficiency while maintaining their home language. Additionally, the academic achievement was at grade level or better as compared to their peers. The success of these programs made the models attractive as alternatives to transitional bilingual education programs in the United States.

Additionally, bilingual education research conducted by Ramírez et al. (1991) suggested that limited English proficient students acquired English and made better progress in academic areas when they participated in late-exit or maintenance bilingual programs with high-quality primary language instruction than students in transitional bilingual or other programs for English language learners. Ramírez (1992) found:

> LEP [limited English proficient] students can be provided with substantial amounts of primary language instruction without impeding their acquisition of English language and reading skills. . . . LEP students who are provided with substantial instruction in their primary language (≥ 40%) successfully continue to increase their achievement in content areas such as mathematics, while they are acquiring their skills in English. . . . (p. 43)

In later studies, which included two-way bilingual immersion programs, Collier (1995) and Thomas and Collier (1997) found that language minority students in maintenance or developmental bilingual programs scored better in English than comparable students in other programs. This was evident only at the end of the elementary grades. They further found that "children in well-implemented one-way and two-way bilingual classes outperform their counterparts . . . as they reach the upper grades of elementary school. Even more importantly, they sustain the gains they have made throughout the remainder of their schooling in middle and high school, even when the program does not continue beyond the elementary school years" (Thomas & Collier, 1997, p. 15). Hakuta (1990) and Willig (1985) reported some secondary benefits of bilingual education, such as motivating students to remain in school rather than drop out and reinforcing important family relationships as children maintain their ability to communicate with their parents and elders.

Two-Way Bilingual Immersion Achievement Outcomes

Studies of two-way bilingual immersion education (Barfield, 1995; Barfield & Rhodes, 1994; Cazabon, Lambert, & Hall 1993; Cazabon, Nicoladis, & Lambert, 1998; Christian, 1996; Christian et al., 1997; Collier, 1995; Genesee, 1987; Lindholm-Leary 2001) found that students' academic achievement, including English language development, was equal to or exceeded that of their peers in transitional bilingual or mainstream classrooms. Though these achievement results varied according to the program type, school characteristics, and student background factors, taken together, they indicate a positive trend in student academic achievement and attainment of bilingualism.

In the most current and comprehensive empirical study of two-way bilingual immersion education, Lindholm-Leary (2001) studied fourteen 90–10 school sites and two 50–50 school sites in California and one in Alaska. Spanish was the target language in all but one school. The one exception used Portuguese and English. Three were magnet school programs, whereas the others were program strands within a school. The schools were in urban, suburban, and rural locations, and participating students were ethnically and socioeconomically diverse. The majority of the 90–10 programs were in schools that had "high ethnic density (greater than 66% minority), and high SES need (more than 20% of EB [English Bilingual] participants on free lunch"; p. 93). While program demographics were very diverse, Lindholm-Leary described the 90–10 programs as following a "relatively similar program model" (p. 94), with regard to important design features such as language separation, language distribution, and the introduction of English literacy during or after third grade. Lindholm-Leary summarized her findings stating:

> The results show that the DLE (dual language education) model is successful in promoting high levels of first-language, second-language and at least medium levels of bilingual proficiency among both language-minority and language-majority students. Further, students can achieve at least as well as their peers who are not in DLE classrooms. By the upper grade levels (grades 6 and 7), students on the average can perform at least at grade level in achievement tests or reading, language and the content areas." (p. 309)

In a prior study, Lindholm (1992) studied a 90–10 program in River Glen Elementary School in San Jose, California. This magnet school program enrolled Spanish dominant minority children and English dominant majority children. She found that those students who, by the end of the second grade, were classified bilingual and students who had initially been classified as English dominant were able to score at or above the 50th percentile in English reading achievement in spite of having been instructed only in Spanish reading. She hypothesized that some of the "knowledge and skills learned through reading . . . in Spanish were available to students in English" (p. 210). She also found that by the third grade, after 1 year of formal instruction in English reading, those students that were categorized as bilingual outperformed the Spanish dominant and were equivalent to the English dominant children in English reading achievement tests. Bilingual students also outperformed both the Spanish dominant and the English dominant children on the third grade reading achievement tests. Lindholm further states:

> There was a significant correlation between English reading achievement and Spanish reading achievement . . . (r = .35, p, 001) . . . the correlation was much higher between English math achievement and Spanish math achievement . . . (r = .65, p, .001). . . . One reason for this difference in the relations across languages in math and reading skills is due to the level and type of language skills required to demonstrate competency in these areas. (p. 211)

Lindholm (1992) argued that the academic language skills required to perform at high levels of achievement, especially for the Spanish-dominant minority children, can only be attained over time:

> The bilingual individual must develop full academic language proficiency in both languages in order for the cognitive and academic advantages to accrue. This means that a bilingual/immersion program needs a full maintenance model that completely develops both languages over an extended period of time to reap the cognitive and academic advantages. (p. 215)

These findings were confirmed in her later study (Lindholm-Leary, 2001), in which she found that "at sixth grade, Spanish-speaking students in all DLE (dual language education) program types (50:50, 90LO, 90HI) scored comparably in English reading and mathematics" (p. 313).

In a comparative study of programs across the United States, Christian et al. (1997) profiled three schools that were implementing variations of two-way bilingual immersion programs, all using Spanish and English as languages of instruction. The programs profiled were Francis Scott Key Elementary in Arlington County, Virginia; River Glen Elementary in San José, California; and Inter-American Magnet School (IAMS) in Chicago, Illinois. River Glen followed a 90–10 model, IAMS an 80–20 model, and Key a 50–50 model. In addition to language distribution percentages, each site differed in the introduction of English literacy: At Key, literacy in both languages was introduced simultaneously; at IAMS, English proficient students first learned to read in English while Spanish proficient students first learned to read in Spanish, and literacy in the second language was introduced in the second grade; at River Glen, English literacy was introduced in third grade. Although identical assessments allowing for direct comparison of student outcomes were not used, the data allowed for some comparisons. Christian et al. (1997) concluded that "the results from all three sites are positive and demonstrate that two-way bilingual immersion programs present a promising and exciting model for promoting bilingualism, biliteracy, and acquisition of average to high levels of content area knowledge for both English and Spanish speakers" (pp. 117–118). They also argued that although the achievement scores compared across these three sites for fourth grade appear to provide evidence that the 50–50 model is more successful than the 90–10 or 80–20, other studies (e.g., Lindholm, 1994), where data covered the sixth or seventh grade, suggested higher student outcomes and in particular "substantial increases in English achievement test scores in 90–10 programs" (p. 117).

Howard and Christian (1997) reported that minority and majority language students achieved higher results of bilingualism and biliteracy in 90–10 bilingual immersion model programs than students in 50–50 model bilingual programs.

Holobow, Genesee, and Lambert (1987, cited in Cloud et al., 2000) found that although participation of African American students in two-way bilingual immersion programs is limited, those who have participated in immersion programs performed on par with the language majority students in the program and better than African American students in the all-English curriculum in the same or similar schools. The study being reported in this book included three African American English dominant students who participated in the two-way bilingual immersion program.

Two-Way Bilingual Immersion Discourse Analyses

Freeman (1996, 1998) studied, using ethnographic and discourse-analytic methods, the two-way bilingual immersion program at Oyster Bilingual School in Washington, DC, which served Spanish and English speakers. Her research focused on issues of language planning and discourse. The program that had started as a grassroots effort by the Latino community challenged dominant U.S. discourses that promoted transitioning to English as quickly as possible. Instead, the community and school gave value to the linguistic knowledge of the community and promoted additive bilingualism. However, Oyster struggled against the mainstream education and

societal discourses and Freeman found that although Oyster school promoted a language policy of "language-as-resource" and the schools aimed
to give all students proficiency in both languages, the two languages were
not distributed or valued equally throughout the schools. She concluded:

> My ongoing ethnographic/discourse analytic research across the multiple
> levels of context in which Oyster Bilingual School was situated allowed me
> to see how the social stratification of Spanish and English in mainstream US
> society could explain the leakage between ideal plan and actual implemen-
> tation that I was observing on the classroom level. . . . What needs to be
> emphasized is the educators' ongoing reflection on their practice, and their
> efforts to work together to find creative ways to reduce the gaps between
> ideal plan and actual implementation. . . . Practitioners in developing pro-
> grams need to understand the complexity involved in designing and imple-
> menting a program that aims to challenge mainstream societal assumptions
> about how to educate a linguistically and culturally diverse student popula-
> tion. (pp. 246–247)

Two-way bilingual programs have the potential for transforming what
Cummins (1994) called "coercive relations of power into collaborative
relations" (p. 319) as both majority and minority students develop bilingualism and biliteracy. Both majority and minority parent and community
groups should see the developing of linguistic assets as a potential that
might result in future educational, social, and economic benefits.

Although there is continuing controversy about the effectiveness of bilingual education, much of this controversy is really about political power,
cultural identity, and social status (Crawford, 1992b) than about the academic performance of bilingual children who have participated in bilingual education. Arias and Casanova (1993) assessed the status of bilingual
research:

> Research has been used through the years to alternatively support and attack
> bilingual education programs. . . . investigations with bilingual populations
> during the last thirty years have enhanced our understanding of language
> and cognitive development and of the cognitive and social implications of
> the pedagogical strategies used in bilingual instruction. (p. xi)

Value Added versus Enrichment Education

Minority language students bring a language other than English to school;
by contrast, the students who study "foreign" languages are for the most

part English monolinguals. Typically, foreign language education begins at the secondary level, whereas bilingual education more often starts at the elementary level. Exceptions to this distinction are the foreign language programs for "gifted" monolingual English students that begin at the elementary level. Perhaps one of the most interesting contradictions in the public's perception of second language learning is that the study of a foreign language is viewed as enrichment for English monolingual students. Yet, minority language students who speak that same foreign language and learn English as a second language are viewed as needing "remedial" education (Saravia-Shore & Arvizu, 1992, pp. 492–493).

In studies conducted in Europe, Grin (1995) found that people who had higher levels of knowledge of second and third languages had higher earnings, while holding constant schooling, profession, age, first language, and other social variables. This was especially the case if one of the languages was English, but having only English did not have a significant advantage in earnings. Skutnabb-Kangas (2000) assessed the world's preoccupation with learning English and the predominance of English:

> There will be too many people who possess that qualification [English]. **High competence in English** will be like literacy skills today and computer skills tomorrow, a self-evident, necessary basic prerequisite, but **not sufficient**. Supply and demand theories predict that when many people possess what earlier might have been a scarce commodity, the price goes down. (p. 264, bold in the original)

For poor Hispanic or Latino children, what constitutes an effective education? Especially when parental economic status and minority or ethnic status are the highest predictors of not only school success but success by other social and economic notions. Although children receive the best education by all the indicators or measures by which we evaluate the quality of education, they still do not gain the advantages that the society promises. Hispanic or Latino children are still a long way from parity in science, math, and technology, and we must continue to improve the teaching and learning in these areas. Many of these students possess a decisive advantage in their potential for bilingualism and biculturalism. The general public and policymakers have no problem understanding that we live in an information society and that the future will belong to those who can participate in the information society. Few people go beyond the sound bites to understand that language and languages play a major role in mediating this new information age.

In this new information age, language can be used to maintain and reproduce the existing socioeconomic and political relations, or it can be used to provide new opportunities. According to García and Otheguy (1994) and Lang (1993), most of the high-level, high-salary jobs of the future will require high levels of competence in more than one language. Capitalizing on the bilingualism potential would give Hispanics a natural advantage as participants in the information age and globalized society. The linguistic capital[11] found in this country, although sometimes unrecognized, is like other types of capital, unevenly distributed and valued. The value of Spanish and Hispanic culture is undergoing a new negotiation because of the number of speakers not only in the United States but worldwide. The numbers, ages, and distribution of Spanish speakers have provided the weight needed to balance the traditionally unequal power relationships in the discussion of language policies. For Mexican American and Hispanic students, knowledge of Spanish and English can be capitalized as the valuable resource that will help us to understand and work with people from other countries and also to compete in the global marketplace.

THIS STUDY

Any examination of the education of children must account for the context in which the education is being delivered, especially, in the case of culturally and linguistically diverse learners, as the Hispanic population is in the United States. The sociocultural theory, which has emerged primarily from the interpretation of Vygotsky's work, provides a perspective for examining the education of these diverse populations that can be an alternative to the dominant research paradigm of comparing the education of these groups with the mythical white English-speaking middle-class population. The sociocultural perspective utilizes the social and cultural con-

---

[11]Bourdieu (1984, 1992) views language as perhaps the most important part of the cultural capital that people acquire and use in a system that he metaphorically presents as an economic system. Thus, he argues that people who possess more linguistic capital, as in knowledge of appropriate discourse norms and forms for a given social context, have more ability to use, produce, and exploit linguistic markets.

text within which children live and learn to examine their participation and outcomes. This perspective attempts to account for the complex human interactions that occur in all learning, including language and literacy development, and the underlying sociocultural beliefs.

According to Vygotsky (1978), all learning occurs in social interaction with others or is socially mediated by the cultural tools, including language and literacy, created by a social group. Thus, the "ways of knowing," "ways of behaving," and "ways of talking" are learned within one's social and cultural group. The systems and institutions that a social and cultural group establishes, like schools, also reflect a particular group's perspective. In a country like the United States with many cultures, these institutions often favor one group's "way of knowing" at the expense or to the detriment of others (Heath, 1983; Philips, 1983; Purcell-Gates, 1995). Over the last 30 years, many lessons have been learned about how institutions can actually be responsive to the needs of the diverse language and cultural communities by attending to the sociocultural context and adjusting school practices (Au, 1980; Heath, 1983; Ladson-Billings, 1994; Moll, 1992).

The context of education in society can also be examined using Bourdieu's (1984, 1992) constructs that view culture and language within a metaphorical "economic system." Bourdieu argued that one gains "cultural capital" by acquiring those experiences valued by particular social groups and that one gains "linguistic capital" by learning not only the standard forms of language but more importantly the socially appropriate language for a given context.

The sociocultural perspective also allows for the examination of how the personal experience and "worldviews" (Freire, 1970; Freire & Macedo, 1987) of students, parents, teachers, and other participants are accounted for in these classrooms. Freire (1970) advocated that education to be relevant for oppressed groups must recognize their right to name the world and name one-self. While the majority, but not all, of the participants in this study are Mexican Americans, including school board members, administrators, teachers, students, and parents, the sociocultural factors— socioeconomic status, religion, language(s), education, family history, sociopolitical views, gender, age—that contributed to each individual's cultural identity determines how each views, interprets, and names the world. Within these two schools, as in most minority communities, members define themselves on a continuum of language and cultural identity. For example, the very term that the majority of participants used to identify their cultural or ethnic identity—*Mexican American*—is at the mid-point on a continuum that must be situated in a sociocultural–sociopolitical context.[12]

By combining a sociocultural perspective with the critical pedagogy of Freire (1970; Freire & Macedo, 1987), and the poststructural constructs of Bourdieu (1984, 1992), a prism was constructed through which I examined the classroom practices and literacy development of the participants in the two-way bilingual program. Through this prism, issues such as the role of participants in decision making, in leadership, in instruction, and especially in the role biculturalism, bilingualism, and biliteracy plays in the lives of students and community members could be discussed and conclusions drawn. This allowed me to focus on how key participants influenced the development of the program, the translation of program elements into classroom practices, and the influence of program elements and classroom practices on Spanish and English language and literacy development. I analyzed how the participants' understanding of their roles, the status of each language, and the programs' cultural identity impacted the access and stances taken by each over time. It is from this perspective and this prism that I conducted the study described in this book.

---

[12]For a discussion of the terms of identity used by the Hispanic or Latino community, see Bean and Tienda (1987).

2

The Community,
School Context, and Students

Morning begins at Storm and Bonham Elementary schools as in thousands
of schools throughout the country. Some children are dropped off by parents in cars, some come by bus, but most walk with older siblings or family members. The children in their uniforms—white shirts or blouses and
khaki pants or skirts—hurry to say goodbye to parents, *abuelos* (grandparents), and siblings as they greet friends and classmates chattering in
English, Spanish, and code switching between the two languages. A child
is heard saying to a grandmother, *"vienes por mí* (come for me) at three,"
another to a younger sister "after school *me esperas aquí* (wait for me
here)." Faces of White and African American children are few; most of the
children are Hispanic—Mexican American or Mexicano as their parents
would self-identify. Teachers, standing by the doors to the classrooms,
greet the children by name, some speaking English, some Spanish, and
some code switching between the two languages. At first glance, it is difficult to distinguish which students are two-way bilingual immersion, developmental bilingual, special education, or "regular" students, as White,
African American, and Hispanic teachers call out greetings and directives,
such as *"buenos días* (good morning), it's a beautiful day," *"qué te pasa*
(what's the matter), why the long face," *"ándale-pronto* (hurry), find your
seat." The number of White and African American teachers' faces appears
to be more than those of the children, but the type of classes that they
teach—two-way bilingual immersion, developmental bilingual, special

education, "regular"—is also hard to identify. Most of the teachers are interacting with the children bilingually. A closer look at these teachers reveals that the majority are also Hispanic—Mexican American as they predominantly self-identify. As the children and teachers move from the hybrid spaces of the sidewalks and hallways into their assigned classrooms, the mixing of codes and use of the community vernacular gives way to "school language" in either English or Spanish.

THE SAN ANTONIO CONTEXT

In San Antonio, the polemics over bilingualism and bilingual education have been similar to anywhere in the United States. The role of Spanish, not only in schooling but in society, has not been appreciated, but the value of the culture, or more precisely the cultural artifacts, has been viewed somewhat differently. Historically, San Antonio has been considered a bicultural city, and the primary industry for the last 50 years has been tourism. Especially since the Hemisphere Fair held in the 1960s, the "city fathers" have promoted and capitalized on biculturalism. The city promotes all things Mexican or Mexican American: food, music, art, dress, and especially *fiestas* (celebrations). The official and unofficial policies that influence the acceptance and use of the Spanish language in public forums have a somewhat more conflicted history. Spanish is encouraged for commerce at the local shopping centers to attract shoppers from Mexico. Several radio and television channels also use Spanish, especially for advertising. However, the ability of Spanish speakers to use Spanish to gain services from the city and county, or to use Spanish in public proceedings, and especially the use of Spanish for public school instruction have been issues and rights that have been controversial and hard fought. A recent story in the *San Antonio Express-News* (Davidson, 2001) titled "Is Spanish Dying?" summarized the historical attitude toward Spanish:

> Anyone who is an adult and Hispanic in San Antonio remembers or has heard stories about children in public schools being punished for speaking Spanish. The stories aren't exaggerated. Until 1969, it was a Class C misdemeanor for a teacher in Texas to use any language other than English as a language of instruction. The English-only law was passed after World War I. It was directed at Germans and German-Americans in Texas but was used more against Spanish-speakers. (p. 1J)

San Antonio is part of the *borderlands,* that is, the spaces where two peoples, cultures, and languages come in contact and interact (Anzaldúa, 1987). Hybridization develops as a product of the borderland interactions. Contemporary theories use the conceptual construct of *hybridity* to describe the borderland synthesis of diverse elements that create new cultural forms, practices, spaces, and identities.[1] In San Antonio, this hybridization has evolved along a continuum of bicultural behaviors that permeate most activities and has some basis of common usage by many of its citizens. In these hybridized spaces, the music, art, and food have integrated elements of both European-American and Mexican cultures to create new forms of creative expression.

The creativity of these people has given rise to *Tejano, conjunto,* and blues sounds that are unique to the region. The Tex–Mex food with all its variety and nuances has gone main-street and is now packaged and distributed worldwide. The arts and cultural expressions, with centers such as the Guadalupe Cultural Arts Center and the Mexican American Cultural Center, have led national and international movements. These notions of hybridity and the borderlands experience have also been given national and international exposure by a number of renowned authors and artists who make their homes in San Antonio.

Sociopolitical movements have also emerged in San Antonio—from legal and voter rights, labor organizing, and community action groups, to alternative political parties—and have provided leadership to national and international causes.[2] The politics, business, and cultures of the city with all its diversity and complexities form the sociocultural context of education in San Antonio.

Language practice has also uniquely emerged within these hybridized spaces. The language mixing, code switching, and the use of what is sometimes pejoratively called "spanglish" or "Tex–Mex" is pervasive throughout the Mexican American community (Lipski & Garcia, 2001). These language practices have emerged in spite of and perhaps because of attempts by European Americans and Mexican nationals to define the

---

[1] For a discussion of the literary theory of hybridity and the development of the new mestiza in the Southwest, see Anzaldúa (1987) and Arteaga (1994).

[2] See Trujillo (1992) for a discussion of the grassroots politics of bilingual education in the region and Rosales (2000) for an analysis of San Antonio contemporary sociopolitical history.

language use of the Mexican American population in the region based on hegemonic ideologies.[3] The English-speaking dominant group rationalizes policies that required Mexican Americans to shift from Spanish to English as a benefit for the group in order that they might participate more fully; meanwhile, the dominant group refuses to examine the structural elements of the societal relationships or power that such policies reinforced. The Mexican nationals, generally upper-class tourists, professionals, or businesspersons, also use a hegemonic perspective to criticize the Spanish language spoken by the Mexican Americans of the borderlands. Here, again the criticism of the norms of discourse of the Mexican American community in San Antonio and the Southwest is more about one group attempting to define another group's social identity than it is about language. These social, linguistic, and cultural pressures have contributed to the evolution of hybrid discourses or language practices—the strategic use of both codes and multiple registers in communicating and making meaning—that defy those that would use language as a mechanism of social control.[4] In San Antonio, the language practices of many Mexican Americans are like those studied by Kalmar (2001). In his study of adult Mexican migrants becoming biliterate in Illinois, he described the hybrid language practices:

> This hybrid sound can be conceptualized in theory as either the union or the intersection of the two sounds. . . . An undocumented alien sound illegally crossing the linguistic border to "pass" for a legitimate sound of a language to which it doesn't "really" belong. (p. 115)

The hybridized discourse of the Mexican American community became a tool for challenging power and political relations. Today, while the polemics as to what is "standard" use of English and Spanish continues,

---

[3] Hegemonic ideologies and practices are beliefs and actions that reinforce power relations and systems of control as they attempt to define or delimit a person's sociocultural and linguistic identity. For a discussion of hegemonic practices in relation to identity and language of minority populations in schools, and the role that schools and teachers play in maintaining this relations, see Erickson (1993) and Cummins (1996).

[4] Kalmar (2001) described the literacy practices of Mexican adults as they attempted to encode English with their knowledge of Spanish. He wrote about the hybrid spaces, alphabets, and discourses used by the men and women he studied. Gutiérrez, Baquedano-López, & Tejeda (2000) also discussed language policies and described the use of hybrid language practices of children in learning.

code switching and other hybrid language practices are more widely used in the media, radio, television, and in everyday community life.

The hybrid spaces and language practices are the context within which Mexican Americans students live and learn. The way schools and school districts are organized, the policies established, the curriculum offered, the personnel hired, and all functions of schooling continue to be influenced by these social, political, cultural, and linguistic pressures.

San Antonio Independent School District

San Antonio Independent School District (SAISD), with 53,700 students, is one of 16 school districts that provide public education to Bexar County and the greater San Antonio metropolitan area. It is the oldest district situated in the Enterprise/Empowerment Zone[5] of the inner city and extends outward from the city-core to include 79 square miles. With 97 schools, 65 of them elementary, SAISD is the second largest district in the county and the eighth largest district in the state of Texas. The district serves a culturally and linguistically diverse student population that is 83% Hispanic, primarily Mexican American; 11% African American; 6% White; and less than 0.5% Asian American and American Indian. Eighty-nine percent (89%) of the students come from low socioeconomic households and qualify for free or reduced-price meals. Seventeen-and-a-half percent (17.5%) of the students immigrated within the last 3 years, and 18% or approximately 9,400 students are limited English proficient (LEP) with Spanish as their home language.

Bilingual Programs in San Antonio District Prior to 1994

Over the years, bilingual education evolved in San Antonio and the educators attempted to deal with wave after wave of political opposition and policy changes. In existence in the late 1980s and early 1990s was an early-exit bilingual program. This program met the minimal requirements of the state transitional bilingual education law and used a concurrent

---

[5]Enterprise/Empowerment Zones are federally designated in economically depressed areas of cities. These zones are targeted for economic revival through grants to small business, tax breaks, and other local initiatives.

language method.[6] Instruction was presented in English or Spanish with immediate translation or interpretation in the other language, with the objective of reflecting the hybrid community language practices. However, as the concurrent language method was implemented in schools, a diglossic[7] situation evolved where different languages were used for different purposes; for example, English was more commonly used for academic discussion and thus was assigned or perceived as having high value whereas Spanish was used to clarify, correct, or discipline and was thus perceived to have low value.

In response to the national as well as local sociopolitical pressures of the early 1980s, the school district changed the name of the bilingual program to the dual-language program. District documents stated that the name *dual-language* reflected the use of the concurrent language method of instruction that was used in most schools. This would later create problems and misunderstandings as to the differences among two-way bilingual education and dual-language programs described in the professional literature and the dual-language program implemented in the school district. The dual-language program implemented in the district in the 1980s and early 1990s was, in fact, not a dual-language program but a modification of the transitional bilingual program which assigned or distributed fewer LEP students to more classes and used the concurrent language method for delivery of instruction. Unlike other dual-language programs, the development of both languages was not a program goal.

---

[6]R. Jacobson (1981) described the *concurrent approach* as the practice where a teacher uses both languages interchangeably; he wrote that it is particularly appropriate in communities in which there is a substantially large bilingual community whose language practices involve natural code switching. Wong Fillmore (1982) criticized the concurrent translation approach, suggesting that children wait for the translation into their dominant language instead of attending to the second language. Another criticism of the concurrent approach by Legarreta-Marcaida (1981) and Milk (1982) suggested that what occurs in concurrent translation is that teachers use much more English and thus interpret that English is the more important language.

[7]*Diglossia* is defined as the situation when two languages or language varieties exist side by side in a community and each is used for different purposes and assigned different values. Usually one is considered or assigned more status, as in the use of official government, media, and education functions while the other is considered or assigned less status. Ferguson (1959, 1962) first introduced the concept in relation to language varieties and Fishman (1965, 1967) developed and expanded the concept to include linguistic aspects of bilingual communities where languages as well as varieties of languages play different roles in communication and thus develop different value.

Prior to the restructuring that began in 1995, the district had been following a policy that had last been revised in 1991. According to the policy statement issued on July 8, 1991, the purpose and goals of the program were as follows:

> Dual-language [bilingual education] education and English as a second language (ESL) programs shall be taught to enable limited English proficient (LEP) students to become competent in the comprehensive [sic], speaking, reading, and composition of the English language. Programs shall emphasize mastery of English language skills and content area concepts and skills so students are able to participate effectively in the regular program. (San Antonio ISD, Policy 015907)

RESTRUCTURING BILINGUAL PROGRAMS

With the arrival of a new superintendent in 1994, all instructional programs in the district underwent a massive examination, justification, and restructuring. Of particular concern and interest to the new superintendent, who had been a bilingual educator in Massachusetts, was the effectiveness and structure of the bilingual and ESL programs. After months of visiting schools and gathering information about the district's efforts in bilingual ESL programming, she determined that an evaluation and restructuring of the programs were necessary. In the fall of 1995, she established the Bilingual Education Task Force. The goals of the bilingual education task force were:

1. to determine the current status of the bilingual education program in SAISD;
2. to explore model programs throughout the district, the state and the nation through research and through exploration at model program sites; and
3. to make recommendations for bilingual education program improvement from prekindergarten through Grade 12.

The subgroup examining bilingual instructional methods refined the third goal as follows:

> to restructure our program so that as a result of our instruction a) our students become biliterate, bicultural citizens, b) our students are able to think

at higher levels, thus become effective problem solvers, c) our promotion rates increase at all levels, and d) our students and our program are perceived as positive contributors to the total San Antonio ISD education program.

At the time, the district had 600 bilingual teachers that were receiving a stipend of approximately $2,000 per year for providing bilingual education to 6,259 LEP students. Part of the superintendent's concern was that LEP students were not receiving appropriate instruction. Small numbers of LEP students were assigned to classrooms where the primary language of instruction was English. The practice of distributing the LEP students in very small numbers had occurred in response to antibilingual sentiment of teachers, administrators, and school board members. The result was that each school organized the education of LEP students in very distinct ways. Thus, few schools had the more traditional K–3 transitional bilingual program with instruction in Spanish for an average of 20 to 22 LEP students per classroom per bilingual teacher. Most schools had the LEP students distributed through all the K–3 grades with as few as 5 to 7 students per classroom. The LEP students were integrated with English dominant students and bilingual teachers staffed the classrooms, but instruction was conducted in English with Spanish used only when necessary and then the instruction used the concurrent translation approach. This lack of a clear program organization definition and the subsequent lack of student academic progress were reasons cited by the superintendent for the need for restructuring.

A second major concern identified by the superintendent was the bilingual teachers' Spanish language proficiency. Although most of the bilingual stipend teachers had the appropriate bilingual certificate issued by the state, many had received their certificates at a time when the state requirements for bilingual certification did not require a high level of proficiency in the target language—Spanish, in the case of most of the San Antonio teachers. In fact, in the 1970s when there was a scarcity of bilingual teachers, the state only required that teachers have 100 clock hours of studying the target language to meet the requirements for bilingual certification. Thus, although many of the teachers certified in the 1980s and 1990s were proficient and well-prepared bilingual teachers, there was a large number of bilingually certified teachers with limited Spanish proficiency. Teachers' bilingual proficiency was a very controversial issue that was forcefully discussed. The bilingual teachers felt that "bilingual teachers were always the scapegoat" and that "the work we do with LEP students is not appreciated by other teachers." They also kept raising issues of LEP student integration and segregation. They argued that all the state-certified bilingual teachers, including those with limited Spanish proficiency, were needed so that LEP students could continue to be integrated. They further argued that this was an "issue of integration," that otherwise LEP students would be segregated in classrooms of only LEP students, and that "segregating students based on any criteria was against the law." Any reorganization proposal that would concentrate students in order to provide more Spanish instruction but would have the effect of reducing the number of classrooms designated as bilingual was opposed. The teacher union representative on the committee kept raising "issues of fairness" and teacher compensation. The fact that state-certified bilingual teachers who had as few as five LEP students received an additional stipend had long been a contentious item in the teacher pay scale. To reopen this issue and to limit the number of teachers that would qualify for the stipend in the future was seen as a "terrible political move" that would further erode support for bilingual education in the district.

The task force read numerous theoretical and research articles on the effectiveness of bilingual programs and program models.[8] The task force members discussed and argued about the results reported in the readings. Some felt that studies could be "found to support any viewpoint" that one group or another was espousing. A few of the task force members argued that the task force should also consider "a strong English as a second language program" as the best recommendation of the committee.

The task force members visited numerous bilingual programs that defined themselves as following a specific program model and had data to show its effectiveness. One principal and a teacher visited the Amigos two-way bilingual immersion program in Massachusetts and described it this way:

---

[8]Readings that were made available to the Bilingual Task Force include Baker (1993), Christian (1994), Checkley (1996), Collier (1992), Crawford (1991), García (1992), García and Baker (1995), Houston Independent School District (1996), McLeod (1994), Molina (1994), Ochoa and Pérez (1995), Ramírez, Yuen, Ramey, and Pasta (1991), National Association for Bilingual Education Report (1995), and National Center for Research on Cultural Diversity and Second Language Learning (1994).

The principal and I went to Boston . . . we visited a school there and looked
at their two-way program and how it worked and we found out that every
two-way program is different. As we were doing the research, we found that
they modified it [two-way bilingual immersion] . . . according to the school,
the population that you have and their needs.

The district's use of the term *dual-language* for the program that was in
place prior to 1994 also caused considerable confusion. Some but not all of
the research literature that they were reading made a distinction between
two-way bilingual immersion bilingual and dual-language bilingual programs. In fact, most researchers make distinctions between two-way bilingual and dual-language bilingual programs, but most practitioners and
some policymakers do not. Other teams of task force members visited
two-way bilingual immersion programs in Ysleta (El Paso) and San Jose,
California, and late-exit maintenance programs in Houston, Dallas, El
Paso, and other districts in San Antonio. They also acquired information
about two-way, dual-language, developmental, and maintenance programs, as well as transitional bilingual programs throughout the country.
The task force members used references from the Texas Education Agency
(TEA) Bilingual Office, the U.S. Department of Education's Office of
Bilingual Education and Minority Languages Affairs (OBEMLA), and the
National Association of Bilingual Education (NABE) to identify which
program in which districts to contact for information.

Another subgroup of the task force examined the skills and distribution
of the bilingually certified teachers in the district. An extensive survey was
conducted that asked teachers to rate on a 5-point scale how much Spanish
and how much English was used in instruction. How were LEP students
served? What types of materials were available in Spanish and English?
What was the status of the bilingual program within the school? What
were the abilities of the teachers to deliver instruction in Spanish? What
were the parents' attitudes toward bilingual education? Were there other
factors that influenced the design and delivery of bilingual education?
Among the findings that the survey yielded were two very important factors that impact the quality of bilingual education. First, numerous teachers did not feel they or their peers had sufficient Spanish language abilities
to deliver sustained instruction in Spanish. Second, most teachers felt that
the way the LEP students were distributed—with no more than six or
seven per classroom with the rest of the children being English speakers—

did not allow for the LEP students to receive substantial instruction in Spanish.

At the end of a long process of surveying, visiting, reading, studying, discussing, and constructing arguments, recommendations were made to the Superintendent. Among the recommendations made were:

1. All bilingual certified teachers who wished to continue teaching bilingually would have to undergo new testing in Spanish to assess their ability to deliver instruction in Spanish.

2. Give schools the option to organize their bilingual programs as transitional bilingual programs or as late exit maintenance programs with the majority of the students in these program classroom being LEP students.

3. Allow the two schools that had been exploring two-way bilingual education to implement that program model as a school within a school in those two schools.

By the time the Bilingual Task Force completed its work and made its recommendations, the superintendent was beginning to have some difficulty with the school board. The Superintendent distanced herself from the work of the committee, and the committee made recommendations directly to the school board. Of particular concern to the superintendent was the recommendation for implementation of the two-way bilingual immersion bilingual program. The superintendent believed that if she was perceived to be the one pushing for this program, the political climate might not permit continuation with the planning and implementation. Instead, the superintendent encouraged the principals and core group of teachers to participate with other task force members in the presentation of recommendation, which included the two-way bilingual immersion proposal to the school board. The board accepted the recommendations of the task force, including the implementation of the two-way bilingual immersion bilingual program at Bonham and Storm schools.

Planning for Two-Way Bilingual Immersion Education

The principals of the two-way bilingual immersion bilingual program schools had been members of the Bilingual Task Force. They had studied and read about two-way bilingual immersion bilingual education, were excited about the potential of this type of education, and wanted, according to a principal, "to go above and beyond what the state required." The principals attended a conference in California where they learned about the success of the River Glen Two-way Bilingual Immersion Program in San José, California. One principal described that experience saying, "We also visited a two-way bilingual conference in California in which we were able to research and learn about the 90–10 model used in California. It was so powerful, the results were so good, we knew that we had to find a way to bring it to our children." Following this California conference, the principals asked Bob Milk, the Director of the Division of Bicultural Bilingual Education at The University of Texas San Antonio (UTSA), to help them organize a retreat to begin the planning. The retreat helped to develop a process for continued study and planning that the principals and teachers took back to their campuses. One principal described this process: "After probably about a long year of research and study and a lot of conversation with the staff as well as the community we implemented it [two-way bilingual immersion]. And that strand is now in the fifth grade." This planning process and the continuous assessment, adjustment, and review that the two schools underwent are described in subsequent sections and chapters of this book.

SCHOOL PROFILES

Storm Elementary School is an old, brick, two-story building situated in a poor, westside neighborhood in San Antonio. The community that comprises the school attendance area is demarked by freeways to the south (these freeways do not have exits or access roads for this area), railroad tracks to the east, public housing and the terminal market industrial area to the north, and a major through-street with a small run-down commercial strip and a catholic church to the west. Thus the community is somewhat isolated with the school at the center. Most of the families live in a mix of small, wood-frame houses and publicly subsidized housing. Between 1994 and 2001, the school had an average enrollment of 500 students, with the latest figures for 2001 being 548 students. Ninety-eight percent (98%) of the student population is Mexican American and more than 50% speak Spanish as a home language. Ninety-nine percent (99%) of the students come from families that the principal described as "working-poor families" and are classified as economically disadvantaged by the state and federal guidelines for assistance to schools. This poverty is accompanied by high mobility, which affects school attendance and continued enrollment. Children enter and leave school throughout the year, or as one teacher reported, "The children come and go and come back," as parents find it necessary to follow jobs, make other arrangements for child care, or lose support for housing. Along with poverty and high mobility comes what the principal described as a "very high crime rate"; however, the parents and teachers described the school as a "safe haven or off-limits to gangs."

Since 1995, Storm Elementary student achievement has improved steadily as measured by the Texas Assessment of Academic Skills (TAAS) and the Texas Education Agency's Academic Excellence Indicator System (AEIS).[9] In 1994, the TAAS scores for all tests taken by all students were at the 18.6 percentile; in 1999–2000 and 2000–2001 the school was "Recognized" when the TAAS scores for all tests taken by all students were at the 80.4 percentile.

Bonham Elementary School is one of the smaller schools in the district and is in the historical core or inner city. The school building is a combination of an old, brick, two-story with more modern additions of a cafeteria and a gym currently under construction. The school is surrounded by a mix of old houses and buildings that have been converted to spaces for small businesses and restaurants. The community that comprises the school attendance area includes small, single-family, wood-frame houses; some public housing; a homeless shelter; and the historic 19th-century King William district. This district has large two-story wood and brick Victorian and German houses with sprawling lawns. Between 1994 and 2001, the school had an average enrollment of 340 students, with the latest figures for 2001 being 341 students; 92% of the student population is Mexican American and 30% speak Spanish as a home language. Ninety-three

---

[9] The Texas Education Agency, Academic Excellence Indicator System includes TAAS scores in Reading and Mathematics for third, fourth, and fifth grades and writing for fourth grade. Bilingual students have the option of taking all tests in Spanish or English. The schools are rated as low performing, acceptable, recognized, or exemplary based on the TAAS performance of students by subcategory (African American, Hispanic, White, and Economically Disadvantaged), dropout rate, and attendance rate. For more information see the TEA web site at www.tea.state.tx.us/student.assessment.

percent (93%) of the students are classified as economically disadvantaged by the state and federal guidelines for assistance to schools. Like at Storm, the families living in poverty experience a high rate of mobility, which affects school attendance and continued enrollment.

Since 1995, Bonham student achievement has improved steadily as measured by the Texas Assessment of Academic Skills (TAAS) and the Texas Education Agency's Academic Excellence Indicator System. In 1994, the TAAS scores for all tests taken by all students were at the 50th percentile, in 1997–98, the school was "Recognized" when the TAAS scores for all tests taken by all students were at the 84.3 percentile, and in 2000–2001 the school was "Exemplary" with TAAS scores at the 93rd percentile.

In 1995, Bonham enrolled children in kindergarten for the first two-way bilingual immersion bilingual program in the city. A school brochure states that the program was implemented in response to the many Spanish-speaking households in the school service area in an "effort to capitalize on this asset . . . the program has been preparing children of this community to become citizens of the world and global leaders in business, communication, arts and sciences."

Storm Elementary opted to spend the 1995–1996 academic year to further study and plan the program. The first two-way bilingual immersion class began kindergarten in 1996. Between 1996 and 1999, the two-way bilingual immersion programs at both schools were part of a Title VII System-wide Improvement Grant. At both schools, the two-way bilingual immersion bilingual programs are K–5th grade strand within the school. At the beginning, each school also offered a late-exit maintenance bilingual program and an English K–5th grade strand. All LEP students and their parents, including special need students, can participate in the two-way bilingual immersion program. English dominant students, including students with special needs, are also encouraged to participate. The processes for informing and recruiting students and parents for the two-way bilingual immersion program are described in chapter 3.

STUDENT POPULATION

The Mexican and Mexican American students in this study share many elements of a culture; that is, they have common features of cultural com-

petence—ways of behaving, interacting, worldview. However, some of
the Mexican American students could also be said to exhibit some elements of U.S. cultural integration and some elements of the hybrid or new
meztizaje; that is, they may exhibit features or traits not found in either
of what is considered Mexican or American cultures. Despite 25 years of
bilingual education in San Antonio, most parents and family members of
the Mexican American student population would be unable to maintain a
long communication only in Spanish, but incorporate a lot of Spanish in
their English communications. Thus, in the two-way bilingual immersion
classrooms, English proficient and Spanish proficient students were in
some ways very similar; that is, they shared elements of a culture, socioeconomic status, and a vibrant bilingual linguistic community. The English proficient speakers, while not being bilingual at the age of 5, 6, or 7
when they entered the program, came from homes and a community where
some Spanish could be heard daily. The Spanish proficient speakers at age
5, 6, or 7 already had been exposed to a lot of English and used isolated
English words in their speech.

A total of 216 children—197 Mexican American, 17 White, and 2 African American—were enrolled in the program in 2001. Ninety-eight students were enrolled at Storm and 118 at Bonham.[10] At each school, the
two-way bilingual immersion bilingual program is a K–5th grade strand
within the school. The number of students by grade level, language, gender, and ethnicity is provided in Table 2.1. In 2000–2001, the program was
staffed with 15 certified bilingual teachers, all Mexican Americans. Their
assignments by grade level are provided in Table 2.1.

Most students began the program in kindergarten in cohort groups. English dominant children were not admitted after first grade. At both schools,
Spanish dominant students were admitted at all grade levels on a space
available basis. Seven special needs or at-risk students participated in the
program.

At Storm, 20% (24) of students that started in the two-way bilingual
immersion program in kindergarten withdrew from the program with 19%
also withdrawing from the school. Nine students were allowed to reenter
the program. These students had attended a transitional bilingual program

---

[10]In 2002–2003, the enrollment in the two-way immersion program at Bonham had
grown to almost half of the 340 total school enrollment.

TABLE 2.1
Two-Way Bilingual Immersion Student Enrollment and Demographics
2000–2001

	K	1st	2nd	3rd	4th	5th
Spanish Dominants	20	27	27	21	20	10
English Dominants	21	17	14	13	17	9
Boys	20	25	19	21	21	11
Girls	21	19	22	13	16	8
Hispanic	37	41	38	29	35	17
Whites and African Americans	4	3	3	5	2	2
Teachers	3	3	3	2	2	1

at one of the other district schools between the time they left the two-way bilingual immersion and their return.

At Bonham, 22% (33) of students that started in the two-way bilingual immersion program in kindergarten withdrew from the program with 20% also withdrawing from the school before fifth grade. Thirteen students were allowed to reenter the program after attending a transitional bilingual program at another school.

The number of students withdrawing from the two-way bilingual immersion was slightly lower than the average for the school as a whole. Nonetheless, the high rate of withdrawals caused both schools to reduce the multiple classes beyond the second grade. In 2001–2002, there was a further reduction and only one school offered two kindergarten and two first-grade classes.

LANGUAGE DISTRIBUTION

The vision and the goal for the two-way bilingual immersion program was to make Spanish a prestige language that would have status within the school so that the social pressure for children to use English would be balanced. After the year of studying and visiting other two-way bilingual immersion bilingual programs, the model selected was the 90–10 model. In the 90–10 model of two-way bilingual immersion bilingual education implemented in these two schools, Spanish was the primary language of instruction for most of the school day at the primary—kindergarten and first—grade level. The teachers were conscientious about their planning so that classroom instructional activities were conducted 90% in Spanish and a variety of strategies were used to assist children to make the language comprehensible. At Bonham the two-way bilingual immersion teacher also provided the 10% of the English/English as a second language (ESL) component of the curriculum. At Storm, the two-way teachers exchanged students with the transitional bilingual teachers for ESL, thus providing a one-teacher-one-language model.

As the children progressed to the intermediate—second and third—grade level, approximately 70%–80% of instructional time was in Spanish. The nature of Spanish language instruction and the strategies for making the language for second language learners more comprehensible became more complex. These classes were self-contained at both schools; that is, the same teacher taught the Spanish and English components of the curriculum.

In the upper—fourth and fifth—grade level, Spanish and English instruction was 50–50. At Storm, these classes were self-contained. At Bonham, the fourth- and fifth-grade classes were departmentalized. The fourth-grade two-way bilingual immersion teacher provided language arts and mathematics instruction in Spanish, and the children went to other teachers for social studies and science in English. At the fifth-grade level, the two-way bilingual immersion teacher taught language arts and social studies, and the children went to other teachers for mathematics and science in both Spanish and English. One of the teachers described this arrangement as "the goal is maintenance of the Spanish communication skills developed in earlier grades and to use it for specific content areas." At this upper-grade level, the amount of support and scaffolding provided to make the Spanish or English more comprehensible was, for the most part, withdrawn, with some exceptions. The exceptions came when teachers introduced new, complex math, science, or social studies concepts. During these lessons, teachers made more of an effort to contextualize the language by using hands-on activities and Total Physical Response (TPR) methodologies (Asher, 1977). The teachers talked about using the Cognitive Academic Language Learning Approach (CALLA; Chamot & O'Malley, 1986) or TPR so the children could understand the new concepts and skills. The instructional context and methodologies used are described in the chapters that follow.

One other significant decision made during the planning year was about the language practices to be used by the teacher and the language practices that could be used and would be accepted from children. Teachers, administrators, and university researchers discussed how the cultural and linguistic borderlands had shaped them, as well as shaped the parents and students who might participate in the program. They debated how this experience had impacted aspects of their and the community's identity and had created the hybridized language of San Antonio. Much discussion took place about the "level" or "standard" of Spanish and English that would be modeled by the teacher and whether children would be required to separate their communications and responses into only Spanish or only English. The discussions and arguments centered around the community practice of code switching as well as the previously used concurrent language approach. After much dynamic vigorous debate, the principals and teachers decided that teachers would be expected to model school language and use "standard American Spanish" and "standard American English"—the standard here being that spoken by the mainstream business and media community. There was much joking and arguing that the Spanish not be "from Mexico City or Spain" as well as that the English not be "that of New York or Boston." There was less disagreement on the language responses that would be encouraged and acceptable from the children. The group almost unanimously decided that children should be encouraged to communicate using all their language systems and registers. Of much concern was that all teachers should be made aware of how to respond, what to say, and what gestures and facial expressions to be careful of when children used code switching. Thus, while the teacher was to model and remain in the language of the lesson, the child's responses would be deemed acceptable in Spanish, English, or code switching, and the teachers would learn a number of strategies for working with children to assist them in understanding their language practices and preferences. Clearly, personal experiences with hybridized language influenced the options that they considered as they affirmed their commitment to the goal of developing students that would become bicultural, bilingual, biliterate persons. This topic is further discussed and illustrated in chapter 4.

As the principals and teachers went through a process of deciding that they wanted to implement two-way bilingual immersion bilingual education, they talked about "going beyond the state bilingual requirements," "giving children advantages," "capitalizing on what children brought to learning," and "preparing children for the future." They also talked about the need for the program to be "model and research driven." They tested their arguments on each other and on the professors that participated with them in some of the discussions as they prepared to communicate their professional recommendations and convince the district administration and the school board. An important early decision was to increase the circle to include more teachers from each of the campuses and to involve parents in the decision-making process. Included in every discussion were issues of curriculum and curriculum materials, instructional methodologies, teacher preparation and staff development, and parent participation. The principals and teachers kept referring back to the professional literature and the data they had collected on their visits to suggest processes and issues for consideration.

CONCLUSION

Evident at the end of this first year of studying and the restructuring work undertaken by the Bilingual Task force was that a core leadership team had evolved and that this core group was convinced that they could and should implement two-way bilingual immersion education. The core group of teachers and principals were likewise convinced that the way to insure the successful implementation and the long-term sustainability of the program was to take care that the model that they implement be rigorous, yield positive student outcomes, and give students added skills that they could not get in other models of instruction.

In chapter 3, I describe why the parents both supported and resisted the idea of making their children bilingual. The process that helped parents imagine new possibilities for their children and the leadership that developed are also described.

3

Leadership and Parents

Parents were gathered to hear about the new, proposed, two-way bilingual immersion program. As the discussion following the school's presentation began, Lydia said, *"Para mí es importante que aprendan inglés"* (For me it is important that they learn English). Another parent at the meeting, Maria, nodded her head in apparent agreement with Lydia and said, "My parents used to say the same thing. They did not teach me Spanish so now I only understand a little but I want my children to know both." From across the room, Julian, one of only three fathers at the meeting, spoke up: *"Saber inglés es importante, pero que no se les olvide el español"* (Knowing English is important but they should not forget Spanish). The discussion this evening began slowly and cautiously with only a few parents speaking up, but as the discussion continued, many more parents expressed opinions about learning English, Spanish, and being bilingual. After a little over an hour of discussion, the parents were told that this was only an information and discussion session and that before any decisions were made, they would have other opportunities to gather information, provide input to the development of the program, and eventually decide for their children whether to participate in the program.

INFORMING PARENTS AND PARENTS' CONCERNS

Numerous parent information and recruitment sessions were conducted every year to inform parents and to provide opportunities for parents to talk with each other and with the school staff about the goals of the two-way bilingual immersion program. Usually the principal or the university researcher in attendance began by stating the program mission. The mission statement changed little over the 5 years; the statement that follows was made during the first year in a parent awareness and recruitment session; in 2001, a very similar statement was made.

Principal:

Nuestra misión es crear un medio-ambiente colaborativo donde los estudiantes alcancen un nivel alto de lecto-escritura y aprendizaje en los dos idiomas en un programa bilingüe de two-way—un programa de doble—sentido y multicultural. . . . Esto será posible con el apoyo de los padres y las maestras que van a valorizar el futuro de los niños. En fin, lo que queremos, son niños que conocen dos idiomas, un programa que nos lleve a un camino de éxito y hacer nuestra escuela ejemplar.

Our mission is to create a collaborative in which students achieve a high level of literacy and learning in two languages in a two-way bilingual and multicultural program. . . . This will be possible with the parent's and the teachers' help who will value the future of the children. Finally, what we want are children that know two languages, a program that will take us on the road to success and to make our school exemplary.

The most dynamic parent information and recruitment sessions were those held during 1995 and 1996, where parents became aware of the uniqueness of the proposed program. These parent sessions were always conducted bilingually and initially the schools relied on the university to provide support. Howard Smith, a university colleague, conducted many of the sessions during the first couple of years. After distributing to the parents brief, written, bullet-style descriptions of the proposed two-way model in both Spanish and English, he would lead a dialogue with the parents about the value of education, languages, and the futures that they aspired for their children. The principal and teachers would always be present to participate in the discussion and to answer questions. Refreshments were served and children of all ages as well as grandparents were often present.

During these information sessions, Spanish-speaking parents and English-speaking parents voiced concerns and opinions for and against the 90–10 two-way bilingual immersion model that was being considered for the schools. The parents' support or opposition did not appear to divide along language competency or Mexicano/Mexican American lines. For example, when told by the principal that "the make-up of the classroom will be 10 or 11 English speakers and 10 or 11 Spanish speakers," one Spanish-speaking parent said, *"pero, los de aquí que ya hablen inglés no van a querer participar"* (but those from here that already speak English will not participate), to which a Mexican American English-speaking parent responded, "I agree about this two-way program, . . . I think it will be better for my child, to know two languages."

Importance of English

At every session, as parents discussed the two-way bilingual immersion program, the teaching of English was a recurring topic with parents making comments such as, *"cuando les van a enseñar inglés"* (when will you teach English), *"quien les va a enseñar inglés"* (who will teach English), and *"yo pienso que les deben enseñar más inglés"* (I think you should teach them more English). The importance of learning English in order to succeed in the United States and the messages that many of these parents had internalized about living in the United States and speaking English were paramount. Although many saw the benefits of being bilingual, parents like Elena were worried about their children learning English and the opportunities that knowing English might provide.

Elena:

Si comparamos las necesidades, el inglés hace mucha falta aquí, sabiendo inglés les da más oportunidades.

If we compare the needs, English is necessary here, knowing English gives [them] more opportunities.

Concerns About Time Allocations

At first, the time allocations described for the two-way bilingual immersion went counter to the theories most parents had about learning languages. For Lupe, the logic of teaching in the primary grades up to 90% of the time in Spanish was counter-intuitive to her ideas about how one learns English and to the importance of learning English.

Lupe:

*¿Si la educación preescolar y la educación primaria—el primero y se-
gundo año—va a ser el 90 porciento en español, cuando van aprender
inglés?*

If preschool and primary education the first and second year will be 90 percent in Spanish, when will they learn English?

An English-speaking parent, Raúl, expressed support for bilingual education and the school, but had questions about the 90–10 model: "I like it
that my child can be bilingual, I am not against my child learning a second
language—Spanish, but I don't know if this 90–10 is the best, I want to
support the school, but I am not sure right now."

Gloria also wanted to support the program but wanted to have a discussion about the amount of Spanish that should be included saying, *"Yo nada
más pienso que los padres deben opinar si están de acuerdo con que les
enseñan tanto español"* (I only think that the parents should voice opinions if they agree with teaching so much Spanish).

To these concerns and questions about the importance of English, the
principal, the teachers, and, in later years, other parents would agree that
English was important and they would share the studies and experiences at
other schools, and would explain that because English is so pervasive in
the culture and community that it was necessary to protect and provide a
strong foundation in Spanish as the children learned English. They assured
parents that from the very first day of school children would be learning
English, but that most of the studies showed the soundness of helping children to learn to read, write, and problem solve in the minority language in
order for them to become bilingual and biliterate.

Whole School versus Strand

Initially the schools, the administrators, and teachers examined and discussed the possibility of all incoming kindergartners beginning in two-way
bilingual immersion classrooms and that over time the whole school might
be involved. A parent, Elisa, spoke up in support of the program and for
the possibility that her children would have advantages that she did not
have by becoming literate in two languages.

Elisa:

Yo sí estoy de acuerdo con esto de dos idiomas—two way-dos-vías—para el futuro de mis hijos. Así no se les olvida el español. El día de mañana ellos pueden hacer lo que yo no puedo que es leer inglés y español. Que lo aprovechen mis hijos.

I am in agreement with this about two languages—two-way—for the future of my children. That way they will not forget Spanish. Tomorrow they may be able to do what I cannot do which is to read in English and Spanish. My children should take advantage of this.

Of the more than 20 parents that participated at one of the sessions, Marta, a parent with children in pre-K and second grade, appeared uneasy about the possibility of the whole school becoming a two-way school. About 30 minutes into the program, Marta voiced her concern and made a suggestion.

Marta:

Yo pienso que deberían de tomar el consentimiento de cada padre de familia . . . para ver quién está de acuerdo con este programa bilingüe. Y que formen un solo grupo de los que estén de acuerdo . . . ya que hay gente que toda su vida vivirá aquí en estados unidos y nació aquí y no muy bien les interesa el español además en todos los trabajos de aquí, los papeles, y todo todo se usa el inglés.

I think that they should consider the feelings of each head of household . . . to see who is in agreement with this bilingual program. And form only one group of those who are in agreement . . . since there are people who will live all their lives in the United States and were born here and may not be interested in Spanish besides, all workplaces here, papers, every- everything is in English.

Marta, while keeping an open mind to the program being proposed for the school and for those parents who might be interested, was also voicing an assessment of the general interest in Spanish. She also appears to echo the mainstream message that in order to work and understand what is happening in the United States, one must know English. Like so many of the other parents, especially the Mexicano parents, she was anxious for parents to have a choice about their children's education and language choice.

It was comments like Marta's, and those of many other parents, that caused the administrators and teachers to reconsider their proposed plan. As the parent meetings continued, the planning committee began to talk more about the two-way bilingual immersion program being a strand within the school.

Helping With Homework

Mariela, an English-speaking parent, voiced a concern that would be brought out at many of the parent information sessions. She began by expressing her concern for the child's possible confusion but later expressed her anxiety about not knowing Spanish and not being able to help her child with her homework. "I don't think it's a good idea. I don't like the idea. I feel that a young child will get confused. I have a child in pre-K . . . if parents speak only English, how will they help their child if the work is in Spanish?"

At another session, as parents were discussing how they would help their children with homework if they were not bilingual, one Spanish-speaking parent shared her experience with helping her child with homework in English and suggested that the English-speaking parents would be able to manage the supervision as she had done.

Elisa:

Aunque yo no hablo inglés, yo me encargo de ver que mis hijos hagan sus tareas. Así lo pueden hacer los padres que no saben español para el bien común.

Although I do not speak English, I take responsiblity to see that my children do their homework. The parents who do not speak Spanish can do likewise for the public good.

School Authority

The parents who came to the parent awareness sessions demonstrated their determination, commitment, and willingness to support the school in the education of their children. For example, one parent expressed her decision-making process as simply a way of supporting what the school staff was recommending: *"La escuela pidió permiso para empezar el programa y yo me animé y dije que sí"* (the school asked for permission to begin the program and I was encouraged and said yes). The parents expressed strong feelings about schooling and learning. Deference to school as an authority figure was also evident as shared by Luisa.

Luisa:

De cualquier manera que se haga estaría bien conque aprendan, que aprendan todo lo necesario y, si es possible, y hay tiempo, que aprendan los dos idiomas.

Anyway that it is organized will be fine as long as they learn, that they learn all they need and, if possible, and if there's time, that they learn the two languages.

The status of teachers as authorities was also voiced by some of the Mexicano parents, like Tila, who expressed confidence in the teachers making the best decisions for the education of their children.

Tila:

Ustedes están ay pa enseñarles lo que necesiten, yo tengo confianza en los maestros.

You are there to teach them what they need; I have confidence in the teachers.

This perspective was not always shared by the Mexican American parents, who tended to ask more questions and generally wanted more information and to be involved in the final decision making.

Value of Bilingualism

Some parents expressed support for the program as a way of developing skills that they assessed might give their children added skills and perhaps an advantage that would prepare them to pursue higher education. For example, Beto, a Spanish-speaking parent of a pre-K child, said:

Yo digo que pa que vallan al colegio es importante que sepan idiomas.

I say that for them to go to college it is important that they know languages.

Other parents expressed their understanding about a possible future relationship between the kinds of jobs and life chances that could be obtained in the United States and the educational achievement of their children.

Pa qué, somos pobres, trabajamos por salarios mínimos, y si ellos aprenden más, las dos idiomas, podrán ganar más y conseguir un trabajo donde no se maten tanto.

For what, we are poor, we work for minimum wages, and if they learn more, the two languages, they will earn more and get a job where they won't kill themselves.

The principals and teachers were very aware of the need to not present themselves as experts of two-way bilingual immersion education to parents. The parents and community members were informed that this was something new that they would be learning along with them and the students, but that the program was based on research on successful programs around the country. They also discussed how the professional bilingual community itself could not agree on the best program model and were careful to point out the limitations as well as the possibilities of the two-way approach. The teachers and principals sought out materials in Spanish and summarized other articles in Spanish in order to share with the parents the existing knowledge in the field as they studied and learned. They invited bilingual speakers, consultants, and trainers to speak to parents and teachers together. Often, the principals and the lead teachers would pose the difficult questions to engage the consultants in discussions about the limits of the knowledge and the possible side effects or criticisms of the two-way model under consideration. Over time, the school gained the support and confidence of the parents.

Sustaining Parent Support

During the initial planning year, there was a general outreach to all parents in the school as the school explored various options in the two-way models and discussed the potential make-up of the classes, entry criteria into the program, and other program planning matters. Teachers and school staff spent many hours calling parents, giving them information about the two-way bilingual immersion model on the phone, telling them about the agenda and the length of the meetings, and assuring them that they could bring their children and other family members to meetings. In subsequent years, after many of the initial decisions about program model were made, the outreach was targeted to parents of pre-K, kindergarten, and first-grade children. However, parents with children in the program often came to the new parent recruitment sessions as a way of keeping up with the progress of the program and to express continued support or raise concerns.

These continuing parents also demonstrated their support by attending these sessions and often helped to explain to the new parents their understanding of the program. For example, one parent attending a session during the fourth year described his observations for new parents who were expressing concerns about children learning and practicing English.

Les dan instrucción en español y en inglés y trabajan en grupos y yo me he fijado que en los grupos [los niños] están hablando inglés con los otros niños.

They provide instruction in Spanish and English and they work in groups and I have noticed that in the groups they are talking English with other children.

The continuing parents time and again asked questions about whether the two-way bilingual immersion program was the best instructional program for their children. For example, Carmen was concerned about her child who was now in second grade but had not begun to read fluently in English.

Carmen:

Yo estoy de acuerdo con el programa, que les enseñen los dos idiomas porque valen por dos, pero yo creo que hay un pequeño problema en como les enseñan porque mi hija está en segundo grado y aún no sabe leer bien en inglés.

I agree with the program, with the teaching of two languages because its doubles the value, but I think that there is a small problem with how they are being taught because my daughter is in second grade and still does not read well in English.

Carmen, as other parents, had agreed to place her child in the program in kindergarten. As the years passed, she and other parents continued to raise questions with the teachers and principals about the appropriateness of the instruction and the soundness of the model. They asked about the proven effect of the model and the research. But even after hearing about the results of dual-language instruction at other schools and other cities, they returned to the primary issue of whether the model and the instruction was the appropriate education for their child in particular classrooms. For example, one parent of a fourth grader was concerned that the child was not bringing home enough school papers that reflected the English curriculum: *"Los papeles que traen son más en español y muy pocos en inglés"* (The papers they bring [home] are more in Spanish and very few in English). Another parent reported that "the bilingual teachers are the best, my child is learning the correct Spanish, and they're teaching us." Parents were generally pleased that the two-way bilingual immersion program encourages children's awareness of their bilingual community and that the classes instill "pride in being bilingual and bicultural."

Both schools developed a close link with the community through sustained efforts, and the fact that many parents walked their children to school daily also facilitated the frequent parent–teacher communications. Each school offered many opportunities for parent involvement, from parenting classes to in classroom involvement. Even though the number of two-way parents involved in school has been higher and has improved greatly over the 5 years, most teachers talked about the need to sustain the interest of the parents and to continue to reach out to those parents who were not as actively involved.

The teachers and schools continuously provided open houses, conferences, and meetings in which they shared the progress as well as concerns about children's learning and the success of the two-way bilingual immersion program. This ongoing contact also provided a vehicle for communication and support for those times when the program would come under more intense scrutiny or political criticism. The parents were informed and able to support the teachers and principals in the ongoing struggle to maintain program viability.

The parents and extended families that had all along recognized the value and importance of learning English for the future of their children came to recognize the value and importance of learning Spanish. The parents understood not only the very complex nature of the society they lived in but also the demands that global societies would exert on their children. They embraced the possibility of bilingualism and biliteracy development for their children and created a very supportive as well as demanding sociocultural context for the two-way bilingual immersion program. The parents' expectations and support influenced many of the programmatic and instructional decisions that were made over the 5 years of the program.

DEVELOPING PARENT AND COMMUNITY LEADERSHIP

During that first year, the principals and teachers did not assume that parents had prior knowledge of the proposed program and made every effort to reach out to parents, especially to parents of preschool children who were the prospective students and parents for the classes that began kindergarten in the two-way bilingual immersion program. As principals, teachers, and university researchers discussed the development and implementation of two-way bilingual immersion education, they continuously involved and checked with parents and community leaders. They were particularly aware of criticisms that schools often receive about not informing key stakeholders, such as students, parents, and families, about instructional and programmatic efforts. During the subsequent program years, while the parent information recruitment sessions continued, the school also focused on involving parents in various committees, instructional activities, and especially in communicating with other parents and the community.[1]

The parents were included in planning task groups with the teachers and administrators as planning decisions were made. Some of these meetings and activities were part of the Campus Leadership Team (CLT) or PTA, but most were special sessions where the teachers and school staff, through extra effort, got the word out and invited parents who did not usually come to school.

Prior to 1995, the principals had explored different ways of increasing parental involvement. They were aware that especially the Mexicano par-

---

[1] Valdés (1996) argued that school officials do not always share with parents the limits of their knowledge: "When an expert presents himself to his own professional community, he is careful to point out the limitations of his approach given existing knowledge in the field. When facing clients, however, the expert will present himself as quite certain of the wisdom of his position. He will not communicate the limits of his knowledge or the possible side effects of the intervention" (p. 198). Jiménez (2000) also raised concerns that students, their families, and teachers are not included when instructional and programmatic decisions are made that address the literacy learning needs of marginalized students. Sigel (1983, cited in Valdés, 1996, p. 199) described parent education programs as following the medical mode where parents are not invited to participate in diagnosing the problem. Valdés argued that parents "must be helped to understand the alternatives in all of their complexity" (p. 203).

ents might not interpret the construct of "parental involvement" in school in the same ways as most middle-class U.S. parents. The principals listened to and engaged with parents to develop an understanding of what parents perceived their role and the school's role in the education of their children. Parents and school staff then began work on redefining parental involvement and parental support within their understanding of each other's roles. With the planning, development, and implementation of the two-way bilingual immersion program, the principals and teachers developed multiple strategies for reaching out to other parents, particularly by those parents with preschool children who were the potential students for the two-way bilingual immersion classes.

Parent education was provided and parent school participation efforts were supported by the activities of the district's Student Support Department.[2] The most requested type of parent education was English classes at various levels. Parents saw the need for English classes not only for their own development but also as a way of supporting their children's education. For example, one parent commented, *"Yo no sé inglés y voy a estudiar para poder ayudar a mí niño en lo que pueda"* (I do not know English and I study so that I can help my child anyway I can).

Each campus had a community liaison or social worker assigned to promote community and parent engagement at the school. The role of the liaison or social worker was to provide support to parents and to create an awareness of the school programs and the benefits of programs, such as the two-way bilingual immersion for the children, parents, school, and community. The liaison facilitated various communications, including the district newsletters and web page, the campus web page, bulletins, and parent letters. Although communications about the two-way bilingual immersion program were always in both Spanish and English, other communications were not equally available in Spanish and English. A good 70% of school communications examined were bilingual and the principals and teachers reported that they kept working with the liaison or social worker and district personnel from different departments to make all of the communications bilingual.

---

[2] The district's Student Support Department provided the Family Support Program, the Therapy and Counseling Program, Parenting Education through the Parent Academy, Parent Volunteer Program, The Children's Creative Response to Conflict Effort, the HOGAR Family Program, and the Homeless Services Program.

Parents also focused on ways that they could support their children's learning. They often reported that they assisted children by making space for and supervising homework, by listening to children read their books and what they had written, by helping them learn new words as for spelling, and by talking about letters, words, and print found around the house and community. The parents' comments concerning their own roles in supporting and reinforcing the bilingual and biliterate development of their children showed that they considered this extremely important and potentially influential in the development of their children's skills. Children also pointed out how the parents would often ask them specifically what homework they had in Spanish and in English. One child reported, "When dad asks where is your Spanish writing or math—I say I only have homework in English—he, he says—I'm going to come talk to your teacher, 'cause it is supposed to be in two, in bilingual, in Spanish and English."

The parents, the principals, and teachers tried to identify and tap into the distinct needs, interests, desires, and identities of the parents as well as school needs. Thus, meetings were held at different times, with the mid-morning and early evening being the most successful meeting times. In addition to the two-way bilingual immersion program information, most meetings included either information on other topics (disciplining children, women's health, cultural traditions), giveaways (consumer product samples, books, raffles), or student presentations. With time and in subsequent years, the parents became involved in the planning and running of the meetings, in making presentations and leading discussions, and in assuming leadership roles in the recruitment of parents and students.

THE SCHOOL-BASED LEADERSHIP

The principals at each school were instrumental in facilitating, promoting, and providing the will and energy that were necessary at the beginning to get the program started and throughout the 6 years in sustaining and continuously renewing the program. Both principals had extensive teaching experience and experience teaching bilingually. In 1995, they were also relatively new in their assignments at each of the schools and were faced with the task of raising student achievement scores, reinvigorating a relatively established teaching staff, and engaging a community that had not been involved, and to a certain degree, not welcomed in all facets of school operations. Each described herself as Mexican American or Chicana and were active in promoting solutions to the plight of the Mexican American and bilingual students. They had experience participating in educational initiatives within the community and professional organizations.

The Campus Leadership Team (CLT) at each school included an instructional coordinator. This position exists at most of the districts' schools. The instructional coordinators at Storm and Bonham assisted teachers with instruction and professional development. Both instructional coordinators were Mexican Americans and had extensive knowledge of bilingual education and reading.

The administrators were very aware of having to make high stakes decisions for their students and they sought out the help of the research community locally, from throughout the state, nationally, and even internationally. Foremost on their agenda was identifying factors that assist Spanish speakers and all Mexican American students as a group to attain high achievement levels in all areas of the curriculum while becoming biliterate.

All instructional decisions, recommendations, and modifications were undertaken through discussion and review by the CLT or site-based decision-making entity. The principal described the role of parents in the CLT:

> Parent involvement is a cornerstone of all instructional initiatives implemented. . . . Parents provide input through various activities such as membership on the instructional leadership team, event chairmanships, town hall meetings, core subject committees and task forces. Perhaps the most significant is the participation on the CLT.

The CLT committee comprised parents, administrators, teachers, community residents, teaching assistants, and other campus support staff. All members were provided leadership training, team building, and team facilitation strategies. The instructional leadership teams were also provided the guidance of district curriculum specialists and the Education Service Center Region 20 and the consultant/researcher support from The University of Texas at San Antonio.

The CLT facilitated the development of the school's campus improvement plan. This campus improvement plan is a living document that summarizes the school's demographics, recent academic achievement, areas in need of improvement, and plans for action for the following year. The CLT plan also contained recommendations on other areas of school life, such as professional development, budgeting, and parent involvement. The campus improvement plans were revised and updated yearly through the CLT. As the campus improvement plans were developed and revised, they were presented to larger numbers of parents at meetings called for this purpose. All the parent meetings were conducted in Spanish and English. One school's vision as stated in their campus improvement plan was that "all students will become independent thinkers and lifelong learners through a student-centered environment that promotes participatory learning and enriches their native language." One teacher spoke about how this new emphasis on helping children become bilingual, bicultural, and biliterate had improved parental involvement. She said, "Parents now feel that when they come, they're not just listening, but will be listened to also. Parents feel more comfortable knowing they can communicate in Spanish. They see that the school, especially this program, encompasses students, parents, and the community."

The school-based leadership team had support from the district-level bilingual department. Within the district level organization, the two-way bilingual immersion programs were part of the bilingual department of the curriculum division. The bilingual department staff consisted of a director and two program facilitators. The staff of the district's bilingual program office were instrumental in providing leadership and support for the school principals, the school-based CLTs, and the parents. They also had the role of monitoring and recommending adjustments that they deemed necessary. There was support but also a certain amount of healthy friction between the district bilingual office administrators and the school based leadership team.

PARENTS AND COMMUNITY MEMBERS INFLUENCING LEARNING

Once begun, the parents, community residents within the school boundaries, and community members and leaders from the business and public sectors provided support for the program. With the support that they provided came a certain amount of influence on the development of the program and on the learning environment. Some of this support and influence was obvious, such as parents and community members participating at school and board meetings, mentoring students, generating publicity, garnering Spanish language books, technology, and other materials; however, other influence was exerted in subtle, unforeseen ways. Perhaps the most unforeseen influence was in the way that the principals and teachers self-monitored and adjusted their practices in order to maintain the support that was being provided by selected parents and some rather influential community members.

The parent and community influence was most directly observable in the proposal to continue the two-way program for students being promoted to the middle school. As the two-way elementary schools approached the District to plan for the continuation of the program at the middle school level, the parent and community support was crucial and became an important factor in the decision making process. Initially, the district had decided that the two-way program would not be implemented at the middle-school level. After much discussion and lobbying by the principals, bilingual department staff, teachers, and parents, the district agreed to reexamine the issue. The principals, while wanting to communicate with all parents of the fifth-grade two-way students who were going on to the middle school, were leery about the high expectations that parents had previously expressed and the disappointment some parents voiced when it appeared that the program might not continue at the middle school. Thus, the principals strategized as to when and how to communicate with all the parents and the community at large while not making any more false starts. Some parents had by this time become very politicized, whereas others had begun to make alternate choices for their children, such as seeking out magnet programs. After numerous staff planning meetings, parent meetings, and meetings with a school board task group, the advocacy of the parents, administrators, and community members was successful in gaining support for the continuation of the two-way program and for further study of the middle school issue.

The business community and public sector embraced the two-way program as demonstrated by the Hispanic Chamber of Commerce's public endorsement of the two-way model at Bonham and Storm elementary schools. Other schools and school districts were challenged to emulate the efforts at these two schools in developing bilingual students and promoting bilingualism.[3] Media coverage of the program created much community awareness and support for the program. Numerous districts throughout the city, state, and nation became aware of the program. Some local and state districts sent teachers to visit these two campuses and were provided onsite training by the two-way bilingual immersion teachers.

SCHOOL BOARD SUPPORT

One school board member who, during the Spring 1996 parent sessions, made the rounds of many of the meetings would ask to speak and would say "the school board members will be voting on this in March. We want to hear from you and your concerns and the last thing we want is to divide the community. This program has already cost us money and it will cost us more money. So we definitely want to hear your concerns. If the community does not want it then we will not have it next year."

The school board was evenly divided in the support of the two-way program. Some of the school board members did not understand the model and were convinced that the research findings could not be duplicated in San Antonio. As they attended the parent awareness session, they became more informed, and as the parents expressed support, they also began to express more support. However, a couple of the school board members continued not only to ask very critical questions, as is their role as elected officials, but to lobby other members and parents to withhold support. During the 5 years, the two-way program came under full review by the school board three times; although board support was not unanimous, the program continues to be supported by the school board members.

CONCLUSION

The parents that came to the parent awareness sessions demonstrated that they valued schooling. They were aware of the importance of learning

---

[3] In 1998, the Hispanic Chamber of Commerce initiated a campaign called "Imaginate" with a series of public service ads in the local media that promoted the advantages of being bilingual. The Chamber made a presentation at the National Association for Bilingual Education Conference in 1999.

English and equated this with being able to succeed not only in school but also for further schooling and for job opportunities. While many voiced valuing Spanish, they often referred to their own limited opportunities and the fact that they wanted more for their children. As parents learned about the two-way bilingual immersion program, they voiced support and opposition based on their lived experiences. Over the years, as the parents continued attending meetings and training, many of the parents became involved not only in the classroom but also in assuming leadership roles. They were particularly instrumental in voicing their support whenever they thought that the program might be in jeopardy. They became comfortable speaking about the program to policy committees and to the school board. In fact, in 2000, when the program was under considerable pressure, the parents mobilized, organized, and made educated and emotional presentations to the superintendent and a task group of the school board. As Freeman (1998) argued, these educators and parents understood "that ongoing communication is necessary for them to negotiate how to work together to develop a shared understanding of what their common goals are, and then about how they can work together to reach those goals" (p. 148). The principals attributed the continuation of the program to the leadership and the political influence exercised by parents of children in the two-way bilingual immersion bilingual program.

4

Oral Language Practices

As the children returned from lunch and put away their lunch bags, toys, and snacks, they chattered in Spanish and English. Sofia asked Mari, "After school will you walk home with me?" Across the room, Michael pushed Tony saying to him, "That sticker is mine, *lo traje de mi casa*" (I brought it from home). Tony replied, *"No es mío, lo sacaste de mi* desk" (No it is mine, you took it out of my desk). Ms. Gallego, a second-grade teacher, walked across the room and said:

Teacher:	*Mientras guardan sus cosas, voy a repasar la lista de permisos para el viaje de la semana que viene. Hay varias personas que no han conseguido o regresado el permiso de sus padres. Ramón, ¿tú llevaste el permiso a casa?* While you put away your things, I will review the list of permissions for the [field] trip for next week. There are several persons who have not gotten or returned your parent's permission. Ramon, did you take the permission home?
Ramón:	*Sí maestra, pero mi mamá se le olvido firmarlo.* Yes teacher, but my mother forgot to sign it.
Teacher:	*Hay que traerlo para el viernes o no podrás ir al viaje de campo de clase. Carla, ¿dónde está tu permiso?* You have to bring it by Friday or you will not be able to go on the class [field] trip. Carla, where is your permission?
Carla:	My mom forgot to give it to me.

The teacher looked up at Carla and waited about three or four seconds; Carla wiggled in her chair and repeated in Spanish:

Carla: *Se le olvidó a mi mamá dármelo.*
              My mother forgot [it slipped her mind] to give it to me.

This common everyday classroom event illustrates the use of oral language and a practice—wait time[1]—that evolved over the years as teachers struggled with stimulating and encouraging children, and especially second language learners, to demonstrate their understanding and to take risks speaking. As the two-way bilingual immersion teachers discussed, planned, practiced, and evaluated ways to assist children with their oral language development, some common practices were shared across the grade levels. While striving to accept children's communicative acts, teachers tried to balance, on the one hand, "not pressuring" for oral production and, on the other, encouraging children to produce oral language, especially the second language. In the preceding example, the teacher initiated the conversation in Spanish, signaling to the children that this is Spanish time. As she began to call on individual children, she allowed enough "wait time" for the children to self-monitor the language of the communication and make switches between languages before she continued.

A major hypothesis of two-way bilingual immersion education is that the presence of students who are native speakers of each language will create the need to use both languages and students will have the available resources in each other to stimulate them to communicate. Thus, children will assist each other in learning the second language. In this chapter, I discuss the communication and oral language practices of these 14 two-way bilingual immersion classrooms. I describe some common communicative and language learning practices that were used across these classrooms, and especially those activities designed to stimulate language learning and oral language production. Some common themes and behaviors emerged that children and teachers utilized for communicating and for making language choices. Children actively made choices about participating in certain activities, about interacting with the environment, and most importantly, about interacting with peers. Many of children's choices appeared

---

[1] Cazden (1988) described how when a teacher uses "wait-time," that is, waiting for three seconds or more, students speak longer and in more detail.

to be related to individual characteristics, for example, social style, communicative need, and risk taking. Children seemed to have less choice about interacting with the teacher although, at the primary level, oral production for second language students was not demanded. Teachers encouraged nonverbal responses in almost all interactions. As in any classroom, there were some instances where children appeared to passively resist participating in certain communications and interactions with the teacher. What follows are descriptions of the sociolinguistic environment, the teacher–student and student–student communications, the struggle to make input comprehensible, and the relation of language and learning in these classrooms.

THE SOCIOLINGUISTIC ENVIRONMENT

Teachers strived to create classroom environments that not only reflected the language policies of the two-way bilingual immersion model but also stimulated language use through social and interpersonal interactions. The aim was to create physical and linguistic spaces that provided multiple opportunities and partners for children where they could develop communicative competence.[2] The expectation was for children to develop the ability to handle the sociolinguistic and discourse aspects of communication in both languages.

Some factors that the teachers attended to in the design of the physical and linguistic environment included (a) creating spaces for small group and peer interactions, (b) making print and materials available in Spanish and English, (c) thinking and being aware of the language levels—semantics and syntax—used for communication and instruction, and (d) informing and sharing language strategies with teachers and staff that provided support activities, such as library visits, physical education, and music.

The physical and linguistic environment of each classroom varied with the personality of the teachers and the personality of the students and evolved over the years. Most teachers described similar goals for their classroom organization. Through careful attention to the classroom envi-

---

[2]Communicative competence within a community of practice, as conceptualized by Hymes (1972), is concerned with both verbal and nonverbal communication within a situated context where form and function are integrally related.

ronments, they hoped to engage children in activity that was accompanied by language, as one teacher said, "to provide opportunities where children can talk or communicate in any way they can." The social settings provided meaningful contacts between learners in which learning of each other's language could take place. Thus, through specific social interactions between students and teachers, among students, students and their environment, and students and texts, children would stimulate language use, practice, and development for each other. In these settings, the children's need to communicate and the children's social styles contributed to their willingness and ability to interact in their first and second languages.

Teachers understood the role of social context, as described by Wong Fillmore (1991), in assisting children to acquire a second language. To promote social interactions among students across language strengths, teachers said again and again, "you have to plan the groups." Teachers often spoke about the social characteristics of children in deciding on their grouping strategies. Some teachers grouped more social children with less social children at the beginning of the year to assure that there would be an initiator of the communication. One primary teacher described her observations and the reason for assessing children's sociability.

> If you put two or three shy children together, sometimes they will communicate with just one word or gestures or work without speaking. But, on the other hand, I have also seen a more talkative child dominate all the conversation. The teacher has to observe and try different combinations.

The primary teachers paid a lot of attention to the physical environment where small groups of children could interact socially and linguistically while working on developmental and academic tasks. They organized centers, such as library, listening, housekeeping, manipulative tools, writing, art, science, and computer. Most of the time in most of these primary classrooms, the children were free to interact at these centers in either language. However, through the placement of materials within these centers, the teachers attempted to signal or stimulate the use of one or the other language. For example, the listening center might for a time have only Spanish tapes of poems, songs, and stories; the computer would have software and virtual books in Spanish; or the writing center would have Spanish alphabet letters, Spanish sentence patterns or story starters, and Spanish text on the center partitions/walls. The center environment provided students with multiple opportunities for oral language development, that is, for talking about what they were doing, role playing, and posing each other questions. For example, as a group of first graders viewed a video in English at the listening/viewing center, Marta commented to Julian, *"son tiburones"* (They are sharks), Julian responded, "Sharks *son tiburones."* Enrique asked, *"¿Cómo se dice* (How do you say) school of goldfish?" Marta responded, *"una escula de pescados"* (a school of fish) as everyone giggled. In some classrooms, students were free to choose centers and partners. Other teachers assigned students in groups on rotation in consideration of students' social skills and to assure that English speakers and Spanish speakers worked at the centers together.

At the intermediate and upper grades, the spaces created for social and linguistic interaction included a mix of some centers and more group work around academic tasks. In some classes, students worked in cooperative groups at centers, tables, or groupings of four or five desks. All classrooms used mixed-language grouping, especially in centers and cooperative learning activities. The cooperative groups were loosely structured; that is, children did not have assigned roles in most cases or most of the time. A third-grade teacher, who used the more structured cooperative groups, reported that "the purpose of the cooperative groups is to stimulate communication as kids do science and social studies projects." The teachers described these cooperative groups and classroom arrangements as spaces that permitted children to explore and display their language use and language strengths across the continuum of both language systems and content areas.

In 2000–2001, the two-way bilingual immersion teachers, working over a number of planning sessions, developed an observation checklist that they considered important for the implementation of two-way bilingual immersion (see Fig. 4.1). The observation checklist incorporates sections dealing with the linguistic environment.

TEACHER–STUDENT COMMUNICATION

Teachers often spoke about their role as "language model" that went beyond the traditional teacher's role. In addition to monitoring social interactions among peers, teachers paid much attention to their role as partner

SAN ANTONIO INDEPENDENT SCHOOL DISTRICT
TWO-WAY CLASSROOM OBSERVATION CHECKLIST

Teacher _____ Date _____

School _____ Observer _____

Number of Students _____ Content Area _____

Time of Observation _____

I PHYSICAL ENVIRONMENT

1 Environment	YES	NO	N/A
a. labels and signs in Spanish with concrete picture cues.			
b. student work displayed (higher order learning is evident).			
c. word walls in Spanish with contextual cues.			
d. display of different texts (genre).			
e. periodic change of environmental print.			
f. print reflects student involvement.			
g. teacher expectations of students are evident through displays (messages, student work, group project).			

2 Classroom Organization	YES	NO	N/A
a. library center			
b. writing center			
c. thematic center (resources/ collections)			
d. space (or plan) for partner and small group as well as large group activities).			
e. listening area/center (recorded books, activities)			
f. manipulative area/ center			
g. space for physical activity			
h. technology and software			

II. CURRICULUM

1 Planning & Assessment	Observed	Not Observed	N/A
a. team planning (grade level, majority/ minority language, special education, support teacher) for assessment (language & achievement) and instruction.			
b. cross-level planning (dual language)			
c. communication and outreach to parents			
d. coordination and organization of teaching objectives & materials (lesson plan book).			

2 Classroom Implementation	Observed	Observed	N/A
a. modeling minority language with staff/parents/ students.			
b. parent lead learning activities (e.g. parents reading to children).			
c. active participation in learning (hand-on, pairs/partners, cooperative groups).			
d. higher-order level questions/ discussion			
e. teacher providing periodic feedback to individual students conferencing).			
f. provide instruction appropriate for grade level, especially at 3rd-5th grade.			
g. periodic assessment of objectives mastery at grade level for all content areas			

FIG. 4.1.   Observation checklist.

III. TEACHER/ STUDENT INTERACTION & COMPREHENSIBLE INPUT

1 Concrete/ Visual	Observed	Not Observed	N/A
a. uses concrete contextual references (visuals, regalia)			
b. uses gesturing and physical expressions to accompany language.			
c. demonstrate and models expected learning (book handling, science thinking).			
d. children will use/interact with classroom labels/ print/roles (meteorólogo).			

2 Language Error Correction	Observed	Observed	N/A
a. modeling in L1.			
b. accepting of L1 and L2.			
c. modeling for error correction.			
d. use of rich vocabulary.			
e. recognize/ respect silent period.			
f. maintaining separation of languages.			

3 Sheltered Instruction for Spanish instruction and ESL.	Observed	Not Observed	N/A
a. preview/ review (topics).			
b. connect to prior knowledge/ experience.			
c. identify/ connect to children's interest.			
d. multiple level questioning (targeted to students).			
e. make connections to culture and cultural schemata.			
f. accept students assistance to each other with language (restating, translating, prompting, etc).			
g. check frequently for understanding.			
h. uses multiple cues (organizers, graphics, examples).			
I. uses wait time for student response.			
j. accepts non-verbal responses (allowing for silent period).			

4 Mediated Learning	Observed	Not Observed	N/A
a. provide multiple opportunities for oral language development (student posing questions, acting out, role playing, readers theater, student partners/ pairing, projects).			
b. provide an environment and activity designs that encourage students to ask questions and carry out research.			
c. demonstrate metacognitive process to provide scaffolding to assist students in making connections.			
d. uses mixed-language grouping especially in centers and cooperative learning activities.			

IV. CULTURE/ COMMUNITY INVOLVEMENT

	YES	NO	N/A
1 create opportunities for families to participate and be visible in school.			
2 work with parents using "funds of knowledge."			
3 use and display authentic literature that reflects and is relevant for the student's culture in the given two-way school.			
4 use local community resources for instruction, mentoring, tutoring, etc.			
5 classroom instruction and interactions should reflect and value the cultural traditions (buenos modales, ser servicial, consejos, family ties, meriendas, celebrations, holidays).			
6 demonstrate awareness and evidence of study of other cultures and identifying universals.			

FIG. 4.1. *(Continued)*

in the communicative acts. Teachers spoke about these communicative acts as separate from language used more explicitly to teach academic content. In these two-way bilingual immersion classrooms, teachers helped children understand language by focusing on communication and the communicative act. They used multiple strategies that were specifically targeted to the linguistic, social, and cognitive needs of the children to accomplish this communicative goal. Because at all times the classroom language was a second language for half of the class, teachers were very much aware of the special need to attend to the social and pragmatic features of the language used for communication. I have organized the practices I observed across the grades around the topics of (a) wait time, (b) say it in any language, (c) think in Spanish/English, (d) ask someone, (e) pass and return, and (f) use of print for oral communication.

Wait Time in Oral Communication

The strategy of creating space for children to respond to a teacher-initiated communicative act that was most widely used by this group of teachers was wait time. After making a comment or asking a question that was often accompanied with gestures, the teachers would allow four to five seconds before repeating or prompting the child to respond. The response that teachers waited for differed based on the purpose of the communication; thus, often the wait time would allow a child to provide a nonverbal response that demonstrated understanding of the language but did not necessarily require oral production. At other times, the communication required oral production and the wait time allowed the child to organize a response, especially if the child was expected to respond in his/her second language.

Wait time was also often used to get children to switch the language of the response to match the language of the teacher; this was a common strategy used by teachers, especially at the primary and intermediate grade levels. In the example at the beginning of the chapter, the wait time allowed Carla to switch languages and to demonstrate competence and performance[3] in her second language. Carla used the reflexive expression

---

[3] *Competence* is used here in the sense that the child is able to create a sentence that demonstrates some internalization of the grammar of the language. *Performance* is used in the sense that the child is able to orally produce or use the language.

se le olvidó (it slipped her mind) followed by the subject; this showed a sophisticated ability to use her second language in spite of the initial hesitation. This expression is part of the everyday discourse of the community and the children in the class. It is possible that Carla learned the sociolinguistic appropriateness of the use of this expression in her social interactions. The wait time allowed Carla to process and organize a response. In this example, Carla does not appear to translate from her English response because she restructured the syntax; that is, had she translated she would have started with "my mom" or *mi mamá*. Instead, the wait time allowed her to find a way of expressing a response that is sociolinguistically appropriate.

Say It in Any Language

In order to create safe environments where children would take risks in their communicative acts, teachers stressed the need to encourage the use of all their developing language skills—in both Spanish and English. Teachers encouraged children to talk and communicate using all their developing language skills. At the primary grade levels, teachers encouraged and scaffold children's attempts and approximations. For example, in a first grade class, the teacher initiated the conversation by saying to Ana, *"Alguien trae un nuevo corte de pelo"* (Someone has a new hair cut). Ana responded, *"tía corto"* (aunt cut), and the teacher said, *"Que bien, te lo corto tu tía"* (That [is] good, your aunt cut it for you). The teacher, by saying *que bien,* reinforced the child's response—perhaps also complimenting the hair cut—and scaffolded by incorporating the child's words into her turn while maintaining a natural conversational tone.

Many nonverbal responses were accepted and accompanied by the teacher verbalizing the response for the child. For example, in a kindergarten classroom, the pet was moved while the teacher and children were at lunch. On returning to the classroom, the teacher asked, *"¿Dónde está la mascota?"* (Where is the pet?). Marcos pointed to a small table in the corner and the teacher said, *"Buen ojo Marcos, esta sobre la mesita"* (Good eye Marcos, it is on the little table). Marcos said, *"Está en la mesa"* (it is on the table). Marcos picked out elements of the teacher's language, changed *mesita* to *mesa,* showing some awareness of the semantic relationships, and practiced oral production. This strategy and the child's response were similar to strategies used by parents with young children in early language development. One teacher reported that "having second language children in the class at all times forces me to focus on communication and meaning. I can't assume that children understand what I am saying so I have to look closely and help children show me what they understand."

The teachers talked about talk in their classrooms. They called children's attention to ways of saying things and alternative responses. The teachers, for the most part, attempted to model standard Spanish and English classroom language, but recognized, encouraged, and reinforced the communicative act and the children's demonstration of their developing language. For example, in a second-grade class, Marcela and the teacher had the following exchange:

Marcela: *Me gusta la historia de Chato.*[4]
I like Chato's story.

Teacher: *El cuento de Chato es divertido, a mí también me gusta.*
Chato's story is entertaining, I like it, too.

Marcela: *La historia de Chato es* funny.
Chato's story is funny

Teacher: *Sí, divertido es* funny*, pero también quiero que pienses porque dices que es historia.*
Yes, entertaining is funny, but also, I want for you to think about why you say history.

The teacher first focused on reinforcing and extending Marcela's language by saying that she also liked the story and used the word *divertido* to describe it. When Marcela used the English word *funny* to show that she understood or guessed the meaning of *divertido,* the teacher accepted and reinforced this but then moved on to challenge Marcela to think about her Spanish word choice for "story." Marcela was quiet for three or four seconds, appeared to be thinking, before responding.

Marcela: *Es cuento pero historia es así como el inglés* story.
It is story but history is like the English [word] story.

Teacher: *Muy bien dicho.*
Very well said.

---

[4] The child is referring to Gary Soto's *Chato y su cena/Chato's kitchen* (1997).

Marcela appeared to evaluate her choice saying that perhaps the more appropriate word was *cuento,* but that her choice *historia* sounded like the English word *story.* The teacher reinforced Marcela's thinking and language saying *muy bien dicho,* without correcting or didactically evaluating her choices.

Think in Spanish/English

As in Marcela's example, teachers often asked children to think about the language choices and language use. Teachers guided children to view language use and meaning making as a cognitive task. They demonstrated metalinguistic processes to provide scaffolding to assist students in making connections. As children progressed to the intermediate and upper grades, teachers often suggested that children think about what they wanted to say in their dominant language and how it might be said in the second language.

This think-in-Spanish/English strategy was used more often in the context of instructional conversations.[5] For example, in a third-grade class during a discussion of the vocabulary following a read aloud, the teacher asked Adriana for a definition. When Adriana said she does not know the word in Spanish, the teacher first used the say-it-in-any-language strategy and then, as the communication proceeded, the teacher used the think-in-the-other-language strategy.

> **Teacher:**   *¿Qué es parientes?*
> What is relatives?
>
> **Adriana:**   *No lo sé en español.*
> I do not know it in Spanish.
>
> **Teacher:**   *Bueno, di lo que sabes.*
> Well, say what you know.
>
> **Adriana:**   *Parientes es* relation or relations *en inglés.*
> Relation is relation or relations in English.

---

[5] Tharp and Gallimore (1988) defined and described the use of instructional conversations for second language learning. The focus of instructional conversations is to use academic or literate discourse within the context of natural or real conversations where students and teachers are working and learning. This would be as opposed to the generally used teacher initiation, response, and evaluation approach to instruction.

Teacher: *Bueno, piensa en español.*
Well, think in Spanish.

Adriana: *Familiares como abuelo, tíos, primos.*
Family [members] like grandfather, uncles, cousins.

Teacher: *¡Muy bien!*
Very good!

The teacher encouraged Adriana to say, or become aware of, what she knew and then suggested that she think about it in Spanish. By first focusing on what she did know, Adriana was perhaps able to turn her attention to how to verbalize it in the second language.

Teachers talked about the need to use and reinforce metalinguistic strategies for helping children to think about language. They hoped that children would use metalinguistic strategies to examine and evaluate their language knowledge. Children in most classrooms were aware of the relationship between the two languages and, like Marcel in the example in the previous section, often discussed the similarities and differences. For example, a fourth-grade teacher, while conducting a rather common calendar classroom activity, called out the name of the month and date and asked if anyone knew the name of the new month.

Teacher: *Hoy estamos estrenando[6] un mes nuevo, ¿qué es?*
Today, we are (starting) a new month, which is?

Carlos: *El primero de* March.
The first of March.

Teacher: *El primero de . . .* [wait time]
The first of . . . [wait time]

Antonio: *Es, marzo en español.*
It is, March in Spanish.

Carlos: *Marzo y* March*, casi suenan iguales. ¿Vienen de la misma raíz?*
March/March, [they] almost sound the same. Do they come from the same root word?

---

[6] The word *estrenar* has a unique cultural referent for which an equivalent word does not exist in English. The old English word meaning "to handsel" is perhaps the closest approximation. In Spanish, the word *estrenar* means to use or to do something for the first time (Pérez & Torres-Guzmán, 2002).

Teacher: *Sí, suenan semejantemente. Tú Carlos, y puedes escoger*
                alguien que te ayude, pueden investigar el origen del nombre
                del mes—marzo.
                Yes, they sound similarly. You Carlos, and you can choose
                someone to help you, investigate the origin of the name of the
                month—March.

Carlos made an observation about similarities in the Spanish and English name of the month and asked if they share a root word or etymology.
The teacher encouraged Carlos to follow up on his observation and to
investigate the linguistic relationship between the two words.

Through the teacher's use of this metalinguistic strategy of asking children to think in the other language, students made connections and made
sense of their developing language system(s). Especially at the intermediate and upper grades, children were challenged and challenged themselves
to detect the regularities and similarities across languages.

Ask Someone

Teachers encouraged children to assist each other with oral production.
Although some younger students were reluctant to produce oral language
and use the second language to communicate with the teacher or among
themselves, by the first grade, most of the students would respond to conversations initiated in the second language. However, when children struggled to respond in the second language, the teachers and children sometimes used the ask-someone strategy. One teacher described this strategy
as a way of modeling for children the expectation for cross-language communication and language brokering. Although many Spanish-speaking
children had engaged in assisting their families with language brokering,[7]
that is, not only translating but interpreting the meaning for parents who
may not speak English, this skill had not been one that most teachers recognized and encouraged. In these classrooms, language brokering was the
expectation. At the primary level, children were often asked *"quieres
ayuda"* and "do you need help," and children could then turn to a buddy or

---

[7] See McQuillan and Tse (1995) and Tse (1995) for a discussion of language brokering.
Many second language learners, even those reported as relatively low school achievers,
engage in translating and interpreting a variety of linguistically sophisticated documents
for parents and other community members.

classmate for help understanding or saying something. However, teachers also attempted to manage the space so the children had enough time to comprehend and organize responses before asking for help. Thus, teachers also discouraged unsolicited help, often saying, *"Espera, no ha pedido ayuda"* (Wait, he/she has not asked for help).

In the upper grades, this strategy was often initiated by children and accepted by the teacher. For example, when a teacher asked a child a question or made a comment she/he did not understand, the child said, *"¿Puedo preguntarle a alquien?"* or "Can I ask someone?" if they were unsure of the communication. Children also used the strategy to communicate among themselves, often asking each other, *"¿Cómo se dice?"* or "How do you say it?" as in the Marta and Julian example at the listening/viewing center described previously in this chapter.

Pass and Return

Teachers attended to personality and social preferences of the individual children. They were aware of the reluctance of some children to speak with the teacher in Spanish or English. Teachers considered children's sociability, communicative need, risk taking, and self-confidence in tailoring their language learning strategies. Thus, all but one teacher included a pass and return strategy in their repertoire. Children could ask for more time before producing an oral response by just saying *"más tiempo," "estoy pensando,"* "pass," "come back, please." This did not mean that children could get out of being engaged in the classroom communication or learning. In most cases I observed, the teacher returned after two or three turns to the child that had passed and provided an opportunity for the child to participate.

Use of Print for Oral Communication

This strategy used classroom print materials, which were often accompanied with pictures or visual cues to help children associate, understand, and produce language for communication. From the start, teachers integrated print and writing in the oral language activities. At the primary level, print and visuals were often used by the children, who pointed more to the picture than the word, but, nonetheless, made the connection between the spoken word and the visual/print referents. At the intermediate and upper grades, the children and teachers often used classroom labels, word walls, and bulletin boards as stimulus for responses.

Table 4.1 gives the tallies of the six strategies described by school and grade level. As I observed the teachers and students using these strategies, it was apparent that many of these strategies had evolved over time and that the children sometimes carried them from one grade level to the next. That is, occasionally a child, referred to how they made meaning, got

TABLE 4.1
Teacher/Student Strategies for Oral Responses
per Observation Segment

Type	Grade Level	Bonham		Storm	
		N	%	N	%
Wait time	K–1	15	30	22	35
	2–3	13	27	15	30
	4–5	5	10	7	15
Say it in any language	K–1	10	20	6	10
	2–3	11	23	10	20
	4–5	10	20	11	21
Think in Spanish/English	K–1	8	16	9	15
	2–3	6	11	8	17
	4–5	12	25	10	20
Ask someone	K–1	6	12	11	20
	2–3	5	10	6	13
	4–5	7	15	7	14
Pass and return	K–1	4	8	4	5
	2–3	5	9	5	10
	4–5	10	20	9	18
Use of print	K–1	7	14	7	15
	2–3	10	20	5	10
	4–5	5	10	6	12

Note. Observation segment here means field notes for a given activity regardless of length of time. Thus, within the same observation field notes, if the activity changed (story reading to math), a new segment would be designated. Multiple strategies are double counted. Percentages are per grade level; thus, grade levels should add up to 100%.

assistance, or spoke in a previous grade. Because the children progressed as cohorts, teachers also reported that sometimes they noticed the children used the same strategy, and they consulted the previous teacher to ask about the practice. What was most obvious was that as children progressed they were synthesizing their language learning from previous years.

INSTRUCTIONAL LANGUAGE

In addition to the language used for communication, teachers focused much attention on the language used for instruction and the language used for learning. The strategies for integrating language and academic content instruction and learning, especially at the primary level, emerged and evolved over the 5 years of the development of the program. Teachers based many of their activities on what they had learned from studying second language theory (Asher, 1977; Cummins, 1981, 1984; Chamot & O'Malley, 1986; Krashen, 1982; Tharp & Gallimore, 1988) and on their own and their students' backgrounds and the uses of oral language in these communities.

Making Language Comprehensible

Although the teachers had studied the literature on second language learning and teaching, the everyday implementation of a model of language learning "emerged" as teachers experienced, discussed, and experimented with numerous techniques and approaches. The teachers attempted to implement their understanding of Cummins' (1981) notion of *contextualized language*[8] and Krashen's (1982) notion of *comprehensible input*[9] in their context. They also integrated language learning with content learn-

---

[8]Cummins (1981, 1984) described communicative proficiency along two continuums: (a) context-embedded to context-reduced—context-embedded communication relying on participants negotiating meaning using situational, linguistic and paralinguistic cues; and cognitively undemanding to cognitively demanding communicative tasks.

[9]Krashen (1982) described *comprehensible input* as meaningful language directed at second language learners in conditions that are optimal allowing learners to make meaning of most of the communication. Comprehensible input should also include new language that can be understood when accompanied by planned contextual strategies, for example, using concrete referents, paralinguistics, or other contextual support.

ing. Teachers' ideas for making input comprehensible and making children aware of ways of talking and using academic language[10] in content learning came to include (a) organizing talk around concrete referents or visual representations; (b) repeating, restating, and paraphrasing often; (c) continuous checking for nonverbal as well as verbal signs of comprehension; and (d) talking about, expanding on, and extending on topics and comments introduced by the children.

An example of how a fourth-grade teacher made input comprehensible was through the adaptation and use of strategies commonly known as Total Physical Response (TPR)[11] as she attempted to make a math lesson taught in Spanish comprehensible for everyone. The teacher reported she did not "consciously" use these techniques every day because "at this grade level they understand almost everything," except that the mathematics lesson she had planned for this day included "new concepts requiring special attention to comprehensible language."

Teacher: *Los conceptos de hoy son translación, reflexión, rotación, y transformación de figuras. La primer muestra es de translación. Una figura se mueve de un lado a otro sin dar vuelta ninguna.*
Today's concepts are translation, reflection, rotation, and transformation of figures. The first demonstration is translation. One figure moves from one side to another without giving any turn at all.

The teacher moved from one side to the other; then, she moved a triangle over a piece of graph paper that was divided into quarters from the top left quarter to the top right quarter.

Teacher: *Tomás, muéstrame translación.*
Tomás show me translation.

Tomás stood and slid a couple of steps over, sat down, and moved his paper triangle across his quartered graphing paper.

---

[10]Cummins (1984) explained the difference between basic interpersonal communication skills (BICS) and the cognitive/academic language proficiency skills (CALPS) and their role in social communication and in academic achievement. For a content-based model of language learning, see Chamot and O'Malley (1986).

[11]Total Physical Response (TPR) is a language teaching method developed by Asher (1977) in which commands are given in the second language and the learner demonstrates understanding through a physical response.

Tomás: *Es translación.*
               It is translation.

Teacher: *Bien, ahora, rotación es cuando la figura da rotación o vuelta*
               de 360 grados.
               Well, now rotation, is when a figure rotates or turns 360
               degrees.

The teacher spun around. Then she rotated the triangle over the graph
paper.

Teacher: *Julia, muéstrame rotación.*
               Julia, show me rotation.

Julia stood and spun around, sat down, and rotated her paper triangle over
her graph paper.

Julia: *Esto es rotación, cuando da la vuelta completa.*
               This is rotation, when it gives a complete turn.

Teacher: *Una vuelta de tres- trescientos sesenta grados.*
               A turn of three- 360 degrees.

Julia: *Rotación es cuando la figura da vuelta de tres-cientos sesenta*
               grados.
               Rotation is when the figure gives a turn of 360 degrees.

Teacher: *Bueno, reflexión es cuando la figura da media vuelta de 180*
               grados, o como que se está viendo cara a cara en un espejo.
               Well, reflection is when the figure gives a half turn of 180
               degrees, or like it is looking face to face in a mirror.

The teacher held her hand out to her side, then brought it up to her face as
if it were a mirror. She then took the triangle and turned it 180 degrees over
the graph paper.

In this example, the teacher created context and organized talk around
visible referents. Both teacher and students combined physical actions
with language use. The teacher repeated with very little variation the same
procedures and language structures, thus allowing children to focus on
understanding the geometry concepts. She often checked children's understanding and prompted for precise use of language, as when she repeats for
Julia *una vuelta de trescientos sesenta grados,* while gradually building on
the concepts.

Attention to second language learning techniques and, in particular, comprehensible input, was much more visible in the primary and inter- mediate grades. The kindergarten and first-grade teachers routinely used objects, pictures, and gestures to accompany language. They also used questions and statements that were shorter and more specific. Even though they used many restatements, these restatements did not significantly vary from the original. For example, in discussing a picture, the teacher pointed to her eyes, then to the picture, and said, *"veo seis personas en el dibujo"* (I see six persons in the picture). She looks around to check for children's signs of comprehension and repeats, *"Yo veo seis personas"* (I see six per- sons). As children's oral language progressed, teachers integrated more talk about learning in ways that helped students to relate the new learning to their experience. As one second-grade teacher stated, "We have decided that asking open-ended questions that require inferencing or synthesis allows children to say what they know—instead of just responding with one word or a phrase—and it also challenges or gets them to use higher order thinking skills." There were many more open-ended questions. Some of these questions required children to make connections to home experiences; for example, in a first-grade classroom, the discussion was about chores and responsibilities and the teacher asks, *"¿Cuáles son algu- nas tareas que los niños pueden llevar en casa?"* (What are some chores that children can have [carry] at home?) Other open-ended questions encouraged children to use the language of the academic activity or text and relate it to their experience. For example, a second-grade teacher asked, *"El texto dice que 'la gente ha construido máquinas para poder viajar más y más rápido' ¿Cuáles de estas máquinas se ven in San Anto- nio?"* (The text says that 'the people have constructed machines to be able to travel more and more rapidly.' Which of these machines can be seen in San Antonio?)

In the intermediate and upper grades, the teachers also used specific second language teaching techniques, such as TPR or preview/review, principally when they were introducing new concepts that they considered difficult. They reported that these techniques actually helped everyone "catch on" more quickly regardless of the language of instruction and whether it was a first or second language for any given child. A third-grade teacher said, "These are just good teaching practices, you provide context, you demonstrate, you repeat, and you check for understanding—all best practices."

Language and Mediated Learning

Teachers often spoke of the need to assist children in becoming aware of how their developing social language could help them to mediate[12] understanding of academic language and learning. They encouraged students to actively monitor their understanding of the language of instruction. Teachers taught children to ask questions, get clarification, restate what they were hearing or reading, and translate for themselves if necessary. For example, in a second-grade classroom, Rosa was working on a set of questions related to the study of turtles at the science center and said to herself, "*tortugas de aqua dulce y tortugas de mar* (freshwater turtles and sea turtles) *aqua dulce* can't be sweet water like *aqua de melon* (melon water). It's, it's ocean turtles and river turtles." Rosa first thinks about her understanding of *aqua dulce* in a sociocultural context, then interprets and clarifies what it might mean in the context of a science activity.

Teachers hoped that as students used their first and second languages to mediate their learning, they would internalize these same language strategies for later learning. For example, in a fourth-grade classroom, some children used their first language to mediate an arithmetic exercise that required the use of multiple operations. The children had a chart with numbers called the "100 chart" and markers. The teacher called out a problem, for example, *cinco por ocho menos siete* (five times eight minus seven), and the children worked the problem, supposedly in their heads, and placed a marker on the number on the chart that answered the problem. The teacher called out the problems at a quick pace, repeating them twice. The children appeared to be very familiar with the routine, all were on task, and there was only one comment from one child who said, "*más despacio*" (more slowly). At the end of the activity the children checked their answers by the design made on the card. Five of the 18 children spoke in audible tones that hinted to the use of language to mediate or process the

---

[12]Mediated learning is used here in the sense of Vygotsky's (1978) notion of mediation between adult and child within formal instruction and the use or manipulation of language as central to the mediation.

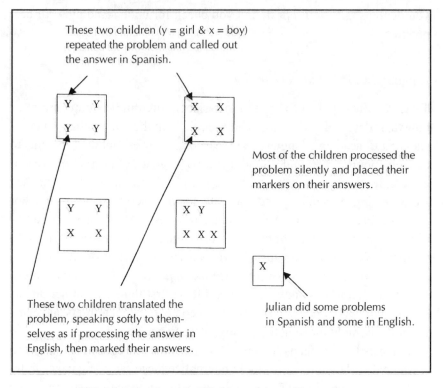

FIG. 4.2.   Fourth-grade 100 chart activity and language use.

information as they arrived at their answers. Figure 4.2 illustrates the organization of the class and how the children sat at tables in mixed-language groups, except for Julian, who sat by himself.

CONCLUSION

In these 14 two-way bilingual immersion classrooms, the presence of students who were native speakers of each language stimulated students to communicate and assist each other in using and learning the second language. The classroom environments reflected the language policies of the two-way bilingual immersion model and stimulated language use through social and interpersonal interactions. Four of the teachers talked about their knowledge of Wong Fillmore's (1991) model of language learning in social context and the need to attend to social context in their classrooms.

Opportunities were provided for students to use both languages socially and for academic tasks. As learning and experience were gained by the students and teachers, they adjusted the nature of the social interactions, the language task, and the strategy was tailored to the specific content. In the primary grades, the most used strategies were "wait-time" and "ask-someone," but as children moved to the upper elementary grades the strategies most used were "say-it-in-any-language" and "think in Spanish/English." Together, this set of strategies helped children develop metalinguistic and metacognitive strategies for communicating and making meaning.

However, one point discussed by Valdés (1997), as well as the Bonham and Storm teachers, was who benefits from the adjustment of the language of instruction. Some researchers and policymakers have been concerned about whether the presence of English speakers, during Spanish reading or math instruction in two-way bilingual immersion classrooms, creates a context where the teacher uses perhaps simplistic language and targets lower level objectives to make instruction comprehensible. I observed two types of activities in these classrooms that provided evidence to the contrary: Spanish speakers and English speakers alike were challenged and benefited from the instruction.

In the first type of activity, the teacher led instruction and encouraged more talk and thus more language development for both groups. Unlike the traditional teacher initiation–response–evaluation (IRE) pattern of lesson structuring (Cazden, 1988) found in many bilingual and mainstream classrooms, these teachers focused on assisting children with oral language production, by using many open-ended questions that could not simply be answered with a word, number, or phrase. The very same questions that required the use of more language also challenged children to think and reach higher level cognitive objectives. The teachers talked about following the strategies suggested by Chamot and O'Malley (1986) and Chamot, Dale, O'Malley, and Spanos (1992) in their content-based second language instruction. The second type of activity focused on creating more contexts for the language of lessons and learning activities. This was evident for both the Spanish and English components. The need to use visual referents, to contextualize the language, and to use physical gestures gave all the students the context for making meaning of the language of instruction. Instead of simplifying the language, due to the presence of second language learners, these teachers created contexts that scaffolded the children's understanding of the rich language exchanges that occurred in these classrooms. The language input provided by teachers and peers facilitated language experimentation and practice. As Wong Fillmore (1991) argued, these "contacts give the learners both the incentive and the opportunity to learn the new language . . . the learners make use of their social knowledge to figure out what people might be saying, given the social situation" (1991, p. 53). By creating meaningful linguistic context, children were provided multiple opportunities to participate in social and literate classroom discourse.

The role of language and communication in learning was central in the everyday activities of these two-way bilingual immersion classrooms. The children developed rich and complex patterns of communication and inter-action and learned when to use each language appropriately. They learned the sociolinguistic rules and the sociocultural values as was evident in their choices and patterns of language use. Although the children's use of language reflected the language practices of the community, especially in the use of code switching, it also differed notably. The children in these classrooms not only developed social communicative skills, but also developed language patterns and practices that were specific and signifi-cant for academic achievement.

5

Developing Literacy

A group of kindergarten children were in a corner of their classroom reading and rereading a big book in Spanish. Among the choral reading, giggling, and discussing who will lead next, Marcos said, *"Yo puedo leer, y* next year *voy a leer más inglés por que ya sé leer"* (I can read, and next year I will read more English because I already know how to read). Marcos stated his understanding of reading and, like most of the kindergarten children in the program, was reading in Spanish and beginning to talk about learning to read in English.

Down the hall in a second-grade classroom, children demonstrated their understanding of reading and meaning making. They talked about their prior experiences and how these experiences assisted them in reading the text. A group of children were attempting to read the book *Pepita Talks Twice* (Lachtman, 1995) in English, the children's second language. The teacher asked, *"¿Qué les ayudó para leer este cuento?"* (What helped you to read this story?). Marcela responded,

> *Si te ha pasado a ti como en el cuento entonces se parece y es más fácil leer. Como Pepita,* I do that, *fue fácil porque yo le digo a mi Mamá que dicen y así como Pepita le hace y- y- como como se siente. Entonces es fácil leer.*

> If the same thing has happened to you as in the story then it is similar and it is easier to read. Like Pepita, I do that, it was easy because I tell my Mother what [others] say and like Pepita does it [translate] and, and like, how she feels. Then it is easy to read.

Marcela, who has engaged in interpreting or language brokering, which is the topic of the text, claimed that her prior knowledge or personal experience with this topic assisted her in making meaning from the text. Another child, Mario, chimed in and said,

Como por ejemplo, yo puedo decirle a una persona que dice who doesn't speak or read English. *Yo sé las dos y es lo mismo pensar que dice en español o* English. It's the same.

Like for example, I can say to a person what [it] says who doesn't speak or read English. I know both and it is the same to think about what [it] says in Spanish or English. It's the same.

For Mario, his knowledge of both languages means that he can interpret a text for someone who does not speak the language; he went on to explain his understanding that interpreting is a metalinguistic and metacognitive skill. He explained that his ability to think and compare meanings across languages helped him and concluded that reading must be the same in both languages.

In the two-way bilingual immersion classrooms, as part of the adopted 90–10 model, children were taught, and they learned, to read and write in Spanish in kindergarten, first grade, and second grade. Although the teacher-directed reading and writing activities in these early grades were almost always conducted in Spanish, the children were exposed to English print and texts during the English language development portion of the curriculum. Thus, many children began to read and write in English before the formal teacher-directed English reading instruction began.

What follows is a discussion of the literacy program prescribed by the district, descriptions of the literacy activities in these classrooms, and descriptions of children becoming biliterate. I discuss (a) the observations and examples that I examined as I sought to better understand the contextual factors that influenced the literacy development of the students in these two-way bilingual immersion classrooms; (b) how the teachers implemented the balanced literacy framework, outlined in Figure 5.1, into everyday literacy practices; and (c) how students responded to literacy instruction. I attempt to identify the basic premise of this instruction, the resultant literate practices and ways of talking and thinking about literacy, and the resultant student and teacher changes that occurred over time.

Kindergarten Read Aloud 10 Minutes Daily	The teacher selects and models reading from a variety of books, including storybooks, theme-related books, Big Books, alphabet, concept, poetry, library books and non-fiction. The teacher introduces knowledge concepts, develops use of book language, and creates an interest in books and a desire to read.
Shared Reading 10 Minutes Daily	The teacher selects poetry for interactive pocket charts and Big Books that children will enjoy and actively participate in reading and rereading. Children are building a knowledge base, an understanding of print concepts, a desire to read, and phonemic awareness. Lap reading can be part of shared reading.
Phonemic Awareness and Word, Letter and Sound Activities 15 Minutes Daily	The teacher uses Hampton-Brown De Canciones a Cuentos (or Phonics and Friends) to build phonemic awareness, introduce letter–sound associations, model decoding strategies, and build emergent reading skills.
Guided Reading 55 Minutes Daily	The teacher works with small groups of 3–5 students. The teacher selects and introduces new books and supports and monitors students reading the text. During guided reading, students are introduced to a new book and reread familiar stories in addition to the new book. The teacher conducts a brief, focus lesson based on the observable needs of the students.
Literacy Centers During Guided Reading	Students not in guided reading group will circulate to literacy centers with activities set up to practice and respond to what was learned in shared and guided reading. Independent reading in centers can be pretend reading, reading pictures, retelling favorite books, rereading books from shared or guided reading. Independent reading centers: Browsing Box, Buddy Reading, Read Around the Room, Pocket Chart, Poem Box, Computer Center, Overhead Projector, ABC Center, Games and Puzzles, Writing Center, Journals, Listening Center, Dramatic Play and Classroom Library (Book Nook).
Content Area Reading	Theme-related and content area books should be utilized during the read aloud and at other times during the day.

FIG. 5.1.   Balanced literacy framework.

First and Second Grades Read Aloud 10 Minutes Daily	The teacher selects books from a variety of genres (fiction, fantasy, folktale, fable, poetry, nonfiction/informational, biography) that challenge listening comprehension and allow more complex comprehension development through discussion. The teacher models reading and thinking.
Shared Reading 10 Minutes Daily	The teacher selects Big Books, poetry for interactive pocket charts, class-created books, or writings displayed on the overhead and invites the class to enjoy and actively participate in reading, rereading, and thinking. The children are building an understanding of many skills and concepts about books and print. When shared reading skills and strategies are secure, the 10 minutes for shared reading can be transitioned into discussion groups following guided reading.
Word Work 15 Minutes Daily	First Grade: the teacher uses Hampton-Brown De Canciones a Cuentos (or Phonics and Friends) to continue to build phonemic awareness, introduce sound–symbol correspondences, model and practice decoding strategies, and apply phonics skills in reading and writing. Second Grade: the teacher uses word walls and other word-making activities to move children from phonemic awareness to fluent reading. The teacher models decoding strategies and teaches application of phonics skills.
Focus Lesson 5 Minutes Daily	The teacher demonstrates a strategy or skill to be used in reading or responding to text. The focus lesson can be done before or during guided reading.
Guided Reading 50–55 Minutes Daily	The teacher works with small groups of 3–5 students who have similar reading needs. The teacher selects and introduces new books and supports and monitors students reading the text by themselves. During guided reading, students are introduced to a new book and reread familiar stories in addition to the new book. The teacher conducts a focus lesson based on the observable needs of the students (if not already done).
Literacy Centers During Guided Reading	Students not in guided reading group will circulate to literacy centers with activities set up to practice and extend what was learned in shared and guided reading. Independent reading takes place in these centers: Classroom Library (Book Nook), Browsing Box, Buddy Reading, Read Around the Room, Pocket Chart, Poem

FIG. 5.1. *(Continued)*

	Box, Computer Center, Overhead Projector Center ABC Center, Games and Puzzles, Writing Center, Journals, Listening Center, and Dramatic Play.
Content Area Reading	The teacher reads from a content area book, demonstrating how to extract and organize information. Cross-curricular materials should be utilized during the time that other areas of study are being taught.
Third, Fourth, and Fifth Grades Read Aloud 10 Minutes Daily	The teacher reads from a chapter book, picture book, or poetry. After reading, students are allowed to free-write, comment, discuss, or just enjoy the experience. The teacher introduces knowledge and concepts, develops the use of book language, and creates an interest in books and a desire to read.
Focus Lesson #1 10 Minutes Daily	Teach students think-aloud strategies before reading the selection. These strategies are visualizing, predicting, questioning, taking notes, and recapping.
Focus Lesson #2 10 Minutes Daily	Taught after reading, teachers will instruct students in the demonstration of a comprehension extension related to the selection.
Guided Reading Rotation 40 Minutes Daily	It is suggested that the teacher divide the class into three separate guided reading groups. During this time, students must read from texts at their instructional level. When the group is not meeting with the teacher, the students should be practicing the strategies independently or with reading partners.
Independent Reading 20 Minutes Daily	Students choose a book, read for an extended period of time, and maintain a log of titles read (optional). Students may share reading experiences through book talks, discussions, or read alouds. During Independent Reading, students can be encouraged, but not required, to select books with a content area or a thematic focus.

FIG. 5.1. *(Continued)*

LITERACY PERSPECTIVE

Teachers and administrators saw the teaching and learning of literacy as crucial to the success of the two-way bilingual immersion program. Thus, next to issues of parent recruitment and participation, decisions about the teaching or reading and writing were the most discussed during the planning period. They reviewed and discussed several research articles: Lindholm (1992) and Lindholm and Fairchild (1990) for the effect of Spanish reading on English reading in two-way bilingual immersion programs; Delgado-Gaitán (1990), Goldenberg (1990), and Goldenberg and Gallimore (1991) for the structure of Spanish reading lessons and parent involvement in early literacy; Barrera, Valdés, and Cardenas (1986) for the relationship between first and second language reading or cross-language processing strategies; Hudson (1982), Langer, Bartoleme, Vasquez, and Lucas (1990), and Moll and Gonzáles (1994) for the role that background or the knowledge a reader brings plays in comprehension; and Durgunoğlu, Nagy, and Hancin-Bhatt (1993) for the transfer of Spanish phonological awareness and Spanish word recognition strategies to English word recognition. The teachers and administrators synthesized this literature through the perspective of Cummins' (1981) interdependence hypothesis.

Initially, the plan developed during the planning year called for the teacher-directed instruction in English reading and writing to begin after the children had attained fluency and second-grade level reading and writing in the district's assessment program. For most children, this occurred by the end of the second semester of the second grade. Two second-grade teachers did not provide teacher-directed English reading and writing instruction although they both used texts, such as poems, chants, and songs, as part of the English oral language lessons and both read English stories aloud to the class. The other second-grade teacher reported that she found most children were eager to start reading and writing in English and that she generally started teacher-directed English reading and writing instruction after spring break, during the second semester of the second grade. Thus, in kindergarten, first grade, and most of second grade, the teacher-directed reading and writing activities were conducted in Spanish.

The teachers fully recognized that children would attempt to read English material prior to the formal introduction of English, reading either by themselves, with other children, or in school activities beyond the two-way classroom, in the library, for example. The teachers decided that they would respond to children's requests, encourage any attempts, and provide materials as children showed interest; however, they would not, as "official policy," lead directed instruction until the children had developed fluency in reading and writing in Spanish. For the teachers, principals, and central office administrators, this was a deliberate, researched decision.

From reading the available literature and from their professional experience teaching bilingual children, the teachers assessed that most children would develop literacy in Spanish by the second grade. They also hypothesized, again from the literature and their professional experience, that if children were reading and writing with fluency and competency at grade level in Spanish, they would be able to begin reading and writing instruction in English at the same grade level. They further hypothesized that the knowledge, skills, and experiences gained in Spanish literacy would transfer to English, especially as the teaching of encoding and decoding—in particular, phonics—was taught in a cycle of reviewing and re-teaching through the third grade. Hence, children would be able to transfer many decoding and encoding skills and would be able to acquire the necessary specific skills for English reading and writing.

A teacher reported that "the balanced literacy approach, which is like an individualized reading approach, accommodates children who are at many different ability levels." Based on weekly and biweekly assessments —running records—teachers matched children with little books that were at their instructional level. Many teachers felt that this empowered them and the students to develop literacy at the children's pace. The techniques and strategies focused on language and literacy and approached skills through a variety of activities. The instruction, according to another teacher was "more teacher directed, instead of teacher centered." Another teacher agreed but added that teachers did not have much decision-making authority, as much of the instruction was "directed by the framework and the suggestions on how to teach particular skills, strategies, and texts. But we can make many decisions about the materials and the reinforcement of the skills and strategies beyond, say, the guided reading lesson."

Other teachers reported that the components of the balanced literacy, such as guided reading or writers' workshop, were beneficial because they did not previously "really understand what these words or methods meant." As teachers studied, observed, and developed experience with the balanced literacy framework, they tested and integrated their previous practices. For some, this meant an emphasis on Spanish phonics, but for most, it meant an integration of literature and content materials into the designated reading and writing language arts block of time. For all teachers, it meant extensive use of small group instruction, cooperative group activities, and individual, independent reading and writing.

SPANISH LITERACY LEARNING

During the early years of the program, there was a good amount of discussion among the kindergarten and first-grade teachers about the methods to be used for Spanish reading and writing instruction. A couple of the teachers wanted to use what they called *el método silábico*[1] (the syllabic method), which focused on teaching the vowels first and then introducing the consonants to make syllable combinations, for example, *ma, me, mi, mo, mu,* then words and sentences, for example, *Mi mamá me ama.* Other teachers wanted to integrate the phonemic and phonics instruction in the reading of a variety of texts. With the development of the district's balanced literacy framework and the State of Texas early literacy assessments—the *Tejas Lee* (Texas Reads) and Texas Primary Reading Inventory (TPRI), which are discussed in chapter 7—a blending of the two approaches evolved. Not only did children interact with whole texts using a variety of trade books (little decodable books and predictable books) and authentic children's literature[2] from the first day in kindergarten, but they also received specific phonemic awareness, phonics, and other skill instruction.

Literacy Environment and Print Awareness

The hallways and classrooms were filled with children's writing, children's art, book covers, charts, and various other types of print in Spanish and English. Much of the print environment exhibited children's works. The teachers incorporated many activities that encouraged literacy to emerge. They read to children daily—this was basically a social interaction in which the teacher and the children constructed the text together

---

[1] For a discussion of methods used in Spanish reading instruction, see Pérez & Torres-Guzmán (2002).

[2] The teachers considered instructional trade books as those which generally controlled language to teach a specific skill. These could be classified in two general categories: (a) decodable texts that focused on phonological elements, such as onset and rime, and (b) predictable books that contained a repetitive pattern that children could either decode or learn and assisted them in being successful in reading the text. Teachers talked about authentic literature as those books that authors wrote for noninstructional purposes and generally did not control either the vocabulary or the syntactic features of the text.

through a combination of reading and discussing the text, based on each participant's experience. Children brought their cultural meanings of the content as well as their developing understanding of the reading process. Teachers talked about what they—the teachers—did as they were reading. For example, one kindergarten teacher routinely announced when she was going to read. After getting a note from the principal's office she said, *"Tengo información de la oficina de la directora, voy a leerla para saber que es lo qué dice"* (I have information from the principal's office, I am going to read it to know what it says). The primary teachers modeled reading as a meaning-making process that tapped the cultural and social practices of the class and the community. They read texts and engaged the children in constructing the text together through a combination of reading and discussion.[3] However, they also routinely called children's attention and reinforced any comments children made about letters, words, and aspects of the symbolic systems, such as punctuation and numbers.

The official texts, which included basals, leveled readers, trade books, and a wide variety of other Spanish language materials had to be adapted to the balanced literacy approach.[4] One teacher stated, "Assessment is used to place students at the level of reading instruction appropriate to their own needs. This is done through the leveled readers."

Kindergarten instruction incorporated phonological awareness and emergent reading and writing, but this instruction also emphasized formal language arts and literacy conventions. One teacher summarized the focus on teaching these conventions during the first semester of kindergarten: "The students were able to explain why their written names began with capital letters, and they learned about word boundaries, punctuation, and the concept of a sentence." The children also learned about book

---

[3]Gee (1991) views literacy as a socially constructed phenomena that is more than the traditional notion of reading and writing. Literacy as social practice describes the complex set of interactions, practices, and abilities that are used by the reader and writer within a specific sociocultural setting to make or recreate the meaning of a text. Other researchers (Adams, 1990; Rayner & Pollatsek, 1989) view literacy from psycholinguistic perspective that requires the reader to use specific knowledge about phonological decoding/encoding as part of the process of word recognition and comprehension of text.

[4]In 1994–1995, the schools used basal materials published by MacMillan/McGraw-Hill and supplemental literature and little books purchased from Rigby, Sunshine, and the Wright Group. In 2000, the schools adopted the basal materials published by Scott Foresman and continued to use trade books purchased from other publishers.

awareness; that is, features of books such as titles, authors, and illustrators.

The first-grade class focused on helping children develop phonics knowledge and beginning fluency in reading. Writing stories, journals, and occasional poems was also a part of the literacy activities in these classrooms. One first-grade teacher would occasionally teach what she called *ortografía* (orthography), the rules of punctuation, accents, and subject–verb agreement. The other teachers integrated the language skills in the context of reading and writing.

Phonological Awareness

Children engaged in a variety of activities that focused on helping children segment and blend syllables, phonemes, and onset rimes. The use of poems, rhymes, alliteration, and songs was used extensively in kindergarten. Spanish and English dominant students developed a sophisticated sense of Spanish phonemes as early as kindergarten. They developed the ability to rhyme, to name things that began with a particular sound, and to distinguish between similar and different sounds. As children developed, they also learned to attend to tasks that required them to group words based on either *onset* (beginning sound) or *rime* (ending sound). Many of these activities required that children group words based on sounds rather than meaning.

Phonological awareness was developed in Spanish and children began to differentiate the Spanish sounds. On occasion, they asked questions and differentiated Spanish sounds from English sounds. Children resolved dissonances between their two emerging phonological systems on a daily basis. For example, a primary teacher was reading an alphabet book in Spanish and associated the sounds of letters to the children's names. We pick up the exchange with the letter *g:*

Teacher: *La ge dice /g/.*
               The g says /g/.

Children: *La /g/ de Graciela.*
               The /g/ of Graciela.

Teacher: *Sí la /g/ de Graciela, y Gustavo.*
              Yes, the /g/ of Graciela, and Gustavo.

The teacher continued reading the text, turning the page to the letter *h*.

Teacher: *La ache es muda.*
               The h is silent.

Heidi: *La ache es mi letra.*
               The h is my letter.

Teacher: *Sí pero la letra de Heidi es la letra en inglés que sí dice algo.*
               ¿Qué dice?
               Yes, but Heidi's letter is the letter in English that does say
               something. What does [it] say?

Heidi: */h/ como Heidi.*
               /h/ like Heidi.

Teacher: *Sí, y si escribiéramos el nombre de Heidi en español*
               usaríamos la jota.
               Yes, and if we were to write Heidi's name in Spanish we
               would use the j.

The teacher turned a couple of pages to show the letter *j,* then turned back to the page with the letter *h,* makes a wide arc with her arm signaling to the group to attend and repeats:

Teacher: *En español la ache es muda no dice nada.*
               In Spanish the h is silent [it] does not say anything.

The teacher assisted the child in making a meaningful connection to her own name. This appeared to be important at this moment, while calling attention to the differences in the sounds of the letter *h* in Spanish and English. The teacher then returned to reinforce the sound–letter relationship for the letter *h* in Spanish.

Phonics Instruction

The teachers integrated systematic phonics instruction in the reading of leveled texts that were either part of the basal series or were sought out for the phonemic elements. Teachers used the syllable as the basic unit of instruction for phonics focusing on blending and segmenting consonant vowel combinations. Most children, both the Spanish dominant and English dominant, appeared to quickly catch on to the whole notion of sounding out words, segmenting on the syllable, and returning to blend syllables to make whole words. Children went through the sequence of studying all the consonant vowel combinations in kindergarten and again in first grade.[5] By the first grade, all but three special needs children were decoding unknown words by using their phonics knowledge. One first-grade special needs Spanish dominant child was having trouble making meaning of the principle of sounding out and struggled with reading. The other two children struggled with the notion of sounding out and phonics, but by the end of first grade were beginning to make progress using a combination of sounding out and having learned a large number of sight words.

Spanish phonetic features and phonics generalizations were also the bases for invented spellings of Spanish used by both Spanish and English dominant children, and the syllables became the basis for segmentation in writing. Most children still struggled with some predictable grapheme–phoneme substitutions in the second and third grades. For example, children used the *c, cu,* or *qu* to spell the /k/ phoneme in Spanish even into the second and third grades. In a third-grade classroom, the assignment was for children to write a text using a word list taken from the reading text that included *alcancen, conocen, encargo, acuerdo* (reach, know, request, agree). The teacher gathered four children around one child's desk, pointing to the word list and to one child's text, and reviewed the phonics rules.

Cuando la vocal a y la vocal o sigue la c se pronuncia /k/, cuando la vocal e o la vocal i sigue la c se suena /s/. Cuando la vocal u sigue la c se suena /q/. Por ejemplo: alcancen—al/k/an, porque sigue la a, y luego alcan/s/en porque sigue la e, /k/onocen porque sigue la o, y cono/s/en porque sigue la e, escuela y acuerdo—se usa la /q/ como es/q/u porque sigue la u.

When the vowel *a* and the vowel *o* follows *c* it is pronounced /k/, when the vowel *e* or the vowel *i* follows *c* it is sounded /s/. When the vowel *u* follows *c* it is sounded /q/. For example: *alcancen—al/k/an,* because *a* follows, and then *alcan/s/en* because *e* follows, *alcan/s/en* because *o* follows, and *cono/s/en* because it follows *e escuela y acuerdo*—uses the /q/ like *es/q/u* because *u* follows.

---

[5]The approach to literacy instruction in kindergarten and first grade was influenced by Goldenberg's (1994) study that compared Spanish-speaking kindergartners who were taught to read using what he termed an *academic code* (which emphasized vowels, consonants, syllables, and words) with those who were taught to read using a more holistic approach storybook reading approach. He found that children benefited from academic code emphasis in kindergarten and a balanced code-literature reading approach in first grade.

Other predictable confusions, that is, common errors made by most Spanish speakers when they are learning to write, which I observed when children were writing, occurred with words such as,

> *soi [soy]* (I am)—using *i* for *y*
>
> *yave [llave]* (key)—using *y* for *ll*
>
> *jente [gente]* (people)—using *j* for *g*
>
> *benir [venir]* (to come)—using *b* for *v*

In most cases, the teachers would review the phonics rule with individuals or small groups of children. Some of these errors continued on to the fourth grade, as illustrated by the children's written texts that I will discuss in chapter 6. These types of phonetic errors are common overgeneralizations that many Spanish speakers make when they are developing writers.

Orthography

Beyond the notions of using phonological awareness and knowledge to decode and encode words, teachers focused on *orthography* (the system of spellings and punctuation of the writing system) within the literacy lessons and activities. Children's attention was routinely called to accents and tildes as important to the reading and writing of words. Children learned to rely on the accents to help them pronounce words when reading. They also learned to use accents in their writing and often discussed among themselves where the accents should go. *"No está bien, le falta el acento, va aquí"* [signaling the *e* in *también*] (It is not right, it is missing the accent, it goes here). The second child said, *"No, va en la e"* (No, it goes on the *e*).

The children almost always identified that the accents went on vowels and seldom placed accents on consonants. They also learned that the accents were used to designate stress when two vowels were together (in what otherwise would be a diphthong) or at the end of words to designate verb tense.

Words and Segmentation

Word lists and word walls were common devices that teachers used to scaffold children's developing literacy skills. Word lists would be used for scaffolding vocabulary use and for spelling. For example, in a primary grade, the children read poems and stories and made their own word list that they were interested in learning for the week. The final list that the teacher put on a wall chart included *cigüeña, desagüe, güero, ladra, ladrillo, padre, piedra, pingüino, bilingüe, madrugada* (stork, drainage, blond, bark, brick, father, stone, penguin, bilingual, dawn). The process that the teacher used for writing the words on the wall chart was to ask the children to call out one of their words. She began writing the word as the other children joined in calling out each syllable.

Child: *Madrugada, ma*
      [A child calls one of his words and the first syllable.]

Teacher: *ma-, y que sigue*
      [The teacher writes the syllable] ma-, and what follows

Children: *dru-, dru-,*

Teacher: *madru-, y*

Children: *ga-, ga-, ga-*

Teacher: *madruga-, y que sigue*

Children: *da, da*
      [Children call out syllables while the teacher writes a syllable at a time and asks what follows]

Teacher: *madrugada, bien. Otra.*
      Madrugada [dawn], good, another.

Child: *desagüe*
      [Another child calls the word drainage]

Teacher: *¿Qué escribo?*
      What do I write?

Children: *de-, de-*
      [The children in unison call out the syllable de-, de]

Teacher: *Vamos a pensar y pronunciar la palabra. ¿Dónde están las sílabas?*
      Let us think and pronounce the word. Where are the syllables?

Children: *de-sa-güe, de-sa-gü-e, no, de-sa-güe . . . des-a-güe.*
      [Several children are calling out different syllable combinations]

Teacher: *Vamos a escuchar a Luis.*
Let us listen to Luis.

Luis: *Se dice desagüe, las silabas son des- a- güe.*
You say disagüa, the syllables are des- a- güe.

Teacher: *Niños, ¿ustedes qué piensan?*
Children, what do you think?

Children: *des- a- güe*
[children segment syllabically in unison]

Teacher: *Bien, ¿qué escribo?*
Good, what do I write?

Children: *des-, des-*

Teacher: *des-, y que sigue*

Children: *a-, a-*

Teacher: *des-a-, y que sigue*

Children: *güe, güe*
[Children call out syllables while the teacher writes a syllable
at a time and asks what follows]

Luis: *Los puntos sobre la u para güe.*
The points over the u for güe.

Teacher: *¿Y cómo se llaman los puntos?*
And what are the points called?

Children: *diéresis*
[The name in Spanish for the diacritic]

Teacher: *¿Y qué hacemos cuando una palabra lleva diéresis?*
What do we do when a word has a dieresis?

Children: *Pronunciamos las dos vocales.*
We pronounce both vowels.

The use of word walls—and the teacher's modeling—helped children
to figure out words and was common throughout the primary grades. Some
variations that occurred in the primary grades were the common practice
of clapping out the syllables to segment. For example, for the word *pajaro*
[bird], the children would clap as they said each of the syllables, *pa* [clap],

ja [clap], *ro* [clap]. As children progressed to the second grade and beyond, the teacher still called the children's attention to the syllable, but used no clapping and less segmentation for scaffolding. According to the teachers, the students who were more successful early on at segmenting the spoken language into phonemic units made faster progress toward beginning to read.

Beginning Writing

In kindergarten, children began to write primarily two types of texts: those that were patterned after some prompt or assignment and those that children produced on their own or with partners at the centers. Texts that were produced as part of an assignment were by their very nature more controlled and varied little; in fact, many children helped each other to create very similar kinds of texts. For example, the teacher prompts written on the board were as follows:

Hoy es _____.   Today is _____.

Me gusta hacer _____.   I like to do (make) _____.

Mario, an English dominant child, followed the pattern but also showed elements of constructing text and developmental errors similar to the Spanish dominant children even when they responded to a formula or prompt. Mario wrote,

> *Hoy es jueves. Megusta [me gusta] ir al parque. Asimos [hicimos] maromas.*

> Today is Thursday. I like to go to the park. We like to do somersaults.

Luis, a Spanish dominant child responding to the same prompt also showed evidence of text construction when he wrote,

> *Hoy es jueves. Megusta [me gusta] muncho [mucho] hacer palomitas. Asimos [hicimos] munchas y comemos.*

> Today is Thursday. I like very much to make popcorn. We make a lot and we eat [it].

As evidenced by Mario's and Luis' texts, children were not just copying the prompts and filling in the blanks but were reconstructing some notions of text. Both children showed some influence of the oral language in their writing in the lack of segmentation between *me gusto*. This is a very common phrase in Spanish that is often blended together in oral language so that in spite of the teacher's having segmented the phrase, when the children wrote it, they were perhaps writing what they heard in their heads rather than what they saw on the board. Both children also wrote the word asimos for *hicimos* (we make); this usage is commonly spoken in their speech community and also showed a common error in the omission of the silent h in Spanish. Finally, Luis' text also showed the influence of the speech community norms for pronunciation or oral language usage in his use of *muncho* for *mucho* (much or a lot), a word that is commonly used in this region by many Spanish speakers. All of the children in this class went beyond the two lines prompt suggested by the teacher; there was much discussion among the children as to who was going to write more, and many elaborated on what they liked to do. Thus, while the teacher gave a prompt and there was an expectation to write to the prompt, the children also demonstrated that it was customary in this classroom to write beyond the prompt. In fact, observations showed that children would often end with a text that was only initially related to the prompt.

"Morning message" was a common routine that teachers used to begin the day. Morning message integrated oral language, writing and reading, and social-cultural sharing. In a kindergarten classroom, a teacher used the morning message as a time for children to focus on Spanish orthography and experience it in a multisensory way. So in addition to the teacher's using Total Physical Response for teaching words, the children also used physical movements to designate punctuation—for example, standing tall with chest pushed out to designate the use of capitals and stooping for lowercase letters; shouting for the use of exclamation points; raising the ending pitch to designate the need for a question mark; and stomping a foot for *punto* or the period. Accents were also accompanied with hand signals, and the tilde (~) was accompanied with the hand and arm wave across the chest.

In most classrooms, the morning message was routine and rather formulaic, but four of the teachers purposely used this time to demonstrate and reinforce the writing process. For example, in a primary-grade level, the teacher and children worked as a whole group and began with a discussion about what they would write about. *"Hoy, ¿de qué vamos a escribir? Vamos a hacer un plan para escribir"* (Today, what are we going to write about? Let us make a plan for writing). The teacher labels the discussion as planning for writing. As the children suggest ideas, the teacher writes key words, making a list *"el tiempo, los Spurs, el mascota"* (the weather, the Spurs, the classroom pet).

The second and third grade used a writing process that was heavily influenced by the TAAS objectives. For example, a second-grade teacher focused on writing as communicative and social practice by writing letters regularly. She said that during the spring semester she "tried to write letters weekly but it was hard with all the TAAS writing that the children had to also do." One day, the class was reviewing the mechanics of letter writing and beginning a new activity. The whole class participated in generating ideas for a semantic map on *cambios a la communidad* (community changes) that was used for children to work in pairs and individually to write and edit persuasive letters to councilman García who visited their school the following week. Figure 5.2 illustrates the semantic map generated by the class.

After generating the semantic map the teacher quickly reviewed the elements of a persuasive letter.

Teacher: *Vamos a hacer una carta persuasiva. ¿Cómo empezamos?*
We are going to write a persuasive letter. How do we start?

Julián: *. . . con un cumplido.*
. . . with a compliment.

Teacher: *Sí, Julián, con un cumplido en la introducción. ¿Y clase luego qué?*
Yes, Julian, with a compliment in the introduction. And class what then?

Vanesa: *El cuerpo de la carta donde, donde escribimos . . .*
The body of the letter where, where we write . . .

Class: *. . . pedimos lo que queremos . . .*
. .. ask for what we want . . .

Teacher: *Razonar por que necesitamos lo que pedimos ¿Y la conclusión?*
Reason why we need what we are asking for. And the conclusion?

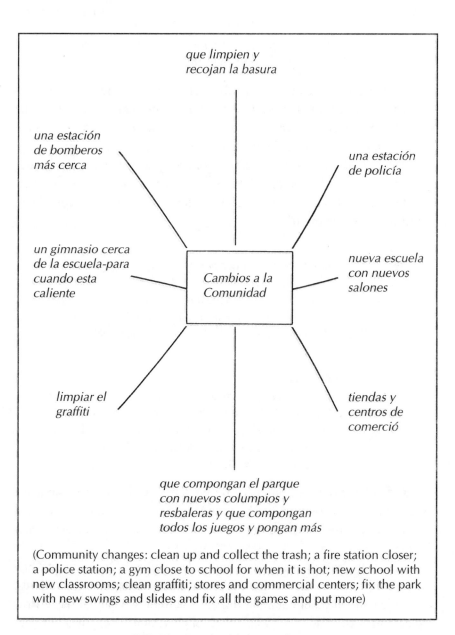

que limpien y
recojan la basura

una estación
de bomberos
más cerca

una estación
de policía

un gimnasio cerca
de la escuela-para
cuando esta
caliente

Cambios a la
Comunidad

nueva escuela
con nuevos
salones

limpiar el
graffiti

tiendas y
centros de
comerció

que compongan el parque
con nuevos columpios y
resbaleras y que compongan
todos los juegos y pongan más

(Community changes: clean up and collect the trash; a fire station closer;
a police station; a gym close to school for when it is hot; new school with
new classrooms; clean graffiti; stores and commercial centers; fix the park
with new swings and slides and fix all the games and put more)

FIG. 5.2.   Letter writing semantic map.

Class: . . . *dar gracias por tomar el tiempo para leer la carta.*
. . . give thanks for taking the time to read the letter.

After the generation of ideas and the review of the elements of a persuasive letter, the children were free to choose the topic either from the
semantic map or some other topic of their interest. The discussion and the
semantic map were done in Spanish, but the children could choose to write
their letters in Spanish or English. Only one pair chose to write this particular letter in English. The first drafts were peer reviewed; all but one pair
selected a topic from the semantic map. The letters were peer edited and
rewritten. A couple of girls wrote,

> *Querido consejero García,*
>   *Gracias por todo lo que usted hace por nuestra escuela y nuestra comu-
> nidad. Hoy escribimos para pedir más ayuda. Nuestra comunidad no tiene
> tiendas o centros comerciales. Solo hay una tienda para comprar comida y
> otras cosas. Nuestra Mamás tiene que ir muy lejos para hacer compras. Por
> favor ayúdenos. Toda la clase lo va agradecer. Gracias por leer nuestra
> carta.*

> Dear Councilman García,
>   Thank you for everything you do for our school and our community.
> Today we are writing to ask for more help. Our community does not have
> stores or commercial centers. There is only one store to buy food and other
> things. Our mothers have to go very far to do the shopping. Please help us.
> The whole class will appreciate it. Thank you for reading our letter.

The teacher explained that because the letters were going to someone
outside the school community, she edited the children's letters and insisted
on the children rewriting the final letter with standard spelling and punctuation.

Many of the early writing assignments, as well as a few of the writing
activities initiated by the children, followed class discussions, read-alouds,
video viewing, or other common full class activities. Many of these writing activities were done in pairs either on chart tablets, overhead projec-
tors, or each child writing on a piece of paper but working together to
decide what to write, how to write it, and often commenting and critiquing
each other's writing. The next example is of a couple of first graders writing an expository text about marine animals. It was typical of the writing
activities observed frequently in first-grade classrooms and occasionally in

second grade. After viewing a video and listening to the teacher read selected passages about marine animals followed by a general class discussion, the teacher told the children to work with their partner—the children had designated partners to work with for writing. The teacher later explained that these pairings were based both on placing children in their "zone of proximal development"[6] and on social needs of children—behavior, shyness, hyperactivity. These two boys chose to write about *"El pulpo"* (the octopus). They wrote on a big chart and took turns writing. They produced a text which is transcribed here as the children wrote it with their line format, spelling, and punctuation.

El pulpo	The octupus
El pulpo tiene ocho brasos.	The octupus has eight arms.
Cambia de colors	Changes colors
Se mueve despacio	It moves slowly
Su cabeza es grande	Its head is big
muy grande	very big
Tiene ojos entodos los	It has eyes on all
lados dela cabeza	sides of the head
El pulpo despide ink, -	The octopus discharges ink,
despide tinta negra.	discharges black ink.
Esto es todo del pulpo.	This is all about the octopus.

The children helped each other create the text. They consulted books as they were writing such as when they were deciding how many *brazos* or arms the octopus had. They looked at the picture, counted the arms, and read the line in the text that said, *"los pulpos tiene ocho brazos"* (octopuses have eight arms); yet, when they wrote their text, the children wrote *brasos* instead of *brazos,* using the grapheme *s* instead of the *z* for the medial position. One child suggested *cambia de colores* (changes colors) while the other child wrote it without much discussion or rereading; thus, they wrote colors instead of *colores,* perhaps showing the influence of English or the fact that children may have seen the English word 'colors' written and it looked okay and they did not reread it in Spanish, which might have caused them to rethink the spelling. The children did not segment *entodos* (on all) and *dela* (of the) showing the influence or dependency on their oral

---

[6] This teacher talked about the notion of *zone of proximal development* and referenced it to Vygotsky's (1978) work.

Spanish where frequently these words are run together or, at least for young learners, they may not have yet developed awareness of the segmentation of the oral language into written words. Finally, the children first wrote the word ink, then decided that ink was English and went looking in the text for the word *tinta* in Spanish. Instead of erasing, which they had done before with the word *despacio* (slow), they decided to leave the word ink but added the phrase *despide tinta* (discharges ink). They also included both a comma and a hyphen after the word ink almost as if to indicate another idea rather than just a correction or clarification of the use of the work ink. The children used periods on selected lines; however, they also capitalized the lines that they apparently perceived as a whole idea or sentence and did not capitalize phrases that were continuations of ideas from the previous lines.

In the text of *El pulpo,* the children show awareness of an audience, as well as some cultural awareness, by adding a final closing sentence. Many Spanish oral and written texts signify the end with a closing phrase or line. Most of the stories children wrote, that I examined, ended with *el fin* (the end), and a few ended with *deseo que te guste mi cuento* (I wish [hope] that you like my story). For example, one third grader wrote the same story in both languages, in Spanish ending it with *deseo que te guste mi cuento, hojala [ojalá] un día tu me puedas decir uno tuyo* (I hope that you like my story, maybe one day you can tell me one of yours), and ending the English story with "Well I hope you like this story."

Writing as Cultural Activity

In the primary grades, children's writing reflected culturally specific topics (*abuelas*), events (*fiestas*), objects (*piñatas,* Spurs *coyote* [the Spurs mascot]), and brief comments or references (such as *apachurrado como una tortilla* (smashed [flat] like a tortilla). They included many other words for foods (such as *tortilla, tacos, frijoles fritos, fajitas, aguas frescas, barbacoa* and barbeque, puffy *tacos,* big red). As the children advanced and gained more instruction, inclusion, and attendance at cultural events, they discussed more complex cultural topics, such as what was meant by *portarse bién, ser bilingüe, respeto* (well behaved, be bilingual, and respect). In a couple of classrooms where the teacher included studies of traditional and hybridized forms of music, art, drama, and dance, there were many examples of discussions and children's writing about *música Tejana, danzas norteñas y* two-step, *los pastores, las calaveras literarias* (Tejano music, dances from northern [Mexico] and two-step, the shepherds [Christmas Shepherd play], and literary skeletons).

Children were encouraged and began to see themselves not only as users of culture but also as active contributors to cultural production. Several teachers often spoke about the hybridized culture of San Antonio and encouraged children to think about new creative combinations. As one teacher voiced it, "We take ideas and traditions from Monterey or New York and we change them and make them our own."

Students' hybridized identities would surface and be used as they selected not only topics and language, but the style of written discourse that children explored. For example, after the teacher directed discussion of *calaveras literarias* (literary skeletons) that are common during *Día de los muertos* (Day of the dead) celebrations, the children were to write poems or short stories based on the genre. A number of students started talking, giggling, and writing. A third grader wrote,

los dulces	the candies
en blanco y negro	in white and black
bailan dulce	dance sweetly
y no asustan	and do not scare
se ríen	they laugh
y se reciben	and you receive them
pa Halloween	for Halloween

She writes with a sense of humor, making fun of the candy skeletons dancing instead of scaring, then she ends her poem with a reference to Halloween, showing the proximity of the celebrations and the cross-cultural influences.

Many children's use of code switching in their written text appeared to be purposeful and used with awareness.[7] Children attempted to show or signal to the reader in some way that they were switching. The most popular ways of doing this were to use dashes or quotes; however, in a second-grade class, children also used their highlighters to highlight the use of

---

[7]For a discussion of bilingual children's limited use of code switching in writing, see Edelsky (1986).

English words in their Spanish text or Spanish words in their English text. Although there was an emphasis on the separation of the languages in almost all the assigned writing, including journals, literature response, read-aloud summaries, and reports, there was limited switching. Code switching appeared more in the informal writing and the texts produced for themselves or to communicate, for example, in notes, cards, and signs. When the teacher suggested they write a thank you note to a community member who had given each child in the class a book, Marcela wrote, *"Sra. López, Muchas gracias por el libro que me regaló. Lo voy a leer* eviriday [every day]" (Mrs. López, Thank you very much for the book you gave me. I will read it every day). Thus, when children saw writing as communicative or having a social purpose, they tended to use more code switching. Children focused on the social communicative process; they used all their language knowledge as they struggled to find ways to express themselves with people about things or topics that mattered to them.

LITERACY TRANSFER

The teachers' view of the process of English literacy learning and instruction was informed by Cummins' (1981) theory of "common underlying proficiency." Cummins views the academic development of bilinguals as interdependent and building on each other. Thus, knowledge gained in one language serves as a foundation and facilitates learning in the second language. Literacy instruction in these classrooms assumed this interdependency relation; that is, that reading and writing instruction in Spanish would result in the rapid development of literacy skills in English. They often cited the work of Lindholm and Fairchild (1990) at River Glen Elementary, which showed a positive correlation of content knowledge and literacy between the first and second language, even for children with as little as 2 years of two-way bilingual immersion program participation.

At Bonham and Storm, children first acquired literacy in Spanish and this had a positive consequence for the development of literacy in English. Children used knowledge of the Spanish alphabet, learned during Spanish reading/writing instruction, and their developing English oral language knowledge to encode and decode English before instruction. Children, as they encountered English or wished to encode something in English, began with a range of possible values within a hypothesized scale for trying out possible sounds or letters that could be used. Whereas the hypothesized scale was limited, for example, within a selected number of consonants or vowels, the range of possible values was a little more extensive. The children attempted three or four different ways to decode vowels as they sought a match in their English oral language and tested their hypotheses.

In kindergarten and first grade, children's quest to make sense of English print appeared deliberate and active. Children experimented with sounding out print with all their acquired knowledge and experience as nascent Spanish readers and writers. Thus, their use of the developing Spanish literacy and the developing English oral language to attempt to make meaning of print and to produce text in English was an exercise of active adaptation and modification of their previous knowledge and frameworks. As they attempted to decode English texts, they focused on previously developed hypotheses about phonemes and segmentation. Some children would also comment on the differences in punctuation— *"le falta la exclamación"* (the exclamation [point] is missing), spelling— *"porqué no hay acentos"* (why are there no accents), and syntax, such as length of sentences. One kindergartner observed, *"En este libro las líneas están más chiquitas"* (In this book the lines are smaller) pointing to the English text. Because most of the English books in his classroom were either big books or low level readers, they had shorter sentences than the wide range of Spanish materials that were available for children in Spanish.

Spanish grapho-phonic knowledge was used by many of the children in attempting to read and write English. As children began to write English, their invented spellings relied more on Spanish orthography for encoding their perceptions of the oral English language words they spoke and heard. It was not until they began to read more English text that children began to use English phonetic features and phonetic generalizations for their invented spellings. By the third grade, most of the influence of Spanish phonics and orthography on English reading and writing had decreased noticeably.

In the primary grades, errors of segmentation were almost always heavily dependent on syllables in Spanish. In English, errors of segmentation tended to be words that were run together, as they were heard in the oral language; for example, "Iam, togo, inthe, enthen" (and then) and others.

Children's writing was characterized by several overgeneralizations or confusions that are typical of Spanish-speaking students. The children's first attempts to write in English, often at centers or integrated in play, were characterized and based on Spanish phonology and orthography. The following examples were taken from texts produced by kindergartners in their drawings and center activities:

Big bari (bari for body)

Jes or No (jes for yes)

I si big dog. (si for see)

Go auey! (auey for away!

In the first grade, children continued to use many of these and other generalizations. The following examples were taken from texts produced by first graders in journals and notes:

I jelp my mom. (jelp for help).

I uen tugo to Fiesta Texas. (uen for want, and tugo for to go).

I sei—dad gimi moni. (sei for say, and gimi for give me)

I jef a neu babi. (jef for have, neu for neu, and babi for baby)

Ai lov llu. (Ai for I, lov for love, and llu for you)

Initial /w/ phonemes presented a special problem for children given that in Spanish this phoneme is used primarily for loan words and most children had not encountered it in their Spanish literacy instruction. Thus, children played with how to encode it, trying out *gua, jua,* and *ua.* For example, children wrote *guant, jaunt* or *uant* for want and *guen, juen,* or *uen* for when. In later years, with English instruction, children began using the /w/ in their invented spelling for when. This is further discussed in chapter 6. Some children pronounced the *r* as a semi-vowel /r/, which posed some interesting dilemmas for the children. For example, farm was often encoded as *faum* and learn as *leun.* A few children also had some occasional use of *cu* or *qu* for the /k/ phoneme, but most appeared to delight with using c or k in English.

Writing English Words in Spanish

Children began to acquire literacy in English in the early stages of oral language instruction in English. Although the instructional program focused on developing literacy in Spanish first through second grade before children began more formal instruction in English literacy, English language activities—primarily oral but many included the teacher's use and production of text—began on Day 1 of the children's entering prekindergarten or kindergarten. Thus, as the children received the designed 10% of the curriculum in English and as children interacted with each other during center and group activities, children began to develop English oral language proficiency. Children began to interact with English print and attempted to read and write in English long before they had oral mastery of the language and long before the teacher led reading and writing instruction in English.[8]

Teachers assumed that phonemic segmentation acquired in Spanish was sufficient and would transfer to learning to read in English. Thus, once the children were reading at grade-level fluency—children in second grade could read second-grade Spanish reading materials fluently—they were introduced to English materials at approximately the same level. The teachers spoke often of carefully screening the English materials that were available for children in English. This was not always to keep these books and materials away from children, but in most cases that I observed, it was to give children strategies or to simply be prepared to tell the child the word if it could not be decoded with the knowledge the child had of the Spanish phonemic system.

The primary teachers used many English oral language activities that focused on phonemic segmentation or phonological awareness—for example, rhyme and alliteration. However, the teachers did not necessarily view these activities as required and did not systematically teach these in English as part of the beginning reading activities in English. Teachers repeatedly said that once students could read in Spanish, they would begin to expose children to reading in English. As part of the balanced literacy program that the teachers were required to follow, they included specific phonics activities in English, beginning in the second grade.

There was a lot of evidence that children used their literacy skills in a bidirectional way and that there was bidirectional transfer of literacy

---

[8] Wong Fillmore and Valadez (1986), Verhoeven (1990), and Lindholm (1992) found that high levels of second language proficiency is a stronger predictor of second language literacy development and recommend that second language literacy instruction should not begin until children have developed high levels of oral second language proficiency.

skills.[9] Children transferred literacy skills learned in one language by hypothesizing, applying, reflecting, and self-correcting as to the possible usage in the second language.

One child said, *"Estudiamos mucho más inglés, pero yo sé escribir bien in español, y es fácil escribir en inglesh"* (We study a lot more English, but I know how to write well in Spanish, and it is easy to write in English). As the child expressed confidence in being able to write because he already knew how to write in Spanish, the child also showed some bidirectional influence of English in his Spanish in the final spelling of "inglesh" (English) using the final *sh* phoneme of the English word.

Teachers assumed that students would transfer their Spanish reading comprehension strategies. Students demonstrated they could monitor their understanding, re-read for clarification, discuss and answer questions, infer and extend from the text, and summarize in English at about the same level of proficiency that they were able to do in Spanish. These were activities they used and demonstrated, whether reading in Spanish or English.

As children responded to a variety of English texts, they often commented on the skills and strategies that they could use to understand or make meaning from the text. When they encountered texts that used code switching, these often produced lively and contested discussions, with one child referring to the real world use of this linguistic alternative, *"Aya afuera cuando vas a la tienda o a los* Spurs *no hablas or lees nomás en* English *o Español, hay mucho todo* mixed and you can read it that way." (Out there when you go to the store or to see the Spurs you don't speak or read only in English or Spanish, there is a lot that is all mixed and you can read it that way).

Children in these two-way bilingual immersion classrooms did not associate literacy with a specific language; they equated literacy as the ability to interpret or encode a text. This reinforces Durgunoğlu's (1998) findings that children's "English word recognition performance (with contextual help) was related to their Spanish proficiencies, such as phono-

---

[9]Manyak (2000), Moll and Dworin (1996), and Verhoeven (1994) found evidence that children transfer reading skills across languages and that that transfer goes across languages in two directions. Verhoeven studied Turkish children in the Netherlands and the others studied Spanish-speaking children in the United States. In all of these studies, children were acquiring literacy simultaneously in their first and second languages.

logical awareness, word recognition, and spelling. Even without formal instruction in English reading and writing, these children had begun to develop basic word-recognition and spelling proficiencies in English with the help of their Spanish literacy proficiencies" (p. 143).

LITERACY RESOURCES

The library was one of the major resources available for children beyond classroom materials. In the library, they not only had access to books but could go on the Internet to find materials in Spanish and English. In spite of multiple efforts to integrate library resources, the library was primarily used to support children doing research or projects in social studies and science. On two occasions, children used it to find information on authors of children's literature when they were doing author studies.

The most common use of the library remained the whole class visits once a week to the library and having everyone select a book to be read during the week and returned the following week. The librarians took a very active role in pointing out to children books at their appropriate grade level and books in Spanish. The librarians also appeared to know most of the children's interests and reading levels and would on occasion call a particular child's attention to a new book that had come in or to another book on a similar topic that the child might find of interest. The librarians described the support the library provided to the two-way bilingual immersion program as not only a resource but also a place where children could develop "social networks and social relations with authors." However, for the most part, children would go to the stacks, browse, advise each other about what was *bueno o interesante* (good or interesting), and make choices. Children in all but two classes were free to choose books in either language. One teacher at the intermediate grade level had the children alternate the language choices, so that one week the child selected a book in Spanish and the next week in English. The other class, an upper grade level, selected books based on the assigned study theme, and these varied over time. When these children were doing a unit study in Spanish, they would check out books primarily in Spanish for 3 or 4 weeks.

CONCLUSION

All the students made the connections between the two languages and multiple literacies, some with more ease than others. As in previous studies (Christian et al., 1997; Lindholm, 1994; Lindholm-Leary, 2001; Verhoeven, 1994), the children who were performing at grade level in Spanish literacy and had attained English oral proficiency performed at higher levels on English literacy tasks (Pérez & Bustos Flores, 2002).

In the early grades, teachers focused children's attention on metalinguistic tasks, and children showed evidence of internalizing this awareness by comparing and analyzing the sounds or phonology of the two languages as wells as other structural aspects of each language. Children attempted to read English environmental print and spell English words with the help of their knowledge of Spanish phonology and letter knowledge. These findings are similar to findings of previous studies (Bialystok, 1997; Bruck & Genesee, 1995; Durgunoğlu, 1998; Durgunoğlu et al., 1993; Galambos & Goldin-Meadow, 1990; García, Jiménez, & Pearson, 1998) that show a certain metalinguistic advantage for young bilingual children related to word recognition in beginning reading. Students as early as first grade were verbalizing some understanding of shared etymology of vocabulary and would challenge each other as to whether some words were cognates or false cognates and generally compared and played with comparisons of words between Spanish and English. These students used similar word recognition strategies and cognate knowledge across languages. Studies by Nagy, García, Durgunoğlu, and Hancin-Bhatt (1993) and Jiménez (2000) and Jiménez, García, and Pearson (1995) examined vocabulary knowledge and cognate recognition in older bilingual students —fourth grade and above—and found evidence that identification and use of cognates contributed to English reading comprehension.

The two-way bilingual immersion students at Storm and Bonham found hybrid learning contexts that encouraged them to use their knowledge of Spanish and English, their prior community knowledge and experiences, their formal and informal ways of communicating and meaning making, and their full identities. Students did not speak of separate skills used for reading or writing in Spanish or English; in fact, often they encouraged each other to say it, read it, or write it in Spanish, English, or code switching and then fix it. They voiced greater confidence in one language or another, but often they referred to this in terms of amount of language, generally voiced as number of words that they knew. Rather than dominate the selection of literacy events and practices the child would participate in, this confidence often became the classroom resource that was used by teachers and students to assist other students in linguistic brokering. This practice resulted in children's learning to use their confidence or strength to continue learning the perceived weaker language.

Children developed ideas about what it meant to be a bilingual, bicultural, and biliterate person; that is, they developed their own notion of a biliterate identity. They assumed particular stances toward text and inductively derived strategic interactions with text. They integrated all their knowledge derived from the literate behaviors learned and practiced in Spanish, English, and real-world code switching.

6

Academic Biliteracy

In a second-grade classroom, children were working in twos and threes consulting a variety of materials in Spanish and English, learning about the solar system, and creating models. Six children were at computers reading and paging through "virtual books" looking for information on the solar system. Each pair or group had been assigned different parts of the solar system. One group was discussing and writing notes, when Felipe said, "How do I write that [orbits of planets] in Spanish, we have to find that in a Spanish book?" Tito responded, "We can write our report in either language, we can even make it bilingual." Lydia said, "But we decided to do it in Spanish, we can find information on the solar system in English and we can translate—*el sistema solar*" (the solar system). The teacher approached and directed the children's attention to resources in Spanish saying, *"Los libros virtuales en el computador tienen texto en español y allí sobre la mesa hay otros libros sobre el sistema solar en español"* (The virtual books on the computer have Spanish text and there on the table there are other Spanish books about the solar system). A review of the final products produced by the children showed that three groups had written their reports in Spanish, two in English, and one bilingual; all were accompanied with a variety of graphics. Each group also made a class presentation in the language of the products.

By the second semester of the second grade, children were reading expository texts in Spanish to learn social studies and science content. As children's literacy competencies became more sophisticated and the demands for content learning increased,[1] children used their literacy skills to learn.

BILITERACY PROGRAM

As children and teachers worked toward the development of biliteracy, they were constrained primarily by time but also by the need to follow the district's mandated balanced literacy framework, described in chapter 5, while attending to the bilingual immersion model as they evolved to a 50% instruction in each language. At the third-grade level, teachers struggled with time and language allocations within self-contained classrooms. At the fourth- and fifth-grade levels, each school took a different organizational approach to this dilemma of time and language. The teachers at Storm integrated more of the content into the literacy timeframe. The Bonham teachers departmentalized the fourth and fifth grade. At the fourth-grade level, the immersion teacher and the transitional bilingual teacher provided the Spanish language instruction integrating the Spanish language arts in science and math, and the teacher of the English program taught English literacy and language arts and social studies. At the fifth-grade level, the immersion teacher integrated Spanish language arts and social studies, the transitional bilingual teacher taught English language arts and integrated science, and the English program teacher taught math.

As children began developing literacy competencies in English, generally during third grade, they also began to use these developing skills to learn content. Thus, in the upper grades, children were using all their literacy skills in both languages to learn content. Children continued to work on their literacy in both languages. As a fourth-grade teacher described it, "We focus on refining the Spanish and English language arts skills, especially spelling and writing as they learn science or social studies." Although

---

[1] August and Hakuta (1997) summarized studies of content learning that point to "fundamental epistemological differences among subject matters" (p. 67) and argued that these require specialized knowledge that is complex and differentiated. They concluded that "it may be that certain disciplines lend themselves more easily to the transfer of knowledge across languages, depending on the structure of knowledge within the domain, but the particular domains to which this would apply to are not readily apparent" (p. 67).

the teachers articulated a pedagogical rationale for this focus on the use of literacy to learn content and writing, they also cited the pressures of the TAAS test as influencing the types of learning opportunities that they provided for their students. Children began taking TAAS reading tests in the third grade, and the test contains reading passages from science and social studies. Children first encountered the TAAS writing test in the fourth grade.

Literacy and Content Learning

The teachers in the upper grades focused on helping the students internalize their language skills while using their skills to learn academic content. The teachers helped students develop and apply certain strategies, such as using details from the text, using context for unknown vocabulary items, accessing and assessing cognate vocabulary, verifying understanding using text information, summarizing and retelling, and translating and transferring information across languages and content.

An example from a fourth-grade classroom illustrates some common teaching and learning practices that helped children use their literacy skills in content learning. After reading silently a passage about fossils, children were asked to write a sentence or two using a specific assigned comprehension strategy. At each child's desk was taped a list of Michael Eaton's suggested comprehension strategies.[2] The teacher quickly assigned children a strategy to use in their written response. After about 3 minutes, in which children individually re-read the text and wrote, the teacher began to randomly call on children to state their strategy and read what they had written. The following are transcriptions from my notes as the children read what they wrote:

Teacher: *¿Julia, cuál es tu estrategia?*
Julia, which is your strategy?

Julia: *Es clave- claves de contexto y la palabra que es- escogí es vestigios. Fósiles son vestigios como- como huellas de animales prehistóricos.*

---

[2]Comprehension strategies were: prefix or suffix; context clues; three details; three events in order; how to follow instructions; where and when; main idea; summarize whole piece; cause and effect; why something happened; predict what will happen; predict what won't happen; draw a conclusion; how the characters feel; realism or fantasy; fact and opinion (Eaton, n.d., p. 18).

It is clues- context clues and the word that I chose is vestiges.
Fossils are vestiges like- like tracks of prehistoric animals.

Teacher: *Bien, clase el texto termina con la pregunta, ¿Cuál era el
eslabón entre los pájaros y reptiles? Usando las claves de
contexto ¿Qué es eslabón?*
Well, class the text ends with the question, which was the link
between the birds and reptiles? Using the context clues, what
is link?

Several children call out link, link, *relación* [relation], *enlace* [connection], link. The teacher shakes her head in agreement and continues.

Teacher: *Muy bien, relación o* link. Norma.
Very well, relation or link. Norma.

Norma: *La mía fue detalles y escribí, los fósiles son de pájaros de
muchos tamaños, de reptiles, y de animalitos del mar o animales acuarios. Los científicos llevan los fósiles a los lab-
laboratorios para estudiar.*
Mine was details and I wrote, the fossils are of birds of many
sizes, of reptiles, and small animals from the sea or water animals. The scientists take the fossils to the lab- laboratories to
study.

Teacher: *Muy bien. ¿Clase qué fue lo que hizo Norma?*
Very well. Class what was it that Norma did?

Several children call out, "She copied." One child says, "She copied the
details. Norma, read it again." Norma re-reads her text, as another child
decides that Norma has not copied but has summarized and says, "No, she
took details from different parts, look, look . . . [pointing to different parts
of the texts]. She copied the details from different parts and wrote her own
sentence." The teacher refocuses the group and restates their analysis in
Spanish.

Teacher: *Norma escribió su propio resume usando los detalles del texto.
Beto.*
Norma wrote her own summary using the details from the text.
Beto.

Beto: *OK, rastrero- rastreramente es la palabra especial. Rastrero- o
rastreramente dice, describe como el- los reptiles caminaban,*

no- no caminaban se movían por el suelo, como como ondas-
ondulando.
OK, creeper- creepingly is the special word. Creeper or creepingly says, describes how it- the reptiles walked, no- not
walked they moved on the ground, like like waves- (waves his
arm) undulating.

Teacher: *Muy bien, Beto. Clase, ¿El texto también dice que estos*
pájaros volaban rastreramente?
Very well, Beto. Class, the text also says that these birds flew
creepingly [low flying].

Class: No response.

Teacher: *Puede ser que volaban bajo muy cerca de la tierra o el suelo.*
It could be that they flew lowly very close to the earth or
ground.

Several of the children begin to flap their arms as they slouch down in their
seats, demonstrating their understanding of the word and how the prehistoric birds might have flown.

Teacher: *Acabamos mañana, es tiempo de guardar sus cosas.*
We will finish tomorrow, it is time to put away your things.

The children read a lengthy and somewhat difficult expository text in
Spanish that contained numerous concepts and unknown vocabulary, but
the text included notes, boxes, and graphics that helped to provide context
and additional information. They learned to use all these contextualized
clues to define words and concepts. Thus, after a brief introduction by the
teacher and silent reading, children were able to write and participate in
the follow-up discussion. It was also apparent that the list of comprehension strategies they were using was a familiar routine. Whereas the strategy was assigned, the children selected sections of text to illustrate the
strategy. Some children selected the most obvious piece of text, but after
the initial sharing, they also challenged each other to find the more obscure
pieces of information contained in the text.

In the previous example, Julia selected the word *vestigios* (vestiges),
which was only used once in the text and once in a caption accompanying
a picture of a footprint. The teacher extended and reinforced the strategy
by choosing another word, *eslabón* (link), which was used in the title

and was not used again until the final question. When children in chorus answered in English, link—link, the teacher waited until someone called out a response in Spanish. She repeated and reinforced both Spanish and English responses. After Norma's response, the teacher asked the children to assess and describe what Norma had done in writing her response. Everyone began to verify whether Norma "copied" from the text and most concluded, and the teacher reinforced, that she wrote her own summary.

Beto did not have a choice as to what to select from the text, as the teacher had previously identified *rastreramente* (creepingly) as the special word for this text and had written it on the board. For the special word, children could use reference materials, such as glossaries and dictionaries. Beto used the dictionary and asked the teacher for assistance to find the root word *rastrero,* which he wrote before *rastreramente.* He began to read his text but also appeared to edit and add as he read what he had written. The teacher again extended the usage by asking the class to interpret a second example, *volaban rastreramente,* but when no one replied, she offered a possible definition. The children showed their understanding through their body movements.

The children were actively engaged in reading, writing and re-reading, but like so much of school learning, the activity was truncated because it was time for the children to go to the library. The teacher reported that when the children restate the strategy that they are assigned, they internalize that strategy.

All of the upper grade classes integrated literacy and language arts skills in the context of other subjects. This integration of literacy and content was most evident in social studies and science in Spanish. But as the children became more proficient in English, they also began to read and write expository texts in English. Children also began to extend activities between the two languages; that is, they would begin a learning activity in one language and continue or extend the activity in the other. An example from the other fourth-grade classroom illustrates this practice. The students had studied parallel lines, line segments, perpendicular lines, intersection, and other concepts about lines and planes during math time, and this work was done in Spanish. A few days later, the teacher integrated the concepts learned in math into a social studies lesson in English about the history and geography of the neighborhood. She introduced the objective that they were to study saying, "We are going to investigate how the cattle industry in Texas and especially in this region had a lasting effect on the development of how your neighborhood looks today." The teacher led a discussion about what remnants of the cattle industry the children noticed in their neighborhood, such as the stockyards, railroad tracks, warehouses, and meat markets. As the discussion progressed, she integrated the previously learned math concepts saying,

> We can use the math concepts to describe the development of the neighborhood when we talk and write about the influence of the cattle industry. For example, we have many little streets that are line segments, that is, they do not span the whole city but they begin at the stockyards and end on Malone or Division or Nogalitos street. Why is that? Or we can say that some major streets are perpendicular to the San Antonio River. Why is that?

As the discussion continued, the children began to integrate the math vocabulary. After about 20 minutes of discussion, the teacher asked the students to write a summary paragraph about one aspect of the discussion and something that they were interested in pursuing, as the investigation of the topic continued over the next few days. The teacher purposely engaged the children in interconnecting what they learned in Spanish in math to the English lesson on geography and history, thus supporting the students in transferring knowledge across languages and content. The process developed students' metacognitive understanding (Brown, 1980) by challenging them to demonstrate what they knew about lines, show how well they knew it by applying that knowledge in social studies, and evaluate and make a plan for actively intervening in acquiring further knowledge.

The children had about 5 or 6 minutes to write before the teacher started calling on children to share their summaries. The following are two texts that are representative of the summaries the children read. These were transcribed from the oral reading.

> I learned that some streets in my neighborhood are diagonal. Diagonal means they do not go east and west or north and south. The diagonal streets are perpendicular to the San Antonio River and some end at the river. I am going to find out if the reason these diagonal streets end at the river is because they were the old paths or *veredas* that cows used to go to the river to drink water.

The second text:

> The railroad tracks and Frio City road are parallel in our neighborhood but down further way past Zarzamora, they intersect. I think the railroad was to bring cattle from far away to the stockyards because the railroad tracks go through the middle of the stockyards. I want to know why Frio City Road is called Frio City, maybe it was the road to a town on the Frio River.

The teacher's choice of a summary text was influenced by the TAAS assessment objectives requiring children to recognize and produce summary statements. There were many occasions when children were asked to produce summaries of discussions. The products of those summaries frequently were listings of events or topics. In the case of the summaries of this discussion, the children were to select one point of interest from the discussion, summarize what they had learned, and describe what they wanted to know more about. They also had to include the math concepts and vocabulary that they had learned and that had been used in the discussion. This example demonstrated how the teachers would teach concepts in one language and would then begin to use them in the other language without directly re-teaching. The teacher was also taking a theme from the fourth-grade curriculum—cattle industry in Texas, and relating it to these children's neighborhood, experiences, and local culture. The teacher demonstrated how to integrate the math vocabulary in the discussion. Once the teacher began to make suggestions of possible reasons their neighborhood looked the way it did and connections between the cattle industry in Texas and their neighborhood, the children actively participated in the discussion and easily produced summaries that integrated the math vocabulary and the social studies topic discussed.

GUIDED READING, LITERATURE, AND SPELLING

As teachers struggled with implementing the balanced literacy framework, they also saw the rationale and usefulness of the framework. One teacher who talked about the difference the framework had made said, "Previously, we delivered reading instruction to the whole classes in each language, and we didn't have an understanding of modeled, shared, guided, or independent reading. Now we plan with the students the kind of reading they're going to do in each language in each of these areas. This has helped."

In the third grade, children's transfer to English reading and writing was assisted, monitored, and assessed daily by the teachers during the guided reading time. Using the hypothesis that children could begin reading English texts that were at approximately the same level as those they were reading in Spanish, the teachers kept testing this by introducing materials, scaffolding the use of the materials, monitoring the students' transfer of skills, and constantly adjusting the materials and the interventions. The monitoring of the transfer occurred during the guided reading time that increasingly was conducted in English. The teacher-directed guided reading lessons included both authentic literature and expository texts from the content areas.

Additionally, the teachers continued to foster the children's Spanish literacy. Children read Spanish literature, listened to read alouds, and responded in discussions and writing in Spanish. There was also a major focus on writing in Spanish and continuing the mastery of the Spanish orthography—spelling, accents, and punctuation.

Guided Reading

As children participated in guided reading, teachers routinely called children's attention to language concepts, such as correct verb forms, antecedents, word origins, and, especially, grapho-phonic skills. Teachers would monitor as children transferred their Spanish grapho-phonic knowledge and oral English as they read English text and would either conduct a phonics lesson prior to reading a particular text or would intervene during guided reading to focus on a particular phonics skill, such as long vowel sounds, or consonant–vowel–consonant–silent e (CVCe, cake, tale, kite) combinations.

For example, during guided reading, Mike read "tall tălé"; tall was said correctly, but he said a short *a* sound and stressed the final *e* in tale. When Mike finished the paragraph, the teacher said, "Let's look at this word [pointing to tale], many words in English that end in *e* are said without sounding that final *e,* and the silent *e* also tells you that the other vowel, this one [pointing to a] it is a long vowel. Let's see if that is the case with this word." Mike said, "tall tăl, no that sounds the same as tall." The teacher said, "Try again use a very long *a.*" Mike's next approximation was almost there as he said, "tall tale." The teacher said, "That is right, tall tale, now say it again with me, tall tale."

Approximately 35% of all the interventions observed during or following English guided reading focused on phonics skills, such as the one previously described. The other 65% of the interventions and discussions following guided reading were about fluency, word meanings, and comprehension. For example, Mrs. Williams often asked, "What do you think the character is feeling?" As the children started giving opinions, she would ask them to use the text to verify their responses. As the children searched and re-read, she would ask, "Read aloud the part that supports your opinion." The teacher reported that this helped children not only with text comprehension but the re-reading and especially the reading aloud helped them with fluency.

Literature

Although children's literature was used less than in the earlier grades, teachers made an effort to continue exposing children to literature in Spanish and English. During the language arts time, most teachers would conduct read alouds and, on occasion, literature studies. Following the read alouds, the most used literature response strategies were writing in ongoing literature journals or writing separate responses on sheets of paper. A third-grade teacher had children write in either Spanish or English in their journals; then as time permitted, the children would share with the class by standing and reading what they had written. Children were free to choose their response; some would routinely summarize, but others frequently related the reading to their own experience. Children's language choice for the literature response was more frequently tied to the children's preferred language, or prior experience, and less to the language of the text. There appeared more occasions—four out of six observations—in which the book that the children were responding to was in English and five to six different children would write in Spanish. The topic and children's prior similar or different experiences appeared to elicit a greater response in Spanish. Only two children on two occasions chose to respond in English when the book that was read was in Spanish.

Other teachers would combine the literature response and TAAS writing objectives by suggesting the children form their own literature responses. For example, when reading *Tomas and the Library Lady* (Mora, 1993), the teacher suggested that children might infer what Tomas was thinking and feeling. Thus, the children were expected to write short paragraphs that discussed what was not in the text but could be inferred based on children's own experiences.

Although there was much good children's literature in both Spanish and English used in these upper grade classrooms, the type of engagement was limited. The three primary ways that children engaged with literature were (a) silent reading of books checked out of the library, (b) assigned readings from trade books or excerpts from literature in their basal, or (c) teacher read alouds from picture books or chapter books. There was little response and engagement beyond the text. For example, all the teachers read aloud to the children, most rotating between English and Spanish texts, but the student responses were almost always to write a paragraph in their journals or on a piece of paper using a TAAS objective, such as fact or opinion. One teacher lamented,

> We know how to do literature circles, character studies or even author studies, but I feel so pressured to prepare them for the TAAS. So we all try to include the literature that children really love but then we do it the way that the TAAS reading and writing will test. This is the only way I have found I can do it.

Spelling

In the upper grades, the focus on spelling in both Spanish and English intensified. Although the children were given spelling words to study and most classrooms employed traditional oral and written exercises asking children to spell the called word and use it in a sentence, the form of testing was updated. The word list generally had a theme and often the word was taken either from the literature or the expository text being studied. On the test date, the children were dictated a sentence or paragraph that included most if not all the words, and the children wrote the dictation. The dictations were checked for spelling—not only for the words on the spelling word list but also for other common words included in the sentence or paragraph. Any misspelling was counted as an error. In the case of

Spanish as in the next example, the accents and the punctuation, as in the inverted question mark, were also checked for accuracy. For example, for the list of words *zoológico, animales, jirafas, camellos, cebras o zebras, víboras* (zoo, animals, giraffes, camels, zebras, and snakes), the children were dictated the following paragraph:

> *Ayer, Lorenzo y la clase del Sr. Murillo se fueron de paseo al zoológico. Vieron unos animales raros y también chistosos. A Lorenzo le gustaba ver a las jirafas, los camellos, las cebras, los monos y las víboras. ¿Cuáles animales te gustaría ver en el zoológico?*

> (Yesterday, Lorenzo and Mr. Murillo's class went on a trip to the zoo. They saw some rare and also funny animals. Lorenzo liked seeing the giraffes, camels, zebras, monkeys, and snakes. Which animals would you like to see at the zoo?)

This contextualized the words for the children and also required that they remember and attend to the spelling of previously learned or encountered words. The same procedures occurred for English spelling.

WRITING, HYBRIDIZATION, AND BIDIRECTIONAL INFLUENCES

The children in these two-way bilingual immersion classrooms did a lot of writing; however, much of it was influenced by the expectations of the TAAS test. Except for children initiated writing and journal writing, most other writing was on assigned tasks that related to either TAAS reading or TAAS writing.

Numerous samples of third- and fourth-grade writing assignments done as part of the TAAS mock testing activities yielded a rich record of cross-linguistic and cross-cultural influences in children's writing. As children became more bilingual, teachers asked children to write on the same prompt or topic in both languages. Fifty-three shorter texts, journals, paragraphs, summaries, and spelling dictations were examined. An additional 69 mock TAAS essays, which were written to a specified prompt and were longer, generally between 150 and 200 words, were also examined. Together these texts provided rich evidence of how children used their Spanish and English language knowledge to make decisions about how to encode sounds and words and how they used their sociocultural experiences to encode their ideas. Many of these words and texts showed a hybrid influence of language and culture and that influence was bidirectional.[3] As children made decisions about what letter to use for what sound and what words to use to convey an idea, especially a cultural construct, they were not constrained or restricted by any need to keep the languages separate and distinct. Often this cross-language influence appeared to be unintended; that is, the children did not leave evidence of the influence being purposeful. For example, Martin wrote "the propositi [purpose] is that we past [passed] the TAAS . . ." and later when assigned the same topic in Spanish wrote, *"El propósito . . . fue que pasamos un hexamen [examen]"* (The purpose . . . was that we passed an exam). Martin's encoding of *propositi* [purpose] was influenced by his knowledge of Spanish, and it is unclear whether he had the English oral word, but he invented or hypothesized that it should be written differently in English. Also, his use of the word *hexamen* [*examen*] in the Spanish text showed the influence of his knowledge of the voiced /*h*/ in English or perhaps overgeneralizing the voiceless *h* in Spanish.

However, the bidirectional influence in many of the pieces analyzed showed that the children were often purposely using knowledge of one language to help them convey a message in the other. Although they knew the word in both languages, they often chose to use a particular word because of the cultural significance. For example, Eva, writing in Spanish about the school field day, wrote, *"Era día de campo, era* field day" (It was field day), and Leo, writing in English about his first holy communion, wrote, ". . . my godfather, my *padrino* called . . ." Both Eva and Leo knew the appropriate words in each language but intentionally used the word from the other language to connote their understanding of what they may consider to be a unique cultural construct. Perhaps for Eva, *día de campo* just did not convey what happens on a school field day as opposed to a day on a camping trip. For Leo, the word godfather perhaps did not have the same feeling or describe the social and cultural relationship that he anticipated with his *padrino*.

---

[3]Hornberger (1989) proposed multilayered biliteracy development continua that included from oral language to written language, from reception to production, and from first language to second language. She also hypothesized that learners progress along these continua bidirectionally, depending on the context and the instructional alternatives.

Children also used numerous words borrowed from one language and adapted or conjugated them in the second language, very similarly to the way the greater language community code switches and uses a hybridized language. For example, Mike, writing about a fishing trip with his father, ended his text with the question, *"¿Qúe cacharías tú si estabas [estuvieras] pescando conmigo?"* (What would you catch if you were fishing with me?). He borrowed the English word *catch* and conjugated it in Spanish writing *cacharías*. Rey, writing in English about his mother's cooking, wrote *"cocining brecfist"* [cooking breakfast]. He borrowed the Spanish word *cocinar* and turned it into an English gerund. There were also numerous words for foods—tacos, hot dogs, nachos, big red, barbeque and barbacoa—that were used bidirectionally as hybridized cultural constructs with ease and confidence and without any need for explanation.

Four Children's Language Usage in Spanish and English Texts

What follows are analyses and discussions of excerpts from four children's Spanish and English texts. These four children, Martin, Mike, Eva, and Dalia, were neither the best nor the worst writers in their classes. Excerpts from their texts were selected because they are representative of the wide range of language usage and errors across all the texts examined. These excerpts share common elements found across numerous children's texts. The children's texts have been transcribed just as the children wrote them. I end the section on writing and bidirectional influences with the analysis of the full texts in Spanish and an English produced by Dalia in response to a TAAS mock testing prompt.

Martin. Martin entered the program in kindergarten as a Spanish dominant student with limited knowledge of English. He wrote an assigned piece about going to the amusement park Fiesta Texas as a reward for having passed the TAAS tests. This assignment was written first in Spanish and then in English and demonstrates the bidirectional influence of his two languages. Although many parts of the two pieces appear to be almost a translation, his English piece is longer: 254 words in English to 213 words in Spanish. Martin's Spanish text has fewer spelling and syntax errors, whereas the English text has more recurring errors. Here are excerpts from Martin's English and Spanish texts:

> . . . we whent [went] to by candy, Sour punch, Hearches [Hersheys], Snickers, Sketiros [skittles] and Lalie [lolly] pop. . . . our groop [group] whent [went] to the rollacouster [roller coaster] . . . they got on the rolacouster [roller coaster] . . . I rod [rode] on the Role causter [roller coaster] one time . . . after that we when [went] to eat hot dog, it meger [measure] like 9 inches . . . When we where in line I saw a frind [friend] Pablo we go the the saim [same] church, we went to the water raids [rides]. . . . the propositi [purpose] is that we past [passed] the TAAS test. By pasing [passing] the test we whent [went] to Fiesta Texas . . . Sometimes you reimember [remember] stuf [stuff].

> . . . fuimos a comprar dulces de Sour punch, hearches, Snickers, Sketiros y una paleta. nuestro grupo fue a la montaña rusa . . . ellos se subieron al la montaña rusa . . . Yo me subí a la montaña rusa del correcaminos una ves . . . después nos fuimos a comer hot dog, el hot dog media como 9 pulgadas . . . Cuando estábamos en línea mire a Pablo, el va a la misma iglesia que yo. . . . El propósito de ir a Fiesta Texas fue que pasamos un hexamen [examen] de matemáticas y lectura . . . Aveces [a veces] no te acuerdas de muchas cosas, pero vale la pena.

At first glance these appeared to be a word-for-word translation first written in one language and translated into the second. However, some phrases such as "I rod [rode] on the Role causter [roller coaster] one time" and *"yo me subí a la montaña rusa del correcaminos una ves"* (I got on the roadrunner roller coaster one time) suggested a slightly different idea. In English, he uses "to ride," which he might have translated to *pasear,* a common word used in the community; however he chooses to use *me subí* (to get on). Because I do not know which he wrote first, the only conclusion I could make was that he might routinely talk about this experience in both languages and uses those words that are more commonly used in each language, although they connote a slightly different meaning. In the Spanish phrase he adds just a little more information, since there are a number of roller coasters at this amusement park he designates which of these, *correcaminos* (the roadrunner), he rode. The fact that the trip was a reward for passing the TAAS is more coherent in Spanish where he expressed it in one sentence: *"El propósito de ir a Fiesta Texas fue que pasamos un hexamen [examen] de matemáticas y lectura"* (the purpose of going to Fiesta

Texas was that we passed a mathematics and reading exam). In English, he wrote essentially the same thought but expressed it in two sentences while explicitly naming the test.

An interesting usage that was a common practice for a number of children and is also a common practice in the language community was using the names of cultural foods in the language of the culture such as Martin's use of hot dog as well as the names of the candy (sour punch, Hersheys, Snickers, Skittles) in English in both texts. The one exception Martin makes is *una paleta* (a lollypop), but he was not clear from his text what prompted his making this distinction, perhaps he has more experiences with *paletas* and although he knows the word lollypop it may not have the same connotation for him.

Martin's Spanish text used many more standard spellings with the exception of the loan words for the names of the candy, which he appeared to have encoded using a combination of English and Spanish phonemes. For example, Hersheys became *hearches,* which demonstrated his attempt at writing this in Spanish; he used the diphthong *ea* for the English vowel controlled by the *r.* He also substituted the *ch* in Spanish for the *sh.* Martin also had not mastered the segmentation of some Spanish words; he wrote "aveces" instead of "*a veces*" (sometimes). He concluded his text with a common cultural phrase used in Spanish, "*pero vale la pena*" (but it is worth the trouble), which he did not include in his English text.

Martin's English text had more errors and demonstrated his developing language skills. He has good control of syntax, verb and noun agreement, and his writing was coherent and cohesive. Martin's various attempts at spelling "went" stood out in his text. He wrote "went" five times in four different ways and wrote it correctly one time. He wrote "whent" three times and "when" one time even though he used "when" appropriately in the phrase "when we where in line." Because the *w* is only used for loan words in Spanish, Martin's errors in encoding the *w* in English showed the influence of instruction and perhaps encounters with the word in English texts in reading. The various ways that he wrote the word "went" showed that he has not yet decided on or internalized one way of writing it. Some of his invented spelling such as groop [group], rod [rode], causter and couster [coaster], frind [friend], saim [same], raids [rides], and reimember [remember] suggest how Martin interpreted the English vowels but do not necessarily suggest that he used Spanish phonemes to encode English.

Martin's invented spellings of some consonants such as meger [measure] and double letters as in stuf [stuff] and role [roller] showed that he was writing these words phonetically using English phonemes. He showed an awareness of conjugating verbs in his use of the word pass, but confused the noun "past" for the past tense of pass—passed, and only used one *s* in the gerund pasing [passing].

Mike.   Mike entered the program in second grade as a Spanish dominant student with limited knowledge of English. Mike seldom wrote the same text in both languages. Even when the teacher assigned the same topic in both languages, he wrote very different texts. Here are samples of his English and Spanish texts. Mike's English text described his experience of going with his father on a construction job to build a house. The text began using a formulaic opening for a story.

> One day at 6:00, mi [my] dad wolk [woke] me up to tell me that I culd [could] gow [go] with hem [him] to work and help him with his gob [job] . . . I help put the bords [boards] an [and] the skrues [screws] on the house, the bes [best] part was wen [when] we were peinting [painting] the house from the insaid [inside] and autsaid [outside] . . . the hardest part was the restrum [restroom] because we deden't [didn't] no [know] were [where] to put the thoylet [toilet] and the tub. Evriting [everything] came perfect . . .

Mike's English text included 167 words of which 28 were not written in a conventional way; this was about 17% of the text. Many of the errors showed some influence from Mike's knowledge of Spanish, such as strit [street], mi [my] aut [out], evriting [everything]; but some of his errors could also be categorized as phonetic spellings of English, such as wolk [woke], wath [what], ther [there], groing [growing], bords [boards], and thoylet [toilet].

Mike's Spanish text included 212 words of which 16 were not written in a conventional way.

> *Algo muy padre o divertido te a pasado en tu vida? A mi sí, te voy a decir todo de lo que paso. . . . Mi papá me llevo a la pesca. Se pasaron 2 horas y pesque uno como el tamaño de mi zapato. Mi papá pesco [pescó] uno como del tamaño de una llanta. Los metimos a la agua y de repente un pescado que tienia [tenía] una nariz muy picuda salto de el [del] agua muy alto come un papalote . . . dospues [después] en el ilo [hilo] demi [de mi] ril*

[fishing reel] *se fue r,r,r,r,r,r, y eso fue cuando yo supe que era elpescado [el pescado] con la naris (nariz) picuda . . . ¿Qué cacharias tu si estabas [estuvieras] pescando con migo?*

Has something really cool and entertaining happened in your life? To me yes, I will tell you all of what happen . . . Two hours passed and I caught one [fish] like the size of a shoe. My dad caught one like the size of a tire. We put them in water and suddenly one fish that had a pointed nose jumped out of the water real high like a kite . . . later on the line of my fathers reel it went r,r,r,r,r,r,r,r and it was then when I knew that it was the fish with the pointed nose . . . What would you catch if you would have been fishing with me?

There were a number of words that were not spelled in a conventional way, for example *dospues* [*después*] (after), *ilo* [*hilo*] (thread), and *naris* [*nariz*] (nose). The spelling of *después* appears to be an encoding of a mis-pronunciation. The lack of the *h* in *hilo,* and the substitution of *s* for *z* in *nariz* are common errors in Spanish orthography. However, most of Mike's errors were errors of segmentation, for example, *ami* [*a mi*] (to me), *elpescado* [*el pescado*] (the fish), and *demi* [*de mi*] (from my). The segmentation errors were not consistent in that the word appeared conventional one time, but later Mike would make an error as if he was writing in a hurry and not re-reading his piece.

For example, in response to a prompt that asked children to write about an amusing or entertaining day or *un día divertido,* Mike opened his essay with a question as suggested by the teacher. He wrote, *"¿Algo muy padre o divertido te a pasado en tu vida? A mi sí"* (Has something very cool or amusing happened to you in your life? [It] has to me). Mike chose the expression *muy padre* in addition to the teacher's suggested word *divertido* (amusing or entertaining). *Muy padre,* although considered slang, is a very common expression in the community and a cultural construct that connotes a really cool experience. The influence of Mike's biculturalism and bilingualism was bidirectional, as he continued writing about the day he went fishing with his father. He referred to fishing rods or reels as *riles de pesca.* In this same piece about fishing, he ended his piece with a question, *"¿Qué cacharías tú si tu estabas [estuvieras] pescando conmigo?"* (What would you catch if you would have been fishing with me?). Here he was again using a word *cachar* common in the language community borrowed from the English word *catch.* He conjugated it in Spanish to the future potential tense writing *cacharías* and correctly accented it.

Eva.   Eva entered the program in kindergarten as a Spanish dominant child with limited English proficiency. Her Spanish text was coherent, cohesive, and had few errors. She appeared to be having difficulty distinguishing the *e* sound in *rendimos* (give up) and *seguimos* (continued). This difficulty maybe attributed to the community language where the pronunciation of these words approximated her invented spelling. Although she used accents more accurately than her peers, her text contained two accent errors. She used some code switching as if to emphasize a cultural construct as in "field day" and "hot cheetoes." She may not know the word in Spanish for "raspberry" or any other word for the proper name sports drink "Gatorade."

> *. . . Hoy era mi día favorito era día de campo, era* field day *. . . mi clase y yo estabamos [estábamos] listos para ganarles a todos. El primer juego era de brincar con una bolsa era muy difícil pero no nos rindimos [rendimos] y ganamos. Siguimos [seguimos] con es estrategia y ganamos . . . Si tenias dinero podrias [podrías] comprar algo afuera como unos nachos con queso amarillo o con jalapeños verdes, unos fritos de hot cheetoes con queso de nacho y un refresco de* gatorade. *Yo compre un* Gatorade *de sabor de rasberry* [raspberry].

In English on the same topic Eva wrote:

> Today was my favorite day it was field day. . . . My class and I were ready to beat all the classes. In the first game you'd have to jump in a bag it was hard, but we did't [did not] give up. Then we won that game!! We kept up that strategie [strategy] and won . . . If you had money you could't [could] buy something outside like crunch nachos with yellow cheese and green jalapenos, hot cheetos with nacho cheese and some Gatorade. I bought a drink it was cherry Gatorade . . .

Eva's English writing included numerous references to Mexican food, for example, she wrote, "crunch (crunchy) *nachos* with yellow cheese and green *jalapenos*" while in Spanish, she wrote, *"nachos con queso amarillo con jalapeños verdes"* (chips with yellow cheese and green peppers). There were a number of words that children used that they identified as generic or hybrid, and not as belonging to a specific language or not needing translations. Here Eva used the words *nachos* and *jalapenos* in both texts without any signaling to the reader whether she understood the origins of the words. However, at other times, she did signal to the reader her understanding of word origin, as in the example of her use of "it was field day . . ." in English and later in Spanish she wrote, *"era día de campo, era field day."* Eva translated "field day" the first time she used it in her Spanish essay, but thereafter she used field day three other times in English throughout the rest of the Spanish text as if the translation did not quite carry the same meaning.

In most of the texts analyzed, the children often used culturally rich words and phrases and code switching in both their Spanish and English texts. Closing phrases in the Spanish texts almost always included some closing words to the reader, *por fin* (finally), *espero que te guste* (I hope you like it), and *vale la pena* (it was worth the trouble). The English texts just ended or used the ending suggested by the teacher.

Dalia. Dalia started the program in kindergarten as a Spanish dominant student. On an assignment to write about an unforgettable day or *un día inolvidable,* Dalia wrote about her school trip to Fiesta Texas in English and about her sister's birthday in Spanish. Dalia's English text contains 231 words and her Spanish text contains 252 words.

Text 1: Unforgettable Day—English

Have you had an unforgetable good day? Well I have and I am going to tell you what happened.
One saturday morning at 11:00 my mom Elva and my dad told me to take a shower and get dressed, so I did it. Then my mom and dad took me to eat in McDonalds and I ate hash brown and strawberry pancake and drank an orange juice. Then we left home and watched a movie for 2 hours. Then we left to Six Flags Fiesta Texas and had

lots of fun. My dad and my mom
Elva got on with me on the super
man róllor coster and it was fun.
Then we ate hot dogs and drank
coca-cola. Then we got on the
mega drop and from the mega
drop I got on the joker revenge
and it was 2 minuets. So we
got off and my mom Elva bought
me 1 pickel and a big red. Then
we went to the castle and we
saw bugs bunny and tweety.
Then it was a maze, we had
to find a way out to go on
the ride that comes with the
castle. My mom Elva and my
dad Feliciano and me got all
wet so we got off. Then we
went home and went to sleep.
I hope you have an unforgetable
day in your life, that will be
a good day.

In spite of the fact that Dalia chained in English and that she started
most of her sentences with "then," her text is coherent, cohesive, and fairly
free of errors.

Text 2: Un día inolvidable—Spanish

un día que nunca olvide

¿Haz tenido un día que nunca

has olvidado? si tu respuesta es
no te contare lo que me pasó a
mí.

Un sábado por la mañana a las
11:30. Mi mamá Elva me lavantó de
mi cama azul, mi mamá me dijo
—Denise ve y bañate—mi mamá me
dijo. Luego me cambie ropa de pantalón
azul y una camiseta blanca. Luego
lave los trastes y salieron tan
blancas como la nieve. Luego mapie
y el suelo estaba tan blanca como
papel blanco. Después mi mamá fue
a la tienda Handy Andy para
comprar sodas de big red y coca-cola
y también compró comida. También
compró cheetos, fritos y doritos.
En seguida mi mamá vino y
me dijo-Denise la casa esta tan
blanca como la nieve y preparó
todo para el cumpleaños de mi
hermana Brandy. Luego el
primero que vino fueron dos
amigos que se llaman Roberto y
Fernando. Entonces yo me quede con
mis dos amigos y mi mamá Elva
fue a comprar un pastel de fresa
y vino. Entonces todos mis amigos y
primos vineron y comenzó la fiesta.
Por ultimo, le regalaron un vestido

azul a mi hermanita Brandy. También
le regalaron 2 pares de zapatos que
son blancos. Luego empezamos a
comer pastel de fresa y estaba
bien rica. Cuando yo mire al reloj
ya eran las 4:30 de la tarde
y le dije a mi mamá- mamá
ya vamos a quebrar la piñata.
Mi mamá le dijo a todos que
ya era tiempo de quebrar la
piñata y yo agarré muchos
dulces.
        Espero que tu te diverdes
cuando tu tengas un día que
nunca has olvidado.

Dalia's Spanish text is more complex. Although she uses less chaining, she frequently uses *luego* (then) to begin five of her sentences. She used relational words such as *despues* (after), *entonces* (and then), *en seguida* (following), and *por ultimo* (finally) to introduce most sentences and she kept the text moving to the next idea. Her Spanish text also included several spelling errors, including accent errors. She used the proper names for Handy Andy, Coca-Cola, and Big Red (a popular soda of the region) without any particular designation that they were borrowed from English. She also used the word *mapie* (to mop), a commonly used word in the language community borrowed from the English word *mop* and used as a verb in Spanish.

The children's writing in these two-way bilingual immersion classrooms reflected the diverse home, community, and classroom influences. The students used the familiar vernacular or community discourse in their writing, which, according to Hornberger and Skilton-Sylvester (2002), is often ignored in school discourse. As children incorporated the specific conventions of their two developing languages, they exhibited a complex understanding of writing as a tool for conveying ideas and relationships (Pérez & Torres-Guzmán, 2002) and demonstrated their developing voice and agency (Gutiérrez et al., 2000). The children's writing, as in the Edelsky (1986) study, was shaped by social and cultural practices as the children hypothesized about the general principles of writing and aspects of writing that they could use across languages. The writing was also constrained by the curriculum and the influence of TAAS.

CONCLUSION

As children used language and literacy to learn more challenging content, the teachers continued to maintain language separation. Often, children chose to respond accurately in either language, then attempted to interpret or translate to match the language of instruction. Rarely did the teachers mix the two languages during instructional time and students typically matched their response to the language of the teacher. I did not observe any significant difference in the pattern of language matching; that is, it occurred as frequently in Spanish as in English.

Although the teachers stressed to each other, to the community, and to the researcher their separation of the languages for instruction, they also articulated the importance of allowing children to communicate using all their language knowledge. The fact that teachers allowed and accepted children's approximations and choices in their use of language was evident in their written texts.

The literacy behaviors of teachers and children incorporated many aspects of the hybridized cultural identity they shared. During numerous lessons, teachers and children made references to their life experiences. They also stopped to add reflections on how these were unique and different from experiences that non-Hispanics might have. They also discussed their experiences as biliterate learners as being distinct from those who were also Hispanic but were only learning in English. As children read content text, they looked for those aspects that related to not only their neighborhood, city, state, but also to Mexican or other Spanish-speaking people.

The teaching of challenging content in Spanish and English through the fifth grade was seen as most important and was given close attention and monitoring by teachers and administrators.[4] In most of these classrooms, teachers were using integrated approaches to teach problem solving through tasks that required complex cognitive activity and the use of literate language. Many of these tasks incorporated technology, fine arts, and the students' personal experiences across their sociocultural contexts. Teachers incorporated and children often made references to their experiences outside of school in their community and in Mexico. Thus, language, literacy, and academic content were acquired simultaneously.

In these classrooms, the teachers were faced every day with situations that challenged their understanding of literacies as situated or literacy as a social practice. They explored with children and with each other what reading and writing meant and challenged each other's understanding of literacy. The teachers drew on numerous theories and understandings, including theories of globalization, literacy as cultural identity, reading and writing as tools of bureaucracies and power relations, literacy as media and technology, the social semiotics of literacy, and the scientific knowledge of literacy.

---

[4]Most studies (Ramírez et al., 1991; Thomas & Collier, 1997; Willig, 1985) of language minority students who are successful in school show that they receive strong literacy, cognitive, and academic development through their first language for 5 or 6 years as well as content instruction through the second language—English. Thomas and Collier (1997) concluded that the students who do receive this type of first language support "are doing well in school as they reach the last of the high school years" (p. 14).

7

Testing Pressures and Student Outcomes

The first-grade teacher began the daily calendar activity saying, *"Hoy es un día nubloso, quiere decir que (a) hay sol, (b) hay nubes, o (c) esta lloviendo"* (Today is a cloudy day, this means that [a] there is sun, [b] there are clouds, or [c] it is raining). The children in unison shout out *"(b) hay nubes."* Later the teacher explained that because of the "pressure to show that I am preparing the children for the different tests," she tried to include the multiple choice format in a variety of activities conducted during each day. The Texas Assessment of Academic Skills (TAAS) has defined success as being able to perform with multiple choice materials that isolate particular skills or asks the child to name strategies as opposed to assessing the actual performance of the child's ability to read, write, and reason for multiple purposes. The state, and thus the district and the campus, requires the TAAS as part of the institutional accountability. It is the TAAS that the teachers and students feel dominates the curriculum and is what their performance will be judged by.

In the first semester of kindergarten, children's language and emergent literacy was assessed; thus, the teachers started to talk to the students about tests and created test-like activities—multiple choice or forced choice questions. The teachers began to worry about tests. As the children progressed to the third grade, these test-like activities intensified as teachers felt more pressure to prepare children for the TAAS. All the two-way classes engaged in instruction in Spanish, and later in English, that was guided by the objectives and the formats of the TAAS.

Preparing for standardized or state tests has become a rite of spring in most schools. For the teachers and students in the two-way bilingual immersion program, this rite assumed major proportions. The pressures of testing, especially the TAAS, were a constant concern for the students and teachers. Especially during the spring semester, as the testing season approached, many of the lessons took on the format of TAAS passages. Even after the TAAS test was administered, the two-way bilingual immersion classrooms continued to be preoccupied with testing.

The influence of the TAAS Test and the psychological pressure that children felt was voiced by Gerardo. Gerardo took the TAAS in Spanish, but later writes about his experience in English. He wrote a long detailed account describing how he found the right answers, checked his work, got restroom breaks, and how the teacher paced while they took the test. He began and ended his story with the following:

> On April 23, 1999 we took the 3rd grade TAAS math test at 8:01 in the morning. . . . Thank you for hiring [hearing] or reading my story of the TAAS and how you are going to be nerves [nervous] when you are in thered [third] grade or higer [higher] youl [you'll] now [know] how it fiels [feels].

EARLY ASSESSMENT

All children are tested as they entered the program to assess their language dominance and were categorized as either Spanish dominant or English dominant based on this initial language assessment. The school district used the IDEA Oral Language Proficiency Tests (IPT-E, IPT-S) to measure and determine oral language proficiency. Four basic areas of oral language proficiency were tested: vocabulary, comprehension, syntax, and verbal expression (includes articulation). The English and Spanish versions were the same with the exception being the language used for administration of the test. Students were tested individually and scored based on six different levels.

At the kindergarten and first-grade levels of the two-way bilingual immersion program, the children were administered the *Tejas LEE,*[1] a

---

[1] *Tejas LEE* is the Spanish version of the Texas Primary Reading Inventory required by the state to be administered in the primary grades.

Spanish primary reading inventory required by the state; the Aprenda, a Spanish achievement test; and the Iowa Test of Basic Skills (ITBS), an English achievement test. In addition to the TAAS test, the district required the use of the Aprenda and ITBS to measure two-way students' achievement. Both the Aprenda and the ITBS were administered beginning in kindergarten.[2] The Aprenda is a norm-referenced, standardized test administered to all students in Spanish. In kindergarten, sounds and letters, word reading, and total reading scores were provided. For first grade, the Aprenda provided reading comprehension, word reading, language, and auditory comprehension subtest scores and a total score. For Grades 2 through 5, the Aprenda had four subsets—reading comprehension, language, vocabulary, and auditory comprehension—plus a total score. In addition, for Grades 4 and 5, the Aprenda provided an English language development subtest score.

The ITBS is a norm-referenced standardized test administered in English. Three subtest scores were provided for kindergarten: vocabulary, language, and reading. For first through fifth grade, subtest scores for vocabulary and reading comprehension and total reading are provided.

THE TAAS AND ACCOUNTABILITY

The Texas Education Agency's Academic Excellence Indicator System (AEIS)[3] is the state's formal report utilized by the school districts to assess and compare their students' performance. In addition, the 1995 Texas Legislature passed an assessment system for limited English proficient

---

[2] Both the Aprenda and ITBS are considered to be reliable and valid indicators of student achievement (see Ochoa, 1998, for a review on Aprenda; see Brookhart, 1998, for a review on ITBS). The Aprenda uses the Stanford Achievement to establish content validity, whereas the ITBS uses the CoGAT for establishing subtest correlations. The Aprenda was normed with a U.S. Spanish-speaking sample and the ITBS was normed with a representative sample across the United States.

[3] The Texas Education Agency, Academic Excellence Indicator System includes TAAS scores in Reading and Mathematics for third, fourth, and fifth grades and writing for fourth grade. Bilingual students have the option of taking all tests in Spanish or English. The schools are rated as acceptable, recognized, or exemplary based on the TAAS performance of students by subcategory (African American, Hispanic, White, and Economically Disadvantaged), dropout rate, and attendance rate. For more information, see the TEA web site at www.tea.state.tx.us/student.assessment.

students.[4] The student's English and Spanish TAAS scores are aggregated by campus and are used as base indicators in the school accountability rating system.

The content standards that are to be assessed by the TAAS are delineated in the Texas Essential Knowledge and Skills (TEKS).[5] Though there is a lot of discussion about whether the TAAS actually assesses the TEKS, the TAAS is used as the accountability system by the state. Thus, as one principal stated, "It drives everything."

Storm's and Bonham's instructional and achievement improvement efforts were focused and guided by the TAAS assessment data. Both schools used mock TAAS tests that were administered every 9 weeks to analyze which objectives students had not mastered and that information was used by the current teacher, as well as shared with the teacher in the next lower grade, to work on those specific objectives. Previous TAAS test versions released by the state were used to compose tests for the mock TAAS tests. The rationale expressed by the principals and teachers for the frequency of the administration of the mock tests was not only to analyze student progress but also to assist children in learning "how to respond to the test format" so that the actual test would accurately reflect students' abilities. The major part of the assessment and evaluation of the school curriculum and instruction was the TAAS test and the mock TAAS tests. Everyone voiced that this was because "the school's performance is judged on the basis of TAAS scores."

The TAAS test influenced, either directly or indirectly, almost all the teachers' instructional decisions. Storm and Bonham teachers examined students' performance for each objective and for each level of assessment

---

[4]Under this legislation, limited English proficient students receiving instruction in Spanish as required by Section 29.055 of the Texas Education Code will take either the TAAS in Spanish or in English at the time of program exit. Students taking the TAAS in Spanish will also be administered a reading proficiency test in English that will identify their level of proficiency in reading English. Students who enter U.S. schools by first or second grade will be required to take the TAAS in English after 4 years. Those entering U.S. schools in third grade or subsequent grades are required to take the TAAS in English after 3 years.

[5]The TEKS Learning Standards for Texas Children have been aligned with the No Child Left Behind statute and a new TAKS test developed. In 2002–2003, schools will be required to use the new assessment, which will be available in Spanish and English through the fifth grade.

and individually as well as collectively made adjustments to their instructional plans based on these ongoing analyses. Teachers reported that this practice focuses attention on individual needs.

> We have gone from talking about meeting individual student needs in instruction to starting to do it and working hard to ensure that it is happening. . . . We are now much more focused. Before teachers would say students are on "third grade level." Now we can talk about specific objectives.[6]

In 1997–1998, as a result of a district mandate that all schools select and implement a research-based school reform model, Storm examined the possibility of implementing the Accelerated Schools model. The school staff received extensive training on the Accelerated Schools model, which they liked because the approach utilized school assessment data as a key element in instructional decision making and the teachers reported, "This was compatible with the school's vision of assessment and instruction." This training helped the teachers and other school staff to analyze assessments conducted at the classroom level to plan instruction. Storm eventually decided not to implement or participate in the Accelerated Schools; however, the training and the focus on assessment data to inform curriculum and instructional choices was maintained and strengthened.

Storm and Bonham staff began using TAAS data to prioritize instructional decisions. For example, low scores in writing had led to schoolwide emphasis on writing, and as a result, writing scores on the TAAS improved. Although the principals and teachers continuously stated that the instructional content and approaches were not selected solely based on the TAAS objectives, one principal said, "Teachers incorporate TAAS objectives into daily instruction . . . they do not teach to the TAAS test, but because the content or the process—like problem solving—is important for children to learn." The teachers also spoke of not teaching to the TAAS test, but also spoke about how difficult it was to monitor and make sure that they were incorporating the TAAS objectives. One teacher voiced her concerns: "How do we do it all? If you teach TAAS [objectives and formats] as something different or separate, it isn't meaningful to kids. You must be able to . . . know how it is asked on the TAAS test and teach that way."

---

[6]Hargett and Murray (1999) and RMC Research Corporation conducted an evaluation of Storm Elementary School and the principal provided me with some transcripts of the interviews conducted as part of that evaluation.

Although there were yearly activities during the professional development days in which the teachers examined and matched the TAAS objectives to their curriculum to identify where every object was being addressed, when it came to the daily work of teaching, it was especially difficult to monitor those objectives that were heavily weighted in the TAAS test and assure these objectives were adequately covered before the testing date. For example, grammar usage as tested in the TAAS writing subtest was worrisome to teachers. Also, teachers reported that they attempted to integrate science and social studies with literacy instruction but did not always feel they covered these content areas adequately. Most teachers reported that the focus was on reading, writing, and math that were tested on the TAAS.

The literature as well as the popular media repeatedly describe and announce how poorly Mexican American and other Hispanic children score on tests, so much so that it has become an accepted truth that even the best teachers who get students to learn and achieve are plagued by self-doubt and feel that the only way to get the children to perform better is to teach a test-like curriculum. In spite of being critical of the testing instruments and the limitations of the state accountability system, teachers for the most part felt their primary responsibility was to equip their students to meet the expectations of the state testing system in spite of the fact that numerous school documents described the school curriculum as being guided by the standards and benchmarks "that are world-class" and espoused those performance competencies identified by the National Council of Teachers of Mathematics, Science, and English, as well as the standards identified by the National Association for Bilingual Education and the International Reading Association.

The teachers communicated their assessment findings among themselves to coordinate instructional planning. Assessment in the two-way bilingual immersion was conducted in Spanish and English. Although the Spanish TAAS test was new and thus old exams were not available for the mock testing, the district office provided translated versions of the English TAAS for the mock testing in Spanish. The bilingual program office had invested a lot of time and energy to ensure that the translations were appropriate, and incorporated feedback from the teachers to assure that the mock tests were fair and appropriate for the students.

Each school had its own method of conveying the assessment information from teacher to teacher as the children progressed through the program. At Storm, they used what teachers called the "little green folder" that contained student assessment information that was passed from grade level to grade level. The teacher at each grade level would add that year's information and that information would follow the child within the school. This assessment information was also available for parents and was often shared with them through conferences.

Even though the focus on the TAAS test and the numerous mock testing events used valuable instruction time, the administrators and teachers felt that the improved results for the school as a whole, and in particular for the two-way bilingual immersion students, provided them with the data they needed to continue the program.

TAAS Assessment Summaries

Both schools made considerable improvements in their TAAS measurements.[7] The two-way bilingual immersion students first took the TAAS test during the third grade along with all other third graders. Children were tested in math and reading in third and fifth grade and in writing in fourth grade. Two-way bilingual immersion students could take the reading, writing, and math in either English or Spanish. The summaries that follow show the initial scores at the inception of the program when the two-way bilingual immersion students were in kindergarten. By 1998, the first cohorts of two-way bilingual immersion students reach third grade and their scores begin to make an impact on the school scores.

Storm Elementary student achievement improved steadily. In 1994, the TAAS scores for all tests taken by all students were at the 18.6 percentile; in 1999–2000 and 2000–2001, the school was "Recognized" when the TAAS scores for all tests taken by all students were at the 80.4 percentile. Storm's TAAS scores for 1994 through 2000 are shown in Table 7.1.

Between 1994 and 2001, Bonham had an average enrollment of 340 students, with the latest figures for 2001 being 341 students. Seventy-eight

---

[7] See www.tea.state.tx.us/PAI/DCR/SP for a technical manual on the Texas Assessment of Academic Skills (TAAS) and the statewide student assessment program in Texas.

TABLE 7.1
Storm Elementary TAAS Campus Data for 1994–2000
Percentage of Students Meeting Minimum Expectations

	1994	1995	1996	1997	1998	1999	2000
All Students							
All tests	18.6	21.6	23.4	28.3	47.3	50.9	80.4
Reading	43.4	43.4	37.2	35.2	59.4	59.1	87.4
Writing	35.2	41.8	46.6	66.7	71.4	78.7	96
Math	23.0	27.5	38	36.6	60.9	69.1	85.0
Two-way students							
Reading							
English	na	na	na	na	61.9	68	87.0
Spanish	na	na	na	na	62	68.6	85
Writing							
English	na	na	na	na	na	86.6	95.7
Spanish	na	na	na	na	na	88	84
Math							
English	na	na	na	na	60.9	68.6	85
Spanish	na	na	na	na	61.4	72	100

Note.   Reading and math scores are for third, fourth, and fifth grades; writing scores are for fourth grade.

percent (78%) of the student population was Mexican American and 30% spoke Spanish as a home language. Ninety-one percent (91%) of the students were classified as economically disadvantaged by the state and federal guidelines for assistance to schools. Like at Storm, the families living in poverty experienced a high rate of mobility, which affected school attendance and continued enrollment.

Since 1995, Bonham Elementary student achievement has improved steadily as measured by the Texas Assessment of Academic Skills (TAAS) part of the Texas Education Agency's Academic Excellence Indicator System. In 1994, the TAAS scores for all tests taken by all students were at the 50th percentile; in 1997–1998 the school was "Recognized" when the TAAS scores for all tests taken by all students were at the 84.3 percentile, and in 2000–2001, the school was "Exemplary" with TAAS scores for all tests taken by all students at the 93rd percentile. Bonham's TAAS scores for 1994 through 2000 are shown in Table 7.2.

TABLE 7.2
Bonham Elementary TAAS Campus Data for 1994–2000
Percentage of Students Meeting Minimum Expectations

	1994	1995	1996	1997	1998	1999	2000
All students							
All tests	50	48.6	67.3	70	84.3	75.6	91.3
Reading	65.4	63.3	77.1	78.7	95.1	82.8	92.3
Writing	84.2	78.6	80	87.9	100	100	97.5
Math	57.1	58.2	80.2	78.7	84	83.9	97.4
Two-way students							
Reading							
English	na	na	na	na	94.7	80.1	91
Spanish	na	na	na	na	94.4	81.8	91.7
Writing							
English	na	na	na	na	na	100	91.1
Spanish	na	na	na	na	na	95.5	93.4
Math							
English	na	na	na	na	82.9	100	95.7
Spanish	na	na	na	na	83.3	89.9	94

Note. Reading and math scores are for third, fourth, and fifth grades; writing scores are for fourth grade.

LITERACY ASSESSMENT

The ongoing literacy assessment was very comprehensive beginning in kindergarten, where many of the teacher assessment activities mirrored the *Tejas Lee,* and continued to the upper grades where, in addition to TAAS-like activities, other assessments were used. For example, beginning in first grade, weekly or biweekly running records were used to match children with little books at their own level.

The testing situation was always challenging the thinking of the teachers and the administrators. The percentage of students that passed the TAAS in each subgroup and in each subject category determined the school's performance rating for the subsequent school year.[8] A major issue

---

[8]TAAS rating system required the following Minimum TAAS passing scores for all students in all categories for each school designation. To encourage schools to meet rising standards, the minimum scores increased from 1994 to 2000. Schools had to make

was the language of the TAAS test because the TAAS was available in both Spanish and English versions and there were different expectations voiced by various central office administrators about which test version should be used for two-way bilingual immersion students. This was continually discussed and one principal summarized the issue as "what language to test while still being true to the model, and to the language of instruction." Because the program model being implemented focused on instruction in Spanish and did not begin a 50–50 language distribution until the fourth grade, which is the second year of state testing, the children theoretically would be better able to perform academically in Spanish. But the pressure of the accountability system both on the teacher and the school raised questions about students performance in each language, about the equivalency and level of difficulty of the testing items in each language, and about the future expectations in later grades when the students would no longer have a language option and would have to perform on the English language testing. One teacher expressed this concern, "The district policy and TEA to test only in English at the fifth grade does not capture what children can do, how do we capture not only what children know but also what we have been teaching in the whole program. . . ."

One of the issues that both teachers and administrators expressed concern with was the policy to admit limited English proficient students at all the grade levels. English speakers were not admitted to the program if they had not started in kindergarten or first grade. Limited English proficient children who entered at different grade levels were included in the testing program as members of the two-way bilingual immersion program. The fairness of subjecting these children to the battery of tests in both Spanish and English that was part of the two-way bilingual immersion program and the reflection of the testing on the program were constant concerns.

The teachers talked about the importance of test data and their observational information, as well as the links between the school vision, the

increasingly higher scores to remain at the same or to improve the school designation in each succeeding year.

School Designation	1994	1995	1996	1997	1998	1999	2000
Exemplary	90	90	90	90	90	90	90
Recognized	65	70	70	75	80	80	80
Acceptable	25	25	30	35	40	45	45
Low Performing	below 25	below 25	below 30	below 35	below 40	below 45	

reform efforts, curriculum changes, and evaluation. Teachers also felt they were pressured to use mock TAAS test results to design action plans and monitor progress in addressing any weaknesses identified in the mock testing.

All classes observed showed evidence that instruction was guided by objectives and items included in the TAAS. For example, during a language arts lesson in a fourth-grade classroom, the teacher explained to the students that the spelling and vocabulary lesson was necessary because "one of our lowest areas on the TAAS was word meaning." Another activity in the language arts, in both English and Spanish and at both the third- and fourth-grade levels, required students to identify and correct errors in sentences provided by the teacher. This activity, called *daily oral language,* mimics a section of the TAAS writing test. The teachers also discussed with the students the results of a mock TAAS test results and reviewed the objectives on which each student had not done well.

APRENDA AND ITBS COMPARISONS

Besides the TAAS assessment data, other major sources of achievement data for the two-way bilingual immersion program came from IDEA (language assessment), Aprenda (language, reading, and math), and ITBS (language, reading, and math). The Aprenda was administered in Spanish and the ITBS was administered in English. Scores for all students for all grade levels were collected, but the low number of students for whom scores were available made analysis difficult except for third grade.

The descriptive results in Table 7.3 show that the Aprenda NCE scores were higher than the ITBS NCE scores for all grades. The Aprenda NCE mean scores for first through third grades were slightly above the mean, whereas the ITBS NCE mean scores were slightly below the mean and the scores are within the average range for both tests.

The initial paired sample two-tailed t-test results (see Table 7.4) demonstrate that for first through fifth grade, the Aprenda scores were significantly different than the ITBS scores ($p < .05$) reflecting the instruction in Spanish. Because of the small numbers (N) for each grade level, only third grade data were further analyzed.

Overall, the Aprenda NCE mean scores (M = 56.877, Sd = 18.924) for third-grade reading were slightly above the mean, whereas the ITBS NCE

TABLE 7.3

Aprenda and ITBS Reading NCEs Paired Samples

	Test/Grade	Mean	N	SD	Std. Error Mean
Pair 1	Aprenda-1	60.896	26	13.152	2.579
	ITBS-1	44.19	26	19.09	3.74
Pair 2	Aprenda-2	61.858	43	14.962	2.282
	ITBS-2	46.58	43	15.03	2.29
Pair 3	Aprenda-3	57.295	57	19.410	2.571
	ITBS-3	41.39	57	16.46	2.18
Pair 4	Aprenda-4	54.767	9	24.325	8.108
	ITBS-4	33.89	9	23.77	7.92
Pair 5	Aprenda-5	58.600	9	19.957	6.652
	ITBS-5	44.78	9	14.06	4.69

TABLE 7.4

Paired Samples T-Tests—Aprenda and ITBS Reading NCEs

		Paired Differences							
					95% Confidence Interval of the Difference				
		Mean	SD	Std. Error Mean	Lower	Upper	T	df	Sig.
Pair 1	A*-1 I**-1	16.704	21.705	4.257	7.937	25.471	3.924	25	.001
Pair 2	A-2 I-2	15.277	17.479	2.666	9.897	20.656	5.731	42	.000
Pair 3	A-3 I-3	15.909	18.165	2.406	11.089	20.729	6.612	56	.000
Pair 4	A-4 I-4	20.878	17.384	5.795	7.515	34.240	3.603	8	.007
Pair 5	A-5 I-5	13.822	14.486	4.829	2.687	24.957	2.862	8	.021

*Aprenda   **ITBS

TABLE 7.5
Third Grade Aprenda Spanish Reading and ITBS English Reading Scores by Language Dominance

Descriptives

Test	*Group*	*N*	*M*	*SD*	*Std. Error*	*95% Confidence Interval for Mean* *Lower Bound*	*Upper Bound*
Aprenda	Spanish	32	61.172	16.156	2.856	55.347	66.997
	English	30	52.297	20.790	3.796	44.534	60.060
	Total	62	56.877	18.924	2.403	52.072	61.683
ITBS	Spanish	31	37.16	16.03	2.88	31.28	43.04
	English	29	44.52	16.46	3.06	38.25	50.78
	Total	60	40.72	16.53	2.13	36.45	44.99

Note. Spanish = Spanish Dominant at time of entry; English = English dominant at time of entry.

From "Biliteracy Development in Two-way Immersion Classrooms: Analysis of Third Grade Spanish and English Reading," by B. Pérez and B. Bustos Flores, in J. V. Hoffman et al. (Eds.), *Fifty-first Yearbook of the National Reading Conference,* 2002, p. 365. Chicago: National Reading Conference.

mean scores (M = 41, Sd = 16.53) for reading were slightly below the mean as shown on Table 7.5. The scores are within the average range for both tests. The initial paired sample two-tailed t-test results demonstrated that for third grade reading, the Aprenda and ITBS scores were significantly different (t = 6.612, df = 56, $p < .001$). This difference is reasonable for the two-way bilingual immersion students given that instruction was primarily in Spanish through third grade. (For further discussion of the results of the comparisons of the Aprenda and the ITBS for third grade reading, see Pérez & Busto Flores, 2002).

Table 7.6 shows a one-way ANOVA of the Aprenda and ITBS reading NCE scores for each grade level by language dominance. Although the Aprenda NCE mean scores were higher for the Spanish group, the only significant between group differences found was for second grade ($p < .05$) and third grade ($p < .064$). Again, the reason for this significant difference may be that the Spanish speakers initially do better in second and third

TABLE 7.6
Third Grade Aprenda Spanish Reading and ITBS English Reading Scores

| | | ANOVA | | | | |
Test	Group	SS	df	MS	F	Sig.
Aprenda	Between Groups	1219.654	1	1219.654	3.548	.064
	Within groups	20625.834	60	343.764		
	Total	21845.488	61			
ITBS	Between groups	810.748	1	810.748	3.073	.085
	Within groups	15301.435	58	263.818		
	Total	16112.183	59			

Note. From "Biliteracy Development in Two-way Immersion Classrooms: Analysis of Third Grade Spanish and English Reading," by B. Pérez and B. Bustos Flores, in J. V. Hoffman et al. (Eds.), *Fifty-first Yearbook of the National Reading Conference,* 2002, p. 365. Chicago: National Reading Conference.

grade because of the Spanish literacy instruction, but as the groups progress within the two-way bilingual immersion program and begin to get more English literacy instruction, these differences are not significant.

For the ITBS reading subtest, those students whose initial language dominance was English had NCE scores that were higher than the Spanish dominant group's NCE scores; between groups the only significant differences found were for second grade ($p < .01$) and third grade ($p < .001$). The ITBS differences found for second and third grade are understandable, given that these scores may reflect higher English language proficiency of the English dominant speakers participating in a two-way bilingual program. Thus, despite being instructed mostly (90%) in Spanish, the English dominant group performed better during second grade than the Spanish group on the ITBS. However, the Spanish group performed within the average range on the ITBS English reading even though literacy instruction was in Spanish.

Together these results indicated that regardless of language dominance, students were achieving well within the average range as measured by the standardized tests in their dominant language and in the second language being learned.

The Aprenda reading NCE scores and language dominance were positive predictors of ITBS reading scores. The Aprenda was the primary, stronger predictor and explained 23% of the variance in the ITBS reading scores, whereas language dominance explained an additional 11% of the variance in the ITBS reading NCE scores. The positive relationship indicated that as the Spanish reading scores increase, so will the English reading scores increase.

The results demonstrated that literacy in Spanish was an influential predictor of English literacy ($p < .001$). For students who entered the program as Spanish dominant, the findings showed that learning to read in Spanish assisted them to acquire reading skills in English. For students who entered the program as English dominant students and initially received literacy instruction in Spanish, were not deterred from acquiring English literacy skills as demonstrated in their ITBS results. Additionally, by the third grade, the ITBS mean results fell within the average range for both groups, which indicated attainment of English language skills. While Spanish reading ability was greater, their ability to read in English was within the average range indicating that the majority of the children were moving toward developing balanced biliteracy. Moreover, the results showed that by the third grade, when instruction was 60% in Spanish and 40% in English, the two-way bilingual program was beginning to accomplish its biliteracy goals. These reading achievement findings are similar to those found for students in other two-way bilingual immersion programs (Cazabon et al., 1998; Christian et al., 1997; Lindholm-Leary, 2001).

THE *TEJAS LEE* AND TPRI

Before the TPRI was available, Storm used the Reading Recovery program and used the Reading Recovery assessment to monitor and adjust its early literacy instruction. In 1998, the school was disappointed with its Reading Recovery test results and implemented a program that focused on awareness of print, including print throughout the school and community, as well as more of a focus on book reading. In following years, the students did well in print awareness, but the TPRI performance identified other areas of weakness, such as rhyming. The teachers again came together to devise a program that would target the weak areas.

Much of the writing program in these classrooms was influenced first by the *Tejas Lee* and later by the TAAS items or prompts. Teachers used

Spanish and English writing prompts and collected numerous student writing samples that were scored using rubrics similar to those used to assess TAAS writing. These rubrics did not always attend to the sociocultural aspects of students' writing, but heavily focused on technical and formulaic criteria for assessment. Thus, texts that included sociocultural experiences, awareness of audience, or other criteria that distinguishes students' perspective did not receive any points on the rubric system used to assess such texts.

The district, through a committee of teachers and administrators, recommended a reading and writing assessment program for the early grades that included testing in syllabic knowledge, reading, comprehension, sight words, and writing. The two-way bilingual immersion students were tested in Spanish using a combination of the *Tejas LEE* or locally developed instruments. The testing schedule for K–2 is illustrated in Figures 7.1 through 7.3.

In kindergarten (Fig. 7.1), the *Tejas Lee* assessment of literacy was primarily an assessment of rhyming, blending, segmentation, other decoding skills, and listening comprehension. The district added knowledge of words and ability to write thoughts. The first grade *Tejas Lee* (Fig. 7.2) continued assessing phonics elements and listening comprehension, and added a running record. The second grade *Tejas Lee* (Fig. 7.3) focused on phonics elements in spelling and writing, and continued with listening comprehension and running records. At both first and second grades, the district added assessment of writing. These assessments, which emphasized knowledge of phonemic/phonics skills and words, influenced the daily literacy instruction that occurred in these classrooms. Teachers spoke often of the conflict they felt between what they considered good instruction and what would be tested.

LANGUAGE ASSESSMENT

Students' oral and reading Spanish and English proficiency was assessed using the IDEA Proficiency Test (IPT). The IPT is a standardized instrument, approved by the Texas Education Agency, which yields data for identifying students for bilingual and ESL classes. The IPT gives a Language Proficiency Level ranging from non-English speaker to fluent

Kindergarten Testing Schedule – English

Date	Assessment	Task	Criteria	Who is tested
May 14-18	Kindergarten TPRI	1. Rhyming*	4/5	Any student who scored SD on Jan. TPRI or corresponding SAISD Assessment
		2. Blending Word Parts	4/5	
		3. Blending Phonemes*	4/5	
		4. Detecting Initial Sounds	4/5	
		5. Detecting Final Sounds	4/5	
		6. Letter Name Identification*	20/26	
		7. Letter to Sound Linking*	4/5	
		8. Listening Comprehension*	4/5	All students take this task
May 21-25	Kindergarten SAISD	Writes Name*	See assessment	Any student who scored SD on the most recent SAISD corresponding assessment
		Sight Words*	10/24	
		Pattern Reading (*Tracks*)*	10/12	
		Using Letters to Write Thoughts*	See assessment	All students take this task.

Kindergarten Testing Schedule – Spanish

Date	Assessment	Task	Criteria	Who is tested
May 14-18	Kindergarten *Tejas LEE*	K.2A Rimas*	4/5	Any student who scored SD on Jan. *Tejas LEE* or corresponding SAISD Assessment
		K.2B Identificación del sonido inicial*	4/5	
		K.2C Omisión del sonido inicial	3/4	
		K.2D Segmentación silábica	3/4	
		K.2E Unión de los sonidos	3/4	
		K.2F Unión de las sílabas*	3/4	
		K.3A&B Reconocimiento de palabras	8/10	
		K.4 Conocimientos alfabéticos*	20/24	
		K.5 Comprensión auditiva*	4/5	All students take this task
May 21-25	Kindergarten SAISD	Writes Name*	See assessment	Any student who scored SD on the most recent SAISD corresponding assessment
		Sight Words*	10/24	
		Pattern Reading (*Puedo leer*)*	10/12	
		Using Letters to Write Thoughts*	See assessment	All students take this task

*Tejas LEE or TPRI tasks with this symbol have corresponding SAISD Assessments and are Kindergarten expectations

FIG. 7.1. Kindergarten reading and writing assessment.

First Grade Testing Schedule – English

Date	Assessment	Task	Criteria	Who is tested
May 14-18	First Grade TPRI	1. Blending Word Parts (onsets, rimes)	4/5	Any student who scored SD on Jan. TPRI or corresponding SAISD Assessment
		2. Blending Word Parts (phonemes)	4/5	
		3. Detecting Initial Sounds	4/5	
		4. Detecting Final Sounds	4/5	
		5. Initial Consonant Substitution*	4/5	
		6. Final Consonant Substitution*	4/5	
		7. Middle Vowel Substitution *	4/5	
		8. Initial Blending Substitution *	4/5	
		9. Blends in Final Position	4/5	
		15. Reading Accuracy- Story 5 * (Reading Level)	Frustrational, Instructional, or Independent	All students except those who have read Story 5 at the Instructional or Independent level previously
		15. Story 5 Comprehension* (listening Comprehension)	4/5	□ Students who score Frust level, on Story 5 have this as Listening Comprehension. □ Students who scored Inst. or Ind. on Story 5 will rely on their own oral reading for comprehension. This score is to be entered under "Listening Comprehension."
May 21-25	First Grade SAISD	Sight Words*	100/100	Any student who has not yet read 100 words
		Writing*	See assessment criteria	All students take this task.

First Grade Testing Schedule – Spanish

Date	Assessment	Task	Criteria	Who is tested
May 14-18	First Grade Tejas LEE	1.1 Conocimiento silábico*	See Tejas LEE criteria	Any student who scored SD on Fall Tejas LEE or corresponding SAISD Assessment
		1.2 Conocimiento de sonidos	20/27	
		1.3 Conocimientos fonológicos A-F	3/4 on each part	
		1.3C Initial Sound Deletion*		
		1.3D Syllable Segmentation*		
		1.3F Syllable Blending*		
		1.4 Unión de sílabas*	8/10	
		1.5 Reconocimiento de palabras	8/10	
		1.6 Comprensión de oraciones	5/6	
		1.8 Lectura en voz alta* "Mis abuelas" (Reading Level)	Frust., Inst., or Ind. (see Tejas LEE criteria)	All students
		1.8 "Mis abuelas" Listening Comprehension*	4/5	□ Students who score Frust. level on "Mis abuelas" have this as Listening Comprehension. (instead of 1.7). □ Students who scored Inst. or Ind. on "Mis abuelas" will rely on their own oral reading for comprehension. This score is to be entered under "Listening Comprehension."
May 21-25	First Grade SAISD	Sight Words*	100/100	Any student who has not yet read 100 words
		Writing*	See assessment criteria	All students take this task

*TPRI or *Tejas LEE* tasks with this symbol have corresponding SAISD Assessments and are First Grade expectations

FIG. 7.2.   First-grade reading and writing assessment.

Second Grade Testing Schedule - English

Date	Assessment	Task	Criteria	Who is tested
May 14-18	Second Grade TPRI	1. Spelling of CVC and CVCe words	4.5	Any student who scored SD on Jan. TPRI
		2. Spelling of Long Vowels	4/5	
		3. Orthographic Patterns, Conventions, and Past Tense	4/5	
		4. Orthographic Patterns, Conventions, and inflectional Endings	4/5	
		(5. Word List)	Skip this Task	
		9. Reading Accuracy- Story 4 (Reading Level)	Frust., Inst., or Ind.	All students who have not previously read and passed Story 4
		9. Story 4 Comprehension	4/5	☐ Students who score Frust. on Story 4 have this read aloud by the teacher and scored as Listening Comprehension. ☐ Students who scored Inst. or Ind. on Story 4 will rely on their own oral reading for comprehension.

Second Grade Testing Schedule - Spanish

Date	Assessment	Task	Criteria	Who is tested
May 14-18	First Grade *Tejas LEE*	2.1 Reconocimiento de palabras (final del año)	14/20	All students
		2.2 Dictado (final del año)	11/15	
		2.3 Lectura en voz alta* "Vamos al parque" *(Reading Level)*	Frust., Inst., or Ind. * (see *Tejas LEE* criteria)	
		2.2 "Vamos al parque" Comprensión	4/5	☐ Students who score Frust. on "Vamos al parque" have this story and questions read aloud by the teacher and scored as Listening Comprehension. (instead of 2.5). ☐ Students who scored Inst. or Ind. on "Vamos al parque" will rely on their own oral reading for comprehension.
		Writing*	See assessment criteria	**All students take this task**

*Difícil = Frust.
A nivel = Inst.
Fácil = Ind.

FIG. 7.3. Second-grade reading and writing assessment.

English speaker. The test is administered each fall and spring to assess children's progress in the development of each language.

SPECIAL NEEDS STUDENTS

The assessment of special needs limited English proficient students who were included in the program was also a major concern. With much consultation with parents and special education support staff, English dominant children who were diagnosed through testing and observation to have any special learning needs continued in the program, but two-way teachers as well as other staff were concerned about whether this was an appropriate placement. The most appropriate placement for limited English proficient students who were have learning difficulties was much discussed in the early years and the decision was made by the teachers, administrators, and parents that the two-way bilingual immersion program was an appropriate placement. All special needs children were provided support services as were their peers in the English-only program. Within the two-way bilingual immersion classrooms, teachers made the necessary instructional adaptations while maintaining the two-way model of instruction. Thus, over the years, the proper assessment, identification, and instruction of seven children who were identified as special needs were continuously discussed.

TESTING AND MIDDLE SCHOOL PLANNING

During a planning meeting for the promotion of the two-way bilingual immersion to a middle school, the principals from the middle schools under consideration, while very interested in the progress the children were making and in sustaining the progress in both languages, also expressed concerns about the organization of the middle school two-way program. Most of the concerns were dominated by the testing and accountability system of the state. One principal voiced the concern, "The testing of social studies, math, and reading at the eighth grade level will be tested in English, therefore these courses should be taught in English."

CONCLUSION

The teachers and students in these classrooms felt pressured to perform on both state-mandated tests and tests that were used to measure progress for the two-way bilingual immersion program. In spite of the reported loss of instructional time to testing and test preparation, most of the teachers felt that the testing reassured them that the program was successful and it provided the data they needed to continuously improve the program and argue for additional support for the program. Genesee (1987) warned of early testing of two-way bilingual immersion students, reporting that in some programs in Canada and the United States, students tested using standardized English language tests during the first three years of immersion programs when instruction in English is minimal results in scores that are lower than control students in an all-English curriculum.

All of the testing showed that the students in the two-way program were performing at or slightly above their peers in each of the schools. Students and teachers were quick to point out that not only were they performing at grade level in most measures, but they were also doing it in two languages.

8

Teachers' Role and Impact

"I have learned to continuously define the model, to describe why I am teaching a certain way and certain content . . . to talk about my practice, and most importantly to be constantly prepared to defend the program," said Mrs. Jurado during a teacher focus group interview. Mrs. Jurado was one of the teachers that had been involved in the two-way bilingual immersion program since 1995. Most of the teachers spoke about the need to always be prepared to explain the program, the program model, and the student progress to visitors, administrators, and parents.

The 14 two-way bilingual immersion teachers were knowledgeable and dedicated to their students and to the program. Like many teachers today, they also reported feeling pressure from multiple sources. The most frequently discussed pressure was an internal one of wanting "to do the right thing" in educating the children. All of the teachers self-identified as Mexican American and, although they felt a strong advocacy for "the right for these children to learn both languages," this did not keep them from second-guessing themselves as to whether the two-way bilingual immersion was the "right way" to educate the poor Mexicano and Mexican American children in their classrooms. The second most discussed pressure was that felt from their colleagues either at their schools or within their professional circles. As bilingual teachers, they had always felt, as one teacher reported, that "other teachers do not appreciate the extra work that it takes to be a bilingual teacher; they think that we have extra perks; they do not understand." Now as two-way bilingual immersion teachers, with the added attention that was given to the program by the district administrators, school board, and public media, some felt that their colleagues in the same school were not always as supportive as they could have been. Another teacher reported, "We have to justify everything," and still another teacher said, "When we have visitors, we have to explain why." The two main external pressures they discussed frequently and vigorously were policy issues, with regard to the status and continuation of the program, and the emphasis on the TAAS test.

In this chapter, after providing demographic information on the teachers, I discuss each of these pressures and dilemmas in turn and the consequences that they had on the teachers over the years. I also discuss what the teachers reported about their professional development activities.

TEACHER DEMOGRAPHICS

In 2000–2001, there were 14 teachers that I observed, interviewed, and interacted with. Of these, three had been teaching in or involved with the program since its inception. In fact, these three teachers had been involved during the planning year when they studied the models and visited two-way bilingual immersion programs throughout the country. They played an important role as keepers of the corporate memory. These three teachers and two others, who had joined the two-way bilingual immersion program in 1997–1998, formed a core group that provided leadership for the program. All of the teachers were actively involved in the continuous planning and advocacy that the program required; however, the core group of five teachers provided the foundation and impetus to motivate the other teachers and to represent the program when necessary.

Figure 8.1 compares the education and experience of the two-way program teachers within each campus. As a group, the two-way bilingual immersion teachers held more Masters of Education degrees than their peers. At both campuses, the two-way teachers were, on average, in the mid range of their careers, with an average of 16 years. At Bonham, the two-way teachers had less teaching experience than their peers, whereas at Storm the two-way teachers had more experience than their peers. All the two-way bilingual immersion teachers met the state bilingual certification standards as well as the district's language competency standards. They received a $2,000 annual stipend given by the district; bilingually certified

Teachers' Experience and Education 2000–2001				
	Bonham		Storm	
	Campus	Program	Campus	Program
Education				
Bachelors	11	2	18	1
Masters	12	7	16	5
Experience				
1–5 Years	4	1	15	1
6–10 Years	2	2	5	2
11–20 Years	3	3	8	3
Over 20	14	3	6	0

FIG. 8.1.   Teachers' experience and education, 2000–2001.

teachers in the district's transitional bilingual program received the same amount.

Over the 5 years of program implementation, six teachers left the program: two transferred to the transitional bilingual program within the school in a restructuring that occurred at Storm in 1998, two went to other schools within the district to begin two-way bilingual immersion programs, one left the district after only teaching in the two-way bilingual immersion program one year, and one teacher left the program and later retired.

As vacancies occurred, the personnel division in collaboration with the principal and two-way teachers at each campus recruited primarily from the district's bilingual teachers. The selection process included interviews in Spanish and English by a team of bilingual program specialists, teachers, principals, and central office administrators.

One of the main reasons for teacher turnover cited by both teachers and administrators was differences in expectations, especially in the teaching of Spanish reading or literacy. The Spanish literacy approach that had been adopted by the two-way bilingual immersion teachers was aligned with the district's balanced literacy model. For some teachers, the adopted approach was too different from the more traditional Spanish literacy teaching philosophy. During the first years of the program, several teachers who had strong Spanish language training insisted on literacy instruction that focused on a bottom-up approach. They used an approach to teaching reading and writing that focused on syllabication, where reading instruction consisted of exercises in syllabication with controlled vocabulary. Although these teachers had a variety of materials that used a variety of approaches, they often used materials that had been published in Mexico or other Spanish-speaking countries that used the syllabic method for reading instruction and, in some cases, they used materials produced in the 1970s and 1980s for use in transitional bilingual programs that also focused on the syllabic method. Differences in philosophy often led to very animated discussions at faculty and in-service meetings. These differences were cited as the reason for two teachers leaving the program during the second year of implementation.

Other reasons for teacher turnover were changes in teachers' family lives and campus personnel conflicts. As with any other group, tensions over workload, fairness, and grievances with administration accumulated over time and were cited as reasons for leaving by two of the teachers. Two other teachers left to work in two-way bilingual immersion programs that were initiated as a result of the success of the two-way programs at Bonham and Storm. These two teachers reported that they felt they could make a greater contribution by helping other schools develop and implement immersion programs. According to the principals, the turnover rate of teachers in the two-way program was less than the turnover rate of teachers at each of the campuses.

TEACHER OWNERSHIP OF PROGRAM

Teachers often talked about not only the two-way bilingual immersion reforms but also the different reforms that they had experienced over the years at their schools. Many felt that they had participated in the choices and decision making about the two-way program and that most of the instructional demands of the chosen model already fit into their philosophy about teaching. They also felt that it was a continuation of previous reform movements that had centered on the principle that all children could learn, except that now, as one teacher stated, "We are assuming a subtle but powerful difference in that we assume that all children are gifted and can become biliterate." One principal described the attitude of the teachers saying,

> From the teachers' standpoint, to see them feel how proud they are to be a part of something that was at one time so negative. To be so proud of the accomplishments it [bilingual education] turned . . . from something negative to something so positive, to see how thankful they are that they were part of that process.

One of the recurring themes voiced by the teachers was the importance that every program teacher be able to articulate the main points of the program. This created internal peer pressures when visitors, the media, and administrators observed classrooms and talked to teachers and students. The teachers would check with each other as to what was asked and what was responded, and these exchanges would be brought to program meetings for discussion. This created a context where most teachers reported that they had learned to "reflect on how and what they were teaching," so that they could answer any questions about how what they were doing fitted into the two-way bilingual immersion model. One teacher described it this way: "Since I feel like we have made a lot of these decisions, I or we have to articulate this process—decision-making process, and defend . . . explain how what I or Martha or Lydia are doing is all part of the two-way model." Another teacher commented that she had the goals of the two-way bilingual immersion model *"muy claros y muy bien definidos"* (very clear and very well defined) and it was this that helped her to articulate not only the practices but also the program accomplishments.

The teachers in these schools gave the agreed on "model" of two-way bilingual immersion an almost ontological significance. That is, they gave it the respect and authority that they would normally reserve for their students. Although they acknowledged the conflicts and frictions that district policies brought to bear on the model, they nonetheless returned time and again to recast their understanding of the model with its unique identity and integrity. Within their learning community, the connective core of all their relationships, with their students, parents, administrators, and each other, was the significance of the "model" itself. The dedication to maintain the model at the core of their learning community created a context of constant awareness and recommitment. Teachers developed and demonstrated sociopolitical sophistication as they continually answered questions about the program and resisted the pressures of experts and policy-makers.

TEACHERS AND LANGUAGE DISTRIBUTION

Because most of the teachers had been transitional bilingual teachers, they often compared their teaching in the two-way bilingual immersion to their previous experience. They talked about the major changes they encountered when they had to "be language models" by consciously separating the languages while attending to contextualizing the communication for the second language speakers. As one teacher reported, "I had not realized what it meant to teach almost everything in Spanish. In previous years, I used English and Spanish throughout the day to talk to the children and for instruction. I had never taught everything in Spanish, this was a scary change."

Teachers often discussed the role of the teacher as language model. They talked about past patterns of success and failure in their classes. They reexamined their own evaluations of students' language practices. They often revisited prior decisions as in the case of the use of a specific language for a specific content for a specified length of time. They routinely assessed and reassessed their language modeling policies.

Although not a change in language policy per se, the teachers felt that after the first year, they had made an accommodation for children's use of code switching and language alteration. The teachers reported that this language accommodation proved to be "creative" for children. Teachers reaffirmed their initial policy that they should not model code switching or language alteration. They reported, and I observed, that they would refrain from using it except in very informal settings away from the classroom. As one teacher said, " We can do it when we are talking to the parents and the kids, outside after school, but we should not do it in the classroom." The accommodation was that children's use of code switching would not be corrected and that, for certain objectives or activities, it would be recognized and encouraged. Several teachers cited acceptable examples as when they read children's literature that included code switching, or when children were writing about events in their family or community life and used code switching. All but one teacher saw these examples as expressions of the community's language use and the creative nature of the use of language by the children and the community. One teacher's attitude to code switching could be categorized as tolerance out of respect to her colleagues, the students, and the community. She stated, "I can see that it is creative, but I think they should learn how to say what they want to say in each language and not mixed." Another teacher talked about how having to teach both Spanish dominant and English dominant at the same time had changed her awareness of her teaching.[1] Ms. Lopez stated, "I have learned to constantly cue, check for understanding, rephrase—I keep trying to find those words that are more closely related in both languages, like cognates, more sophisticated, *por ejemplo vamos a construir, en vez de hacer* (for example, we are going to construct instead of make). This is essential." Frequently, the teachers openly talked about the challenges, their accomplishments, and their frustrations.

TEACHER ACCOUNTABILITY

The issue of accountability, the TAAS test, was always present at the conscious level for most of the teachers and the learning community. The teachers consistently voiced belief that they could be true to the two-way bilingual immersion model while addressing the accountability issues. To meet the TAAS objectives and other accountability issues, such as the *Tejas Lee* in the primary grades, the teachers drew from disparate theoretical orientations of instruction. They frequently revisited a wide range of instructional approaches from contextualized second language strategies to direct instruction. For literacy, they used strategic reading skills but also included language and meaning intensive literacy experiences for their students. As the norms for accountability in the state and district changed and evolved, the teachers took up the challenge and were able to justify their constant adherence to the two-way model in disciplined, public, and compelling ways. They maintained a dynamic conversation within their

---

[1] Many of these teachers exhibited Palmer's (1998) description of teaching. "Teaching . . . is actually an intricate patterning of life, with rhythms, textures, and shapes we must attend to, a kind of creative chaos we can learn to enjoy" (p. 147).

learning community; they monitored student progress and especially students' performance on the TAAS; they kept testing their understanding of methodologies and discovering new insights. They did all of this without deviating from their commitment to the model. These teachers knew how to observe and to reflect and to speak and to listen with passion and with discipline.

Teachers mentioned that their primary accountability was to the students and the parents. The teachers felt that they were the main point of contact for parents with the school and that parents had a high level of confidence in them. They found that the two-way parents made more of an effort to connect with them and often asked about their children's progress. These teachers reported that they had to believe and show that the two-way bilingual immersion was the best way for children to learn because that was the way that they had represented the program to parents.

PROFESSIONAL DEVELOPMENT

During the first couple of years (1995–1997), the teachers participated in monthly Saturday sessions that focused on the two-way bilingual immersion model, the theory, research, and instructional practices. Many of the sessions that focused on instructional practices elaborated on the specific approaches for providing context and making the instructional input comprehensible across the content areas. All teachers attended a minimum of five staff development sessions required each year. Several school documents stated that the objective for the required professional development was "teachers will acquire proficiency in the use of research driven instructional strategies designed to improve the academic performance of LEP students and non-Spanish-speaking students attempting to become bilingual." These required five sessions were linked to receiving the bilingual stipend.

The most important and recurring themes of the professional development sessions for the bilingual teachers were strategies, activities, techniques, observation checklists, and other topics related to second language learning. At many of these training sessions, teachers were provided opportunities to develop observation checklists, rubrics for cooperative learning groups, group project design, and authentic assessments criteria for classroom use. Teachers also requested and were provided training on working with two-way parents. They held many discussions on developing appropriate parent engagement activities so that parents would be knowledgeable and could support their children in their homes as they participated in the two-way bilingual immersion program.

The two-way bilingual immersion teachers also participated in training each year that went beyond the staff development days required by the state. Stipends were provided for teachers participating in this additional training. Additionally, several of the faculty and teaching assistants in the two-way program participated in teacher certification and Masters-level programs through the bilingual systemwide Title VII grant. The district provided a tuition reimbursement program for community teaching assistants seeking degrees in education with bilingual teacher certification.

The district's bilingual department provided the support and much of the staff development through a systemwide Title VII grant. The systemwide Title VII grant provided training for teachers of limited English proficient students, including the two-way bilingual immersion teachers. The topics for these Title VII supported sessions included, (a) informal assessment of two-way or LEP students, (b) providing comprehensive input, (c) how oral proficiency differs between limited English proficient and non-limited English proficient students, (d) identifying informal instruments to assess literacy, (e) development of mathematical skills and concepts in Spanish, (f) instructional strategies to implement the district's Estrellas bilingual curriculum, (g) the use of technology instruction and concepts in Spanish, (h) teaching content area concepts in Spanish, and (i) strategies and assessment across the content areas and languages.

In the fall of 1998, as part of a district wide implementation of the restructured reading and writing curriculum that was called "balanced literacy," the district required all teachers including the two-way bilingual immersion teachers to participate in the balanced literacy training. As part of this balanced literacy training, teachers were observed implementing the strategies learned in the training sessions and feedback was provided. The instructional guide at each campus and district office area consultants, including bilingual consultants, conducted these observations. Some of the two-way teachers were called on to provide peer observations and feedback as they implemented the balance literacy curriculum in their classrooms.

Over a 6-year period, the two-way teachers reported that they attended staff development sessions that were specifically designed for their needs and requests.[2] The staff development sessions ranged from those specific to assisting them with the understanding and implementation of the model and second language strategies (previously listed) to more general topics of instruction. These more general topics included cooperative learning, balanced literacy, literacy development across the curriculum, process writing, thematic lessons, interdisciplinary and expeditionary learning, performance and portfolio assessment, uses of technology, multiple intelligences, critical thinking, learning strategies, inclusion and strategies for TAAS.[3]

Each school had campus specific training on analysis of TAAS objectives. This training helped them to identify where students had not done well in the previous TAAS test or where students were not doing well on the mock TAAS assessments that were conducted periodically. Each campus hired consultants to conduct training for specific grades and specific TAAS objectives where students were weak. These sessions often included many handouts that specifically illustrated how the teachers could teach to specific TAAS objectives. For example, using contextual clues for defining words. Various techniques were demonstrated; the teachers discussed how they could implement these techniques in their classrooms. The two-way bilingual immersion teachers participated in these sessions although often the material would not be available in Spanish. Nonetheless, they discussed how they could adapt the techniques for the two-way bilingual immersion setting.

One common complaint of the two-way bilingual immersion teachers with regard to professional development was that when they were required to attend sessions that dealt with content materials and strategies (e.g., when the math curriculum changed), the sessions focused on how to use

---

[2]According to Thomas and Collier (1997), "students who attended classes taught by teachers who had been through intensive staff development in these current approaches to teaching made faster long-term progress than students attending more traditionally taught classes" (p. 50).

[3]Numerous TAAS preparation meetings, workshops, and activities were conducted each year, and many teachers reported that these were repetitive and often offered very little new to their teaching. The principals and administrators reported that it was necessary to have these sessions for everyone so as to emphasize the importance of the TAAS on all the teachers.

the materials and strategies with English-speaking students and did not address the needs of the bilingual teachers. They felt that they were always expected to adapt and modify on their own. After attending one such session, a third-grade teacher stated:

> I realized again that I was going to have to take these math in-services and workshops and just do it all in Spanish. Sometimes is it a little overwhelming, but you know, I had other resource materials and we [two-way teachers] get together and provide each other assistance.

Professional development resources were available to teachers through the University of Texas at San Antonio, the Region 20 Educational Service Center, and other outside consultants. The professional development sessions had to meet the district's requirements, and, on request, consultants were available through the district for specialized help on such topics as cooperative learning and classroom management, balanced literacy, everyday mathematics, two-way language instructional strategies, parent involvement, and technology. Yearly professional development plans were developed as a result of "taking stock," based on teacher critical reflection on their teaching and the needs of their students. The staff came together to discuss the common needs and plan for the following year.

The dedication of the faculty to the bilingual program model was demonstrated in the high degree of participation in staff and professional development programs. The two-way teachers were also active in providing professional development to their peers. The teachers, because of their advanced levels of proficiency in the two-way model, saw an opportunity to hone their professional skills and contribute to the knowledge base of two-way or dual-language programming. Numerous teachers conducted sessions for faculty from other campuses. They also made presentations at local, state, and national meetings. They reported that these presentations were the best professional development for them, as they had to reflect, evaluate, and disseminate their understanding of the program and its progress.

PARTICIPATION AND ROLE OF SUPPORT PERSONNEL

Even though the teachers often talked about tensions with peers, they also talked about the support they got from most of the school personnel. The teachers at both campuses reported having strong support from the principals and instructional guides. One teacher described her principal this way:

Because she was from the Latino community, she was knowledgeable about home and community cultural practices, and she drew from this knowledge in her interactions with students and parents and with us. She saw students' Spanish language and literacy skills as resources on which to build. She also clearly leaned toward a structured teaching environment, and she explicitly talked about teaching students concepts, vocabulary, and skills they would need for success in academic English. She made demands but she provided the support.

Teachers pointed to the instructional guide at each campus as providing the assistance that they needed to implement much of the training that they received at professional development sessions. The instructional guides facilitated their being able to observe other teachers who were successfully implementing strategies. The guides would also provide feedback to teachers as they attempted to apply those new strategies. The school's instructional guide was also the person the teachers contacted concerning new ideas or needs for further professional development. The guide also provided technical assistance to teachers and organized training customized to the school site. The instructional guides were also key to the analysis and interpretation of assessment data. The teachers reported that the instructional guides helped them to "come up with plans for targeting their instructional approaches based on the students' needs."

The teachers considered the instructional guides a valuable resource and, as another professional, the guide served as an in-house consultant to work out possible solutions to their teaching questions. One teacher described the instructional guide as, "Often I just go to him and he listens —sounding board—and I work out the problem with his input."

The counselors, special education support staff, and the bilingual staff worked closely at one school and with a certain amount of friction at the other. Because most of Storm and Bonham students have special needs and because the school conducts almost all its business bilingually, there was a need for everyone to work very closely together. Issues of how and when to assess two-way bilingual immersion students who were also special needs students created some contentious discussions. Some of the issues in conflict were attributed to district policy; for example, teachers cited that they were having difficulty getting the English dominant students assessed because of a policy that required that children receive instruction in an appropriate placement prior to being referred to special education. Supposedly, the district special education personnel did not consider the two-way program as an appropriate instructional placement for English dominant children. Thus, if children were having difficulty learning, the special education department wanted them transferred to the English program; then, if they were still having problems learning, the students would be assessed for special services. These kinds of interpretations of policies created some tensions at one school and were under constant negotiation at the other. However, one of the special education support staff observed that the school's two-way program was supported: "We believe in it, we bought into it. . . . We have a lot of hard working teachers, but sometimes we were not working smart. Now we're working smarter. We do care about children and we care about what we do, and because we care about what we do, our strength is that we're willing to change also."

Another member of the special populations support team commented on the effects the two-way efforts had on the campus as a whole saying that in the last 7 years, attitudes toward teaching low-income Mexican American students have changed dramatically. "We have expectations of ourselves too. We look at ourselves and continue to grow."

Much of the literature[4] asserts that any school innovation in order to be successful must include a wide range of school staff and must permeate and be supported by the school culture. Thus, the role of other teachers, the librarian, the nurse, the counselor, the administrative staff, food service providers, janitors, and even bus drivers were thought to be significant to the success of the two-way program. Teachers talked about the need to inform all these personnel and to gain their support. During the first years, training of the extended staff was done in earnest with everyone being engaged in discussions of the linguistic, academic, and social goals of the two-way bilingual immersion model and the importance of giving this program status and support. However, as the years passed and staff changed through retirements, transfers, growth, and contractions, the training of these new folks on the campuses did not always occur.

---

[4]See Bizar and Barr (2001) for a discussion about cases in urban reform of schools and school innovations.

Although there was a recognition that the larger school environment would remain for the most part an English-speaking institution, it was agreed on by most—although there were a small number at each campus that held out as long as they could—that children would not be extolled about the primacy of English and would, whenever possible, be addressed and encouraged to communicate in either Spanish or English and that code switching would be viewed as a communicative community practice.

TEACHERS' STANCE TOWARD THE STUDY

Participating in research in classrooms involved a number of difficulties and dilemmas for the teachers and the researcher. The mere presence of an outsider changes the very thing that the researcher wishes to study, that is, everyday practices. All but one teacher welcomed me into their classrooms after only a very brief explanation of the purpose of the classroom observations. The one "hold-out" teacher not only required numerous explanations but also continuously forgot to inform me of changes in the instructional schedule, most of which she did not control. When I attempted to reschedule for a different day and time, she reported other conflicts. Thus, I was able to observe in her classroom only twice.

Most teachers participated in several discussion sessions and all freely responded to my many formal and informal interview questions. They also participated in feedback sessions where I shared with them some of my observations. All were eager to discuss not only my observations but to also raise possible explanations and conclusions.

CONCLUSION

The teacher plays the most important and instrumental role in whether children learn in any school setting. The teacher as the key player in the school community also influences any school reform or effort to increase student learning. The teacher is the center cog of the wheel around which the other spokes rotated, including program implementation and school change. The teacher, her knowledge, experience, and beliefs determined the instructional decisions that directly affected program implementation and, more importantly, student learning.

Most school reform efforts have failed or produced disappointing re-sults when these reform efforts have not engaged or empowered teachers.[5] This group of two-way bilingual immersion teachers represents a wide range of beliefs about many issues but a very firm commitment to the two-way bilingual immersion model of instruction and to the success of their students. This commitment translated into action in the form not only of producing student learning results but also in their participation in the school and teaching community through their participation and leadership in professional development. Though the principals at each of these two campuses provided strong instructional leadership, it was the ability of teachers to articulate and defend their practices that sustained the program through numerous policy reviews.

---

[5] See McLaughlin and Oberman (1996) for a discussion about the role of teacher and teacher learning in school reform.

9

Politics, Policy, and Theory

On May 18, 2000, teachers, parents, principals, bilingual administrators, and community members were called to make a two-way bilingual immersion program presentation to a committee of the San Antonio Independent School District school board. The two-way bilingual immersion presentation was particularly crucial because the new superintendent announced that the review was made necessary by a budget shortfall and all programs considered enrichment programs were under scrutiny. Throughout the spring, the superintendent visited district schools and, while at the two-way bilingual immersion schools, the principals and teachers reported:

> He [the superintendent] asked us to describe the program and then he would focus on the fact that two-way programs were considered enrichment programs. It was not until later that we realized that what we meant by enrichment was not what he meant. His definition of enrichment—that it was not mandated or compensatory—meant it could also be considered to be cut if necessary because of budget or political problems.

The differences in interpretation of the two-way bilingual immersion program as enrichment, especially for a predominantly Hispanic population, became a key point for reflection and redefinition of the program. Thus, the presentation before the school board committee was viewed by the two-way bilingual immersion group as crucial to the continuation of the program. In preparation for the presentation, the principals, parents, teachers, and university faculty clarified and redefined the purpose and goals of the two-way program. The discussions that preceded and followed the presentation again raised the level of political consciousness and commitment to the program. The prior work that the staff and parent leaders had done with the program parents and the community played a pivotal role. The participation of parents at this meeting demonstrated how knowledgeable they had become about the program and how satisfied they were with their children's progress.

As the discussion evolved that late spring and into the fall of the next academic year, the teachers, parents, and administrators who had previously voiced notions of "effective education," "linguistic capital," and "enrichment," with regard to two-way bilingual immersion education, began to reexamine their understanding of these constructs and also focused on other terms, such as *linguistic rights, reclaiming language and cultural heritage,* and *value-added education.* They began, in particular, to question whether the way that the professional literature described two-way bilingual immersion, as "enriched education" (Cloud, Genesee, & Hamayan, 2000; Valdés, 1996) was appropriate for their setting. The literature uses the term *two-way bilingual immersion* to focus on the promotion of the acquisition of English and the target minority language by both minority and majority students. Because the programs in their schools, though balanced between English-dominant and LEP students, served mostly Hispanic students with only a few majority or Anglo children, they began to question whether "enrichment" adequately described the purpose of the program. The teachers and principals began to ask the "why" questions (Palmer, 1998). They began to grapple with questions such as why Hispanic children no longer spoke the language of their parents and grandparents; why assisting Hispanic children to learn to communicate with their extended families was considered enrichment; why giving Hispanic children an education that gave them a linguistic advantage in the global marketplace was considered enrichment; and why preserving and protecting Hispanic children's language and cultural rights was considered enrichment education. As the principals, teachers, and parents discussed these questions, they began to talk about two-way bilingual immersion education as a way of giving poor and minority children the kind of education that not only met the state educational standards but that also protected their cultural and linguistic rights and gave them a competitive educational and future economic advantage.

REASSESSMENT AND RECOMMITMENT

Over the years, as the program took on challenge after challenge, the central office administrators, teachers, and parents saw these challenges as opportunities to examine the discrepancies between the ideal model, the research, and even the prior decisions about language distribution and standards for the use of Spanish and English. By redefining the two-way bilingual immersion plan over time and explaining it to the multiple levels of policymakers and community groups, they clarified for themselves the evolving program context. Administrators and teachers attempted to account for the discrepancies between the ideal and the actual implementation of the model.

At each campus, the staffs constructed and reconstructed multiple social, cultural, and linguistic contexts for all learning, but in particular for the two-way program. These contexts were grounded in and reflected each school's unique history and community. For example, Bonham continuously expressed having to account for factors, such as historical preservation, changing demographics, and regentrification of the neighborhood, as they discussed the future of the two-way bilingual immersion program. At both schools, the major contributing factor in every reexamination process was the confidence accumulated from the experiences gained in implementing two-way bilingual immersion programs. The teachers, parents, students, and administrators participated in this evaluative and constructive process. Each contributed to the evolving program from their own unique role and personal perspective, often in ways that bridged roles and expectations.

This process of constant renewal helped each school to remake itself in its physical appearance, in its relation to each particular community, its curriculum, and its staff. Teachers and parents recounted that only a few years prior to the implementation of the two-way program, which also closely coincided with the start of the tenure of each of the principals, many teachers had low expectations for students at Storm and some students at Bonham. Now teachers, parents, students, and all school staff shared the expectation that students would meet high standards and, for most students, to do so bilingually.

Parent Participation

Parent support and advocacy was apparent in the long-term success of the program, as discussed in chapter 3. The early identification and cultivation of the leadership of a few parents at each school played a key role in defending the program politically and in involving more parents. However, as in most school programs, even though the number of two-way parents actively involved was larger than for other school programs, it did not motivate or include the total number of families served by the program. Nonetheless, the parents were crucial to sustaining the program.

Teacher Commitment

A core group of teachers with very strong professional beliefs about the pedagogical soundness of the program provided the backbone and rigor at every reassessment and recommitment point in the development and implementation of the program. The principals had always understood the nature of schooling as a political activity. The teachers, on the other hand, came to understand not only the political nature of teaching and schooling, but also assumed stances and articulated positions that demonstrated and advanced their political skills.

Each time the program came under question and review because of changes in administration or policies, the teachers interpreted this as a political threat to the program and mobilized political resources to defend the program. With each succeeding defense of the program, the program model, vision, and goals were redefined and reinforced. Teachers joined with parents and recommitted themselves to the program. The constant reviews and defenses of the two-way program also attracted much publicity that generated additional support from a wider spectrum of the community and interest from other schools and communities for starting similar programs. Thus, a number of two-way bilingual immersion teachers were recruited to begin two-way bilingual immersion programs at other schools. Teachers saw this as a way not only to disseminate what they believed to be the best practices for Mexican American and Mexicano children, but also as a way of developing a broader sociopolitical support for two-way bilingual immersion education.

LANGUAGE, IDENTITY, AND HYBRIDITY

Bonham and Storm adopted language policies for the two-way bilingual immersion program that at face value appeared to favor norms of discourse that were hegemonic (Erickson, 1993). Administrators and teachers had decided on a model that separated languages for instruction and used "standard" forms of school discourse in each language despite knowing that, for most children, their home discourse included a range of practices that did not separate the two languages, Spanish and English. Administrators and teachers agreed that the existing body of research and theory suggested that the separation of languages was the way to achieve their goals of bilingualism and biliteracy. Over time, the teachers came to question whether the separation of the languages favored the development of particular forms of language that focused on meeting students' future needs at the expanse of valuing home discourses.

Teachers, administrators, and parents often engaged in discussions about the norms of discourse used for each language and whether the two-way bilingual immersion program was preparing students to participate in the greater educational, cultural, and economic systems. Parents, in particular, were concerned about the standards or norms for Spanish discourse. Additionally, parents repeatedly raised concerns about the rate of English language acquisition. In almost all cases, parents were concerned about their children using code switching and language alteration. Parents wanted children to achieve high standards of bilingualism because they felt that would give their children the most advantages.

Some teachers, but not all, questioned whether teaching "standard" forms was contributing to the imbalances in power and social justice that existed in the community or whether this would give the students linguistic advantages permitting them to fully participate in the larger global society. They recognized that focusing on particular forms of language reinforced existing social, political, and power influences. In this way, the teachers assumed what Foucault (1984) described as "disciplining of discourse"; that is, they decided on teaching certain language forms, for example, middle-class discourses over student's community discourses, because they perceived it met society's expectation for their students without challenging the imposed standards that are often based on the needs of the powerful, such as businesses and future employers.

Teachers were aware of children's needs for their home and community discourses to be recognized and valued. Over time, teachers began to create spaces where children would feel safe to use and develop these home and community discourses. Through the selection of study topics in science and social studies and through the selection of literary works that required the use of community knowledge and experience, the teachers and students gave voice to the community discourses. In this way, all but one of the teachers encouraged children to participate and contribute to the cultural production of new linguistic expressions in the form of hybridized discourse (Anzaldúa, 1987; Arteaga, 1994; Gutiérrez et al., 2000; Kalmar, 2001). Teachers did this in three ways. One was in oral and written responses to children's literature containing code switching, dialects, or language alteration which encouraged children to write from their own experience and using their home as well as school discourses. The second way was when teachers selected lesson content that focused on a social-historical period requiring the acknowledgment and use of different discourses. The third more ordinary but yet more powerful way that teachers created space for hybridized discourse was in the social context of the classroom. Teachers created mixed-language student group activities where cultures of linguistic collaboration evolved. These activities encouraged students to participate in cross-linguistic communication that required the sharing of sociocultural and linguistic resources. Within these groups and activities, children used hybrid language and literacy practices. They blended Spanish and English, used their home and school registers, and used their home and school cultural knowledge for communication, meaning making, and learning. The teachers acknowledged, encouraged, and celebrated these hybrid moments and the knowledge created by this interaction and blending.

Anzaldúa (1987) and Arteaga (1997), literary and cultural studies scholars, have developed complex theories of hybridity and defined spaces where languages and cultures come in contact as borderlands in which Mexicanos, Mexican Americans, and Chicanos negotiate ethnic, cultural, and linguistic identities. In educational settings, Kris Gutiérrez and her colleagues (Gutiérrez, Baquedano-López, Álvarez, & Chiu, 1999; Gutiérrez et al., 2000) have used theories of hybridity and borders to examine pedagogical spaces where children systematically blend English and Spanish language and home and school knowledge and culture to construct or reconstruct their learning, their identity, and to generate new worldviews. The educational environments of these two-way bilingual immersion classrooms did not stand in opposition to the creation of these borderland spaces; thus, children's acquisition of identities as competent academic and literate members of their social groups flourished. As students negotiated ethnic, cultural, and linguistic identities in the two-way bilingual immersion classroom communities, they engaged in multifaceted, ingenious hybrid practices and expressions.

In the borderland spaces of these two-way bilingual immersion classrooms, children were not only participating members in their culture but were contributing to the creation of new cultural expressions as they integrated, reflected, and extended their experiences. The children brought the experiences from their world—ways of doing, thinking, behaving as well as reading, writing, and talking—into the classroom. They brought their community discourse, mastered through enculturation in the community sociocultural practices, into the school. While community discourses were not overtly taught in the schools, they were accepted and not socially stigmatized. Children learned each other's community discourses while they were learning the school's Spanish and English discourses. Through their use of the community discourses and the school discourses, the children demonstrated Gee's (1991, 1997) notions of *discourse* as *identity kit* as they defined themselves as bilingual, biliterate learners. Children incorporated knowledge of their world into the classroom learning and interpreted learning based on their view of the world. The cultural tools of literacy, the ways of school reading and writing in either language, were hybridized not unlike what they observed and experienced in their world. This occurred in spite of a conscious policy and effort by the school to separate the languages and teach standard forms of each language. While the children demonstrated that they could assume the behaviors of the dominant culture and perform at high standards on school tasks and tests in each language, they, nonetheless, took the literacy cultural tools and hybridized them as they saw fit. The children did not see certain language and literacy functions as legitimate or illegitimate; thus, they used, created, and recreated their language, literacy, and biliteracy in ways that served the functions and needs in their worlds.

As discussed in chapters 5 and 6, children in the program spoke and wrote about their understanding of their linguistic heritage and their emerging and evolving sense of identity with confidence and conviction. They spoke with determination about the comfort, usefulness, and advantages that being biliterate was already bringing into their lives. They also spoke of the richness of being able to engage in the cultural activities of various groups and of their own sense of contributing to cultural production in the hybridized spaces of San Antonio. Thus, these students and their teachers saw the possibility of contributing "to new features in the ethnic minority's culture, so that it develops specific cultural traits not found in any of the source cultures" (Skutnabb-Kangas, 2000, p. 132).

The linguistic and literacy behavior that these children engaged in and the confidence with which they spoke about their bicultural, bilingual, and biliterate development provides an indication of the children's thinking about group membership and reflects a dual, hybridized identity construction. These children were linguistic brokers (Tse, 1995) that not only translated the spoken words and text but also skillfully interpreted the nuances of language and cultural meanings. Children often made distinctions about which meanings were relevant to the cultural borderlands of San Antonio and which language and references might be more relevant elsewhere, say Mexico, New York, or English language television. This was not a new skill for many of these children, as immigrant children often engage in linguistic brokering where the responsibilities are demanding and the stakes are high. What was new was that linguistic brokering was recognized and rewarded in school as a valued skill and that children added complex literacy skills to their interpreting repertoire.

BILITERACY DEVELOPMENT

The teachers in these schools used existing research evidence to make decisions about the biliteracy practices that were offered to the children in these two-way classrooms. Thus, they designed a program where formal literacy instruction in kindergarten, first grade, and second grade was in Spanish. Formal English literacy instruction began in the third grade. From the third grade onward, both Spanish and English reading and writing were taught and used for all content learning. However, whereas formal literacy instruction in English did not occur till third grade, there was much evidence that children began reading and writing in English before the third grade.

The development of biliteracy by the children in this study adds to the evidence that supports several theoretical notions as well as findings of previous research (Bialystok, 1997; Bruck & Genesee, 1995; Durgunoğlu, 1998; Durgunoğlu et al., 1993; Galambos & Goldin-Meadow, 1990; García et al., 1998). In particular, the role of underlying language and literacy proficiencies (Cummins, 1981) available to children as they build on their conceptual understanding of literacy developed in a first language as they are exposed to print and opportunities to use literacy in a second language. The study also contributed to biliteracy theory by questioning notions of transfer, especially the continued focus on attempting to identify the optimum time for providing overt literacy instruction in the second language. Even though the teachers were careful not to begin formal literacy instruction in English until third grade, these children began from kindergarten to use their developing Spanish literacy knowledge to make meaning from English texts. Once children understood literacy as a cultural tool or behavior that assisted them in interpreting texts in their everyday lives in classrooms and schools, they began to participate in as many of the literacy practices as their developing knowledge and skills could embrace. They saw written language in Spanish and English as functional and brought all their developing language and literacy skills to interpreting it within their sociocultural world.

As demonstrated in chapter 4, the teachers in this study made Spanish language and literacy comprehensible, as in Krashen's (1982) notion of comprehensible input, in the early grades to enable all the children to become fluent readers and writers of Spanish. This foundation in Spanish literacy became the common underlying proficiency (Cummins, 1981) that children drew on to begin reading and writing in English. By the third grade, all the children in this study were biliterate. As children progressed, their literacy skills in both languages became more sophisticated and they exhibited bidirectional (Hornberger, 1989; Hornberger & Skilton-Sylvester, 2002) influences of the languages. Children demonstrated, in many cases, that their knowledge of one language helped them communicate or solve linguistic problems in the other language. Although teachers and students felt pressured by the prospect of future testing in English and also by the possibility that the children would not be able to continue their studies in two languages in middle and high school, they resisted pressures to focus on English literacy at the expense of Spanish and they maintained their commitment to the development of balanced biliteracy for all students.

These schools attended to the criticism about bilingual children's progress only being evaluated in English by documenting results in both English and Spanish. They were committed to the understanding that both languages, as Skutnabb-Kangas (2000) argued, "in the students' repertoire are equally important and the development of all of them have to be taken properly into consideration" (p. xxii). The schools used the Aprenda and the ITBS to document children's literacy progress in both languages. And, the children's third-grade reading scores on the Aprenda and the ITBS provided evidential support for the teachers' initial decision to focus on Spanish literacy first. These scores also provide additional evidence to support the theory of underlying proficiencies for the children's scores in Spanish were predictive of their performance in English.

Academic Achievement

The students at Storm and Bonham, as other dual-language students studied by Linholm-Leary (2001), performed academically at grade level or above in reading, writing, and mathematics when compared to their peers on the Texas statewide testing program TAAS. An analysis of language and reading performance at third grade on standardized tests also showed that students were performing at or above grade level in both Spanish and English. Chapter 7 provided data that demonstrated that children's language proficiency at the time of entry into kindergarten did not significantly affect children's performance on Spanish or English reading at third grade. However, children's Spanish reading performance did have a significant effect on children's performance on English reading at third grade. These findings are similar to studies (Durgunoğlu, 1998; Durgunoğlu et al., 1993; Verhoeven, 1994) that examined the influence of L1 reading on L2 reading. However, these findings are different from other studies (Lindholm, 1992; Lindholm-Leary, 2001) that have associated higher levels of bilingual proficiency with higher levels of reading achievement and had concluded that this strengthens the correlation between reading achievement in English and Spanish. At Bonham and Storm, students' performance on TAAS mathematics was slightly above their peers, while analysis of students mathematics performance on standardized test was not performed, other studies (Christian et al., 1997; Lindholm, 1992; Lindholm-Leary, 2001) have found a significant correlation between reading achievement and mathematics achievement in the two languages. According to Lindholm-Leary (2001), "Clearly 90:10 programs have the advantage of promoting higher Spanish and bilingual proficiency . . . higher levels of bilingual proficiency were associated with increased performance in reading, and higher scores in reading were linked with better performance in mathematics" (p. 314). Students in these two schools were performing at grade level or above on all academic measures and were beginning to acquire the levels of bilingualism that have been associated with cognitive advantages (Cook, 1997; Cummins, 1981).

Continuing Challenges

A major challenge of any program that targets poor and immigrant students, and that affected this program and study as well, is the high rate of mobility. Although the rate of mobility was slightly lower for the two-way bilingual immersion program when compared to the general student population at each school, it was nonetheless a problem. The students come and go, often re-enrolling in the same school three or four times in their very short elementary school years. This makes it difficult for the students to have a continuous learning environment that meets their needs. The high rate of mobility also makes it difficult to assess the effects of the program model in ways that are definitive for the very populations that these programs are suppose to serve. Nonetheless, even those students with high mobility appeared to adjust to the classroom environment, perhaps because of the high level of skills the teachers exhibited and because of the cooperative, collaborative context that two-way bilingual immersion classrooms provided.

Another major limitation of the two-way bilingual immersion programs at these two schools was the response to special needs children. Although the policy for children who entered the program and were later identified as having language and learning needs that could not be met by the program was in place, it was not clearly understood by all the teachers and staff on the campus. This created confusion and loss of time in testing and referral of children; thus, the program did not serve either language group well. The discussion about the initial identification was always complicated because of the initial placement in the two-way program. Some school personnel blamed what they considered an inappropriate placement as contributing to the learning problems the child was experiencing and to compounding the factors that had to be assessed and sorted out in order to identify the appropriate support for this placement. Lindholm-Leary (2001) cites parent support for the inclusion of special needs students in dual-language programs stating,

> We have observed many instances in which children were identified with special education needs and the DLE [dual-language education] program was blamed for the problems. The student was then pulled from the program and put into an English mainstream program, and the parent returned the following year asking for re-admittance into the DLE program because the children had the same problems in English. The parent then felt that the child received more stimulation and a better learning environment in the DLE program. (p. 327)

IMPLICATIONS

As discussed in chapter 1, the increase in the number of Spanish-speaking children continues to challenge schools to find programs that meet their language and educational needs, and the continuing controversies over language and language policy creates a sociopolitical context that further complicates the educational options. Thus, according to Lindholm and Fairchild (1990) and Christian (1996), who have studied and evaluated two-way bilingual immersion programs in California, many schools with large numbers of language minority populations are turning to dual-language programs as viable alternatives. This, in fact, has happened in Texas as more schools look to two-way or dual-language education as alternatives that have demonstrated higher achievement rates for language minorities. The two-way bilingual immersion programs at Storm and Bonham have served as model sites for schools throughout Texas to visit, study, and emulate. The design and success of the two-way program at these two schools has heavily influenced two-way or dual-language education in other San Antonio and Texas schools.

Program Design and Implementation

The 90–10 two-way immersion model implemented at Storm and Bonham was a value-added model of bilingual schooling that contrasted greatly with the compensatory transitional bilingual models of the past. The teachers and administrators worked diligently to implement and maintain the features of the model as they understood them. The continuous evaluation and renewal also assured the integrity of the model. Here, as in many other schools implementing two-way bilingual immersion, the politics and the student population influenced the ultimate implementation of the model. Thus, as school sites undertake the task of identifying the most appropriate model, the realities of their sociopolitical context will impinge on the implementation of that model. In selecting a model, it is necessary to examine the local social, cultural, political, and population (availability of language minority and language majority speakers) factors. However, ultimately the success of any model will depend on the development of ownership by parents, teachers, and administrators.

Linguistic Capital

Spanish became more than a communicative or learning tool on the way to learning English, it became a commodity, an outcome that would provide advantages in the larger global society. Thus, children who by fate, geography, or state policy had been relegated to school systems who interpreted the school's role as the transmission of English and majority cultural norms could now have an alternative: an education that not only provided the skills and knowledge required to meet the state educational standards, but also provided certain advantages through the development of bilingualism and biliteracy. Two-way bilingual immersion education is providing policymakers concerned about minority education additional evidence that supports a value-added approach to minority education.

In these classrooms, the goal was not to "fix" students who were perceived as having a language problem or being disadvantaged. The program was not compensating or remediating for deficits. The focus of the program was academic success for all students through the implementation of an intellectually challenging program that respected and valued the students' and community's linguistic and cultural experiences. The linguistic, cultural, and social capital of the community was an important resource for the classroom and the school. The community perceived the program positively and students succeeded academically. As other schools attempt to replicate the model at their sites, attention must be given to the linguistic, cultural, and social contextual factors that are specific and varied across school communities.

Language Policy

Language policy and planning issues, which in the past had denied bilingual education for Hispanic, English-dominant children, were also challenged by Storm's and Bonham's stance of value-added bilingualism. The ideal and actual language use in the dynamic context of two-way planning and implementation at these two schools challenged the notion of the symbolic domination (Bourdieu, 1984) of English. By reassessing school success to include bilingual and biliteracy proficiencies, not just for those limited English proficient students but also for the Mexican American English speaking students, these two schools sought to create advantages these children might enjoy in their futures. By redefining the cultural and linguistic capital that these schools provided, they sought to break the dominance of school practices that reproduce the social arrangements, including the preeminence of English, in the lives of these children and schools.

The teachers and administrators faced and continue to face resistance in their efforts to transform language politics and ideologies. Their educational stance reflected an enlightened view of language, which challenged policies that served to perpetuate the prejudices against the learning of Spanish. They promoted the equal status of Spanish as an important tool with social capital, and they especially challenged prevailing views of language mixing with valued stances on the use of hybridized languages. The children and teachers in this study provided many concrete examples of courageous practices as they constructed alternative discourses that enabled students to develop cultural and linguistic capital. Thus, students, teachers, and administrators created spaces and practices from a synthesis of the diverse elements in their sociocultural context that added value to the learning, language, and lives of all involved in the two-way bilingual immersion program.

These bilingual teachers had become aware of the political dimensions of their work and had to incorporate political stances about language planning and language policy. Their instructional decisions impacted student learning. While they saw it as their duty to teach children English, they also saw their duty as safeguarding the linguistic rights of their students to maintaining and renewing their Spanish ancestral language. They argued against the forcible language transfer and maintained constant vigilance to assure that space was provided for full expression of both languages. These collective experiences changed their understanding of languages and literacies that are a part of everyday community life and caused them to rethink the role and value of school literacies.

Appendix

RESEARCH METHODOLOGY

During the years that I collected data for this study, I was a participant observer and researcher. The primary tool for data collection and analysis was ethnography. The use of ethnography, as most broadly defined, can yield a rich description of the culture of a community (Spindler, 1963; Cole et al., 1971) and of the context (Hymes, 1982). My goal was to describe the broader cultural context as well as the two-way community culture that emerged and evolved as the participants engaged in learning, teaching, and decision making. In most ethnographic studies the researchers are not insiders to the culture; thus, they make an effort to understand and describe the cultural practices while claiming a certain degree of objectivity. Recently, a number of researchers have conducted studies within their own culture (Valdés, 1996; Ladson-Billings, 1994; Valenzuela, 1999). When the researcher shares a culture with the participants being studied, the researcher has a special burden to strive to make the familiar strange or unfamiliar in order to study it and understand it. I share an ethnic culture and am bilingual (Spanish/English), as were many of the participants in the study. I am also a teacher educator, and have extensive elementary public teaching experience and share in the culture of schooling with some of the participants. Thus, it was particularly crucial for me to attempt to make even the most casual or passing events as unfamiliar as possible and to use multiple lenses; that is, I questioned and interpreted every event from multiple perspectives.

I have discussed my own sociocultural theoretical lens for conducting the research in the Introduction. The Introduction also includes the guiding questions that emerged from the questions that teachers, parents, and administrators posed during the beginning restructuring activities. No research is truly free of bias; however, I have made every effort not to direct the data collection or interpretation in any preconceived way, by allowing the guiding questions, participants, and data to inform the research. Because I was totally immersed as a participant observer in the local actions, accounts, practices, and statements of belief of participants, it was often challenging to maintain the substantive focus on the guiding questions of the study while also maintaining an awareness of my own presuppositions. Of course, the guiding questions were adjusted and modified in response to the perspectives of the participants and the relationships of the events over time. I used a variety of methods appropriate to the guiding questions to collect the data, and I employed constant cross-analysis to minimize bias and to strengthen the validity of the findings.

The need to make sense and synthesize complex interactions, and to find a way to make a coherent and meaningful whole, led me to *grounded theory* as an appropriate tool for this study. According to Strauss and Corbin (1990), grounded theory can be used and may be ideal for examination of complex phenomena. It allows for context to not only be accounted for, but also for the social phenomenon being studied to be situated in the context where it occurs. Grounded theory assumes that complexities in the field will be explored and allowed to influence the guiding questions of the project. By using grounded theory, I was able to entertain multiple viewpoints while being a participant observer in the study and taking an active role in engaging teachers, parents, administrators, and students in interpreting their world.

I consulted and considered perspectives from multiple bodies of literature for the theoretical frameworks that could inform discrete phenomena. The categories and themes that emerged from the ongoing analysis of data collected from several sources were assessed in terms of these diverse existing theoretical frameworks. The emerging themes that evolved over time led me to continuously consult the literature of two-way or dual language education, second language learning, biliteracy, and sociocultural theories. As I sought to make sense of the emerging findings as a whole and to account for context, I was led to further consult the literature of critical theory, social capital, language policy, hybridity, and borderland studies.

Participant Observation

The primary modes of data collection I used were participant observation and open-ended interviews with individuals and small groups. I used a number of observational tools and techniques, including prolonged contacts with parents, teachers, and students of the study group. I participated in various groups' activities (parent meetings, faculty meetings, training sessions, classroom interactions, work sessions, open houses, celebrations, and field trips). I also conducted interviews and captured data from formal and informal conversations with participants. This approach allowed me access to the culture of the schools and to examine the nexus between the espoused adopted model—two-way bilingual immersion—and the behaviors and attitudes of participants; that is, students, teachers, parents, and administrators. Through these prolonged face-to-face contacts with members of the community I was studying, I attempted to ensure that the perspective of the participants was represented.

As a participant observer, I participated in numerous school and community meetings and activities over the 6-year period. My field notes record a wide range of school-related functions; classroom interactions; and casual conversations with students, parents, counselors, teachers, administrators, and community leaders. Over the years, I was a frequent observer in the classrooms and schools as the implementation of the program progressed through the grade levels. But in order to fully describe the classroom practices and how the model was interpreted at the classroom level, I spent a year as a participant observer systematically gathering data in the classrooms. During most weeks of this year of intensive observation of classrooms, I would spend Tuesday mornings at Bonham and Thursday mornings at Storm, visiting 3 or 4 classrooms for each observation visit. Observations ranged from a minimum of 30 minutes to a maximum of 90 minutes, depending on what was occurring in the classroom. The teacher's instructional schedules guided my observation times and I looped my observations, always starting in a different class in order to observe as wide a range of language and literacy activities as possible. I took extensive field notes while observing in the classroom, and dictated additional details to a small tape recorder after leaving the classroom. I tried to note and record the speakers' words exactly as they had been spoken, and attempted to describe gestures, postures, and other accompanying details to create as close an account of the actual interaction as possible. After each day of participant observation, the field notes and tape recordings were transcribed, and the transcribed accounts were expanded into a fuller, more detailed account as I filled in context, impressions, and details. This strategy proved to be a very effective means of accurately recollecting and reconstructing classroom events. My observations and field notes of class-room practices and classroom discourse focused on patterns of language use, teacher–student interactions, student–student interactions, student–text interactions, and the general ecology of the classroom.

Analysis

Table A.1 provides a summary of the types of methods used in collecting the data and the types of data collected. As I examined the data, I developed categories and themes based on an ongoing analysis of data drawn from several sources and assessed in terms of existing theoretical frameworks. The major themes that emerged over time pertained to: context of schooling and success; the place within schools for social, cultural, and linguistic community resources; first- and second-language issues and maintenance; beliefs about the two-way model; school leadership and parent roles; and language development and literacy instructional practices. As I identified each major category and theme, I subjected it to cross-analysis (Miles & Huberman, 1984). The cross-analysis entailed comparing successive cases (whether of individuals or groups of individuals) to establish the support for the emerging themes found earlier. (See Table A.2 for examples of the categories and themes used for initial analysis of data.) Through this highly reflexive process (Hymes, 1982), I became attuned to the complex social and cultural worlds of the participants. The research process of making the familiar unfamiliar helped me to hear and see nuances and contradictions as I evaluated emerging themes and attempted to test existing theory.

The open-ended nature of the data gathering provided ongoing opportunities for self-correction during the study. As in other ethnographies, questions that seemed essential at the start of the study changed as the inquiry unfolded and new categories, themes, and topics emerged (Cazden et al., 1972; Edelsky, 1986; Hymes, 1982). I continually checked my interpretation of events with participants, discussed other possible interpretations, and discussed whether the observed behaviors were a shared belief among the community being studied, or particular to individual members of the group. Discussions with teachers and administrators helped me gain a sense of their perspectives, and added multiple perspectives to my conclusions.

The quantitative data was also obtained from multiple sources. I relied on documentary evidence collected from the Texas Education Agency, from the school district's administrative offices, from the school, and from some individual classrooms.

The final analyses yielded the thematic categories that evolved into chapters, chapter headings, and subheadings in this book. Throughout the data collection and interpretation, as categories and themes emerged, I had numerous conversations with teachers, administrators, and some parents. In one faculty meeting and a couple of teacher workgroups, I presented my findings, with many examples, to teachers and administrators. Some voiced confidence in the findings, others took the examples and made use of the findings to modify their instruction, and a few engaged in long discussions about alternate interpretations. Some teachers and administrators read drafts of the manuscript, giving me feedback as I was writing and revising; however, in the end any errors of interpretation or of the subsequent implications that I drew are mine.

TABLE A.1
Summary of Types of Methods and Data

Type of Method	Type of Data	Sources of Data	Collection Time	Purpose/Use
Report collecting	School/program policies and procedures, program goals, community context factors	TEA & Title VII grant applications, school board meetings, *School Zone* newsletter, *Insider* newsletter, minutes of meetings, meeting agendas, Vision 2005, Texas School Performance Review, TEA Snapshot	1994–2001	To describe the community context; process of decision making about model; sociopolitical, linguistic, and socioeconomic situation in community
	School/student/teacher demographics	SAISD Website (www.saisd.net)		
Record collecting	Test scores, student participation, language classifications, socioeconomic status	TEA AEIS campus data (www.tea.state.tx.us/cgi) and (www.tea.state.tx.us/student.assessment/results/), standardized assessments, school/class reports	2000–2001	To describe students' and grade-level educational histories, students' language dominance, and performance
Participation	Field notes and anecdotal notes (written after events)	Bilingual task force meetings, parent awareness sessions, faculty/school meetings, School Board meetings, Vision 2005 meetings, in-service meetings/sessions, consultantships, and interactions with district personnel over several years	1994–2001	To describe the circles of contexts; change and decision-making process; relations among program, administration, and community

Observation	Field notes, map of school location, map of class, list of materials, map of community	Two schools, fourteen classrooms, and two school communities	September–October 2000	To describe the community, school and classrooms; print environment; and use of classroom materials
Participant observation	Field notes, audiotapes, materials shared by teachers and students	Thirteen two-way classrooms, 2 others in bilingual program	October–May 2000–2001	To describe classroom context, student–teacher and student–student interactions, and language and literacy practices
Writing samples collection	In-class writing, notes, journals, reports, letters	Thirteen two-way classrooms	October–May 2000–2001	To describe students' written language
Open-ended interviews of school personnel	Field notes, audiotapes, and transcriptions	Fourteen teachers, 5 administrators, instructional coordinators, librarian, counselor, 2 instructional aides	2000–2001	To present teacher/school personnel beliefs, roles in two-way program, and involvements with parents
Conversations and open-ended interviews with parents	Field notes	Ten parents	March–April 1995 & February–March 2001	To present parents' beliefs about the two-way model, their participation, and involvement

Note. Adapted from Edelsky (1986), pp. 20–21.

TABLE A.2

Categories and Themes Used for Initial Analysis of Data

Categories	Themes/Topics	Examples
Circles of context	Sociopolitical	If the city leaders support the program the board will too.
		The board's review is their way of trying to cut the program.
	Community/identity	*Somos Mexicanos* (We are Mexican).
		Take pride in being bilingual and bicultural.
		I am Mexican American but I think the teacher says she is Chicana.
	Socioeconomic	Parents are working hard for a better life.
		Families move to better housing; they follow jobs.
	Institutional	*Un medio-ambiente colaborativo* (A collaborative environment).
		Support from the teacher organizations is needed.
Language issues	Value of English	*Para mí es importante que aprendan inglés* (For me it is important that they learn English).
		Cuándo les van a enseñar inglés, para mí que diez por-ciento es muy poco (When will you teach English, I think 10 percent is very little).
	Value of Spanish	*Que no se les olvide el español* (They should not forget Spanish).
		They get lots of English on TV; we need to make sure they practice Spanish.
	Language separation	Can you think of that word in the other language?
		My child is learning the correct Spanish, not Tex-Mex.
	Language assessment	I don't think they should test English if they are not yet learning English.
		We keep assessing oral English even though they are only getting 10 or 20 percent.

Language of TAAS	As a parent I think they should take the TAAS in Spanish, to show what they have learned.
	We have to make a decision and I think the third grade can take the TAAS in Spanish.
Two-way model	
Teachers' beliefs	
Exemplary practice	They have had powerful results with two-way at other sites.
	These are just good teaching practices; you provide context, demonstrate . . . and check for understanding.
Value added	The program goes beyond what the state required.
	We capitalize on community language and learning.
	Giving children advantages is important.
Enrichment	For children who do not have family that speaks Spanish, this is enrichment.
	The two-way gets a lot of attention and more resources.
Parents' beliefs	
Value added	The program gives us pride in being bilingual and bicultural.
	Es importante para el futuro de mis hijos (It's important for the future of my children).
	I wish that I had learned to read and write Spanish.
	I think they are going to have more opportunities because they will know how to read and write English and Spanish.
Enrichment	*Les da ventaja a los de aquí que ya hablen inglés* (It advantages the ones from here that already speak English).
	I want my child to be able to compete.
Children's beliefs	
Value	*Yo sé las dos y es lo mismo pensar que dice en español o* English (I know both [languages] and it is the same to think what does it say in Spanish or English).
	I am going to get a better job because I am bilingual.

(Continued)

TABLE A.2 (Continued)

Categories	Themes/Topics	Examples
Leadership	Parent decision making	*Esta información me va ayudar hacer la decisión* (This information will help me make the decision).
	Parent support	I can call other parents to ask what they think, to come out, and learn about the program.
	Participatory/consensus building	I [principal] suggest and suggest until I begin to get buy-in. After a long year of a lot of conversations with the staff and the community. The CLT tries to build consensus.
	Parents' voices	*Los padres deben opinar si están de acuerdo* (Parents should voice their opinion if they agree). *Deben de oír el consentimiento de cada padre* (They need to listen to the feelings of each parent).
	Teachers' voices	We researched all the models and we felt the 90–10 was the best. Teachers do not have much decision-making authority [about literacy instruction].
Classroom learning Oral language[a]	Communication environment	If you put 2 or 3 shy children together, sometimes they will communicate with just one word, or gestures. Asking open-ended questions that require inferencing or synthesis allows children to say what they know. New concepts require special attention to comprehensible language, like TPR.
	Teacher/student information	*Esta palabra es un sustantivo* (this word is a noun).
	Relating/expanding	*Líneas paralelas son como que* (Parallel lines are like what).
	Motivational	*Son los más listos* (You are the smartest).

Directive	*Siéntate* (Sit down).
Assistance	
Among students	Sharks *son tiburones, cómo se dice* (Are sharks, how do you say). *Espera, no he pedido ayuda* (wait, I [child] have not asked for help)
From teacher	*Busca la palabra esta en ese libro* (Look for the word, it is in that book).
Comparisons	
Student initiated	*Marzo y* March, *casi suenan iguales* (Marzo and March sound alike).
Teacher initiated	*Parientes es* relation or relations *en inglés* (relation is relation or relations in English). *Es cuento pero historia es así como el inglés* story (It's story but history is like the English story).
Self-mediation	*Agua dulce* (sweet water) can't be sweet water like *agua de melon* (melon water). Children translating for themselves in just-audible voice.
Context/gestures	Marcos points after having been asked *¿Dónde está la mascota?* (Where is the pet?). While waving arms, Beto says, *"como ondas- ondulando"* (like waves undulating).
Code switching	
Child E/S phrase	After school *me esperas aquí* (wait for me).
Child S/E word	*Lo sacaste de mi* desk (you took it out of my desk).
Child reflection	*Aya afuera . . . no hablas o lees nomás en* English *o español, hay mucho todo* mixed (out there . . . you don't speak or read just English or Spanish, there is a lot mixed).
Teacher E/S phrase	Settle down, *el nuevo escenario* (the new scene).
Teacher S/E word	*Ándale, pronto* (hurry), find your seat

(Continued)

TABLE A.2 (Continued)

Categories	Themes/Topics	Examples
[Classroom learning] Oral language[a] (Continued)	Separation	
	Teacher model	I am a language model; in the classroom, I don't mix the languages.
	Student awareness	When I cannot say it in Spanish . . . the teacher gives me clues so I can think or someone helps me.
Literacy[b]	Print awareness	Child pointing to classroom chart, "¿A ver qué dice?" (What does it say?)
		Teacher read a note from the office saying, "Voy a leerla para saber que es lo qué dice" (I am going to read it to know what it says).
	Prior experiences	Si te ha pasado a ti como en el cuento entonces se parece y es más fácil leer (If the same thing has happened to you as in the story then it is similar and it is easier to read).
		Voy a escribir de cuando yo era bebe (I am going to write about when I was a child).
	Syllabic awareness	Children/teacher call out each syllable in ma dru ga da (dawn).
		Children clap the syllable in words like pajaro (bird).
	Phonological awareness	
	Spanish	La /m/ o eme de Martin (the /m/ of Martin).
		La ge dice /g/ (the g says/g/).
	English	Teacher: light and night rhyme.
		Try again, use a very long a.

	Cultural referents	*Apachurrado como una tortilla* (Flattened like a tortilla).
		Barbacoa is different from barbeque.
		Calaveras literarias (literary skeletons).
		I like to dance the two-step.
	Cognates	*Historia es* history.
		Respect is like *respeto*, it just has a *c*.
Writing	Orthography/spelling	
	Spanish approximations	*asimos [hicimos]* (we make).
		brasos [brazos] (arms).
		siguimos [seguimos] (next).
	English approximations	*eviriday* [everyday].
		auey [away].
		Ai lov Ilu [I love you].
	Mixed S/E approximations	*hexamen* [examen or exam].
		"*cacharías*" for catch.
		"*cocining brecfist*" for cooking breakfast.
	Punctuation	Shouting for exclamation points; hand signals for the tilde.
		Porqué no hay acentos (Because there are no accents).
	Literary devices	
	Genre	*El cuento de un día inolvidable* (The story of my unforgettable day).
		Voy a leer mi poema (I am going to read my poem).
		Sr. García le escribo esta carta (Mr. García I am writing this letter).
	Setting/time/place	*Un día en mi casa* (One day in my house.
		El domingo en la iglesia (On Sunday at the church).
		On a field trip to Fiesta Texas.

(Continued)

205

TABLE A.2 (Continued)

Categories	Themes/Topics	Examples
	Characters	*Un animal espantoso* (A scary animal). My uncle is enormous and has a big black beard.
	Story grammar	The baby was lost and he was crying and crying. . . . A lady said, "I will help you find your mami."
	Audience awareness	*Deseo que te guste mi cuento* (I hope you like my story).
Academic content	Mathematics	*Los conceptos de hoy son . . . transformación de figuras* (The concepts for today are . . . transformation of shapes). Many little streets that are line segments.
	Science	*El sistema solar* (The solar system). *El eslabón entre los pájaros y reptiles* (The link between birds and reptiles).
	Social studies	We are going to investigate how the cattle industry . . . had a lasting effect on . . . your neighborhood.

[a]Themes were further refined into the teacher/student strategies reported in chapter 4.
[b]Themes were further refined into constructs and strategies reported in chapters 5 and 6.

References

Adams, J. J. (1990). *Beginning to read: Thinking and learning about print.* Cambridge, MA: MIT Press.

Andersson, T., & Boyer, M. (1970). *Bilingual schooling in the United States.* Austin, TX: Southwest Educational Development Laboratory.

Anzaldúa, G. (1987). *Borderlands/La Frontera: The new mestiza.* San Francisco: Aunt Lute Books.

Arias, M. B., & Casanova, U. (1993). *Bilingual education: Politics, practice and research.* Chicago: National Society for the Study of Education, University of Chicago Press.

Armas, G. C. (2001, August 6). Foreign languages popular at home: Census survey offers look at immigration. *San Antonio Express-News,* p. 5A.

Arteaga, A. (1994). *Another tongue: Nation and ethnicity in the linguistic borderlands.* Durham, NC: Duke University Press.

Asher, J. (1977). *Learning another language through actions: The complete teacher's guidebook.* Los Gatos, CA: Sky Oaks Productions.

Au, K. H. (1980). Participation structures in a reading lesson with Hawaiian children: Analysis of a culturally appropriate instructional event. *Anthropology and Education Quarterly, 11*(2), 91–115.

August, D., & Hakuta, K. (1997). *Improving schooling for language-minority children: A research agenda.* Washington, DC: National Academy Press.

Baker, C. (1993). *Foundations of bilingual education and bilingualism.* Clevedon, UK: Multilingual Matters.

Barfield, S. (1995). *Review of the ninth year of the partial immersion program at Key Elementary School, Arlington, VA, 1994–95.* Washington, DC: Center for Applied Linguistics.

Barfield, S., & Rhodes, N. (1994). *Review of the eighth year of the partial immersion program at Key Elementary School, Arlington, VA, 1993–94.* Washington, DC: Center for Applied Linguistics.

Barrera, B. R., Valdés, G., & Cardenas, M. (1986). Analyzing the recall of students across different language-reading categories: A study of third-graders' Spanish-L1, English-L2, and English-L1 comprehension. In J. A. Niles & R. V. Lalik (Eds.), *Thirty-fifth yearbook of the National Reading Conference* (pp. 375–381). Rochester, NY: National Reading Conference.

Bean, F. D., & Tienda, M. (1987). *The Hispanic population of the United States.* New York: Russell Sage Foundation.

Ben-Zeev, S. (1977). The influence of bilingualism on cognitive strategy and cognitive development. *Child Development, 58,* 1009–1018.

Bialystok, E. (1986). Factors in the growth of linguistic awareness. *Child Development, 57,* 498–510.

Bialystok, E. (1997). Effects of bilingualism and biliteracy on children's emerging concepts of print. *Developmental Psychology, 33*(3), 429–440.

Bialystok, E., & Hakuta, K. (1994). *In other words: The science and psychology of second-language acquisition.* New York: Basic Books.

Bizar, M., & Barr, R. (2001). *School leadership in times of urban reform.* Mahwah, NJ: Lawrence Erlbaum Associates.

Bloom, D. E., & Grenier, G. (1992). Economic perspectives on language: The relative value of bilingualism in Canada and the United States. In J. Crawford (Ed.) *Language loyalties* (pp. 445–459). Chicago: University of Chicago Press

Bourdieu, P. (1984). *Distinction: A social critique of the judgement of taste.* Cambridge, MA: Harvard University Press.

Bourdieu, P. (1992). *Language and symbolic power.* Cambridge: Polity Press.

Brisk, M. E. (1998). *Bilingual education: From compensatory to quality schooling.* Mahwah, NJ: Lawrence Erlbaum Associates.

Brookhart, S. M. (1998). Review of Iowa Test of Basic Skills. In J. C. Impara & B. S. Plake (Eds.), *The thirteenth mental measurement yearbook* (pp. 539–542). Lincoln, NE: Buros Institute of Mental Measurements.

Brown, A. L. (1980). Metacognitive development and reading. In R. J. Spiro, B. C. Bruce, & W. F. Brewer (Eds.), *Theoretical issues in reading comprehension* (pp. 453–481). Hillsdale, NJ: Lawrence Erlbaum Associates.

Bruck, M., & Genesee, F. (1995). Phonological awareness in young second language learners. *Child Language, 22,* 307–324.

Casanova, U., & Arias, M. B. (1993). Contextualizing bilingual education. In M. B. Arias & U. Casanova (Eds.), *Bilingual education: Politics, practice, and research* (pp. 1–35). Chicago: National Society for the Study of Education.

Cazabon, M., Lambert, W. E., & Hall, G. (1993). *Two-way bilingual education: A progress report on the Amigos Program* (Research Report No. 7). Santa Cruz: University of California, National Center for Research on Cultural Diversity and Second Language Learning.

Cazabon, M. T., Nicoladis, E., & Lambert, W. E. (1998). *Becoming bilingual in the Amigos two-way immersion program.* Santa Cruz: University of California, National Center for Research on Cultural Diversity and Second Language Learning.

Cazden, C. (1988). *Classroom discourse: The language of teaching and learning.* Portsmouth, NH: Heinemann.

Cazden, C. B., John, V. P., & Hymes, D. (Eds.). (1972). *Functions of language in the classroom.* New York: Teachers College Press.

Center for Applied Linguistics. (2002). *Directory of two-way bilingual immersion programs.* Washington, DC: Author. www.cal.org/twi/directory

Chamot, A. U., Dale, M., O'Malley, J. M., & Spanos, G. (1992). Learning and problem solving strategies of ESL students. *Bilingual Research Journal, 16*(3–4), 1–33.

Chamot A. U., & O'Malley, J. M. (1986). *A cognitive academic language learning approach: An ESL content-based curriculum.* Washington, DC: National Clearinghouse for Bilingual Education.

Checkley, K. (1996). Keeping native languages alive. American Association Curriculum Development. *ASCD Education Update, 38,* 2.

Christian, D. (1994). *Two-way bilingual education: Students learning through two languages.* Santa Cruz, CA: National Center for Research on Cultural Diversity and Second Language Learning.

Christian, D. (1996). Two-way immersion education: Students learning through two languages. *The Modern Language Journal, 80*(1), 66–76.

Christian, D., Montone, C. L., Lindholm, K. J., & Carranza, I. (1997). *Profiles in two-way immersion education.* Washington, DC: Center for Applied Linguistics.

Cloud, N., Genesee, R., & Hamayan, E. (2000). *Dual language instruction: A handbook for enriched education.* Boston: Heinle & Heinle.

Cole, M., Gay, J., Glick, J. A., & Sharp, D. W. (1971). *The cultural context of learning and thinking.* New York: Basic Books.

Collier, V. P. (1992). A synthesis of studies examining long-term language minority student data on academic achievement. *Bilingual Research Journal, 16,* 187–212.

Collier, V. P. (1995). A synthesis of studies examining long-term language-minority student data on academic achievement. In G. Gonzáles & L. Maez (Eds.), *Compendium of research on bilingual education* (pp. 231–243). Washington, DC: National Clearinghouse for Bilingual Education.

Cook, V. (1997). The consequences of bilingualism for cognitive processing. In A. M. B. de Groot & J. F. Kroll (Eds.), *Tutorials in Bilingualism* (pp. 279–300). Mahwah, NJ: Lawrence Erlbaum Associates.

Crawford, J. (1991). *Bilingual education: History, politics, theory and practice.* Los Angeles: Bilingual Education Services.

Crawford, J. (1992a). *Hold your tongue: Bilingualism and the politics of English only.* Reading, MA: Addison-Wesley.

Crawford, J. (1992b). *Language loyalties: A source book on the official English controversy.* Chicago: University of Chicago Press.

Crawford, J. (1997). *Best Evidence: Research foundations of the Bilingual Education Act.* Washington, DC: National Clearinghouse for Bilingual Education.

Cummins, J. (1981). The role of primary language development in promoting educational success for language minority students. In *Schooling and language minority students: A theoretical framework* (pp. 3–49). Los Angeles: California State University, Evaluation, Dissemination, and Assessment Center.

Cummins, J. (1984). *Bilingualism and special education: Issues in assessment and pedagogy.* Clevedon, UK: Multilingual Matters.

Cummins, J. (1994). From coercive to collaborative relations of power in the teaching of literacy. In B. Ferdman, R. M. Weber, & A. G. Ramírez (Eds.), *Literacy across languages and cultures* (pp. 295–331). Albany, NY: State University of New York Press.

Cummins, J. (1996). *Negotiating identities: Education for empowerment in a diverse society.* Ontario, CA: California Association for Bilingual Education.

Cummins, J., & Swain, M. (1986). *Bilingualism in education: Aspects of theory, research and practice.* London: Longman.

Davidson, J. (2001, January 14). Is Spanish dying?: Speech patterns in region raise debate among linguists, others. *San Antonio Express News,* p. 1H.

Delgado-Gaitán, C. (1990). *Literacy for empowerment.* London: Falmer Press.

Díaz, R. M. (1985). The intellectual power of bilingualism. *Quarterly Newsletter of the Laboratory of Comparative Human Cognition, 7,* 16–22.

Díaz, R. M., & Klingler, C. (1991). Towards an explanatory model of the interaction between bilingualism and cognitive development. In E. Bialystok (Ed.), *Language processing in bilingual children* (pp. 167–192). Cambridge, England: Cambridge University Press.

Dolson, D. P., & Mayer, J. (1992). Longitudinal study of three program models for language minority students: A critical examination of reported findings. *Bilingual Research Journal, 16,* 105–158.

Durgunoğlu, A. Y. (1998). Acquiring literacy in English and Spanish in the United States. In A. Y. Durgunoğlu & L. Verhoeven (Eds.), *Literacy development in a multilingual context: Cross-cultural perspectives* (pp. 135–145). Mahwah, NJ: Lawrence Erlbaum Associates.

Durgunoğlu, A. Y., Nagy, W. E., & Hancin-Bhatt, B. J. (1993). Cross-language transfer of phonological awareness. *Journal of Educational Psychology, 85,* 453–465.

Eaton, M. (n.d.). Power Builder PreK-2. Carrollton, TX: Michael Eaton Associates.

Edelsky, C. (1986). *Writing in a bilingual program: Había una vez.* Norwood, NJ: Ablex.

Erickson, F. (1993). Transformation and school success: The politics and culture of educational achievement. In E. Jacob & C. Jordan (Eds.), *Minority education: Anthropological perspectives* (pp. 27–51). Norwood, NJ: Ablex.

Ferguson, C. A. (1959). Diglossia. *Word, 15*(2), 325–340.

Ferguson, C. A. (1962). Problems of teaching languages with diglossia. *Monograph Series on Languages and Linguistics, 15,* 165–177.

Fishman, J. A. (1965). Who speaks what language to whom and when? *La Linguistique, 2,* 67–88.

Fishman, J. A. (1967). Bilingualism with and without diglossia; Diglossia with and without bilingualism. *The Journal of Social Issues, 23*(2), 29–38.

Foucault, M. (1984). The order of discourse. In M. Shapiro (Ed.), *Language and politics* (pp. 108–138). New York: New York University Press.

Freire, P. (1970). *Pedagogy of the oppressed.* New York: Seabury Press.

Freire, P., & Macedo, D. (1987). *Reading the world and the word.* S. Hadley, MA: Bergin & Garvey.

Freeman, R. D. (1996). Dual-language planning at Oyster bilingual school: "It's much more than language." *TESOL Quarterly, 30,* 557–582.

Freeman, R. D. (1998). Bilingual education and social change. Clevedon, UK: Multilingual Matters.

Galambos, S. J., & Goldin-Meadow, S. (1990). The effects of learning two languages on levels of metalinguistic awareness. *Cognition, 34,* 1–56.

García, E. E. (1992). Linguistically and culturally diverse children: Effective instructional practices and related policy issues. In H. C. Waxman, J. Walker de Fleix, J. E. Anderson, & H. P. Baptiste, Jr. (Eds.), *Students at risk in at-risk schools: Improving environments for learning* (pp. 65–86). Newbury Park, CA: Corwin.

García, G. E., Jiménez, R. T., & Pearson, P. D. (1998). Metacognition, childhood bilingualism, and reading. In D. J. Hacker, J. Dunlosky, & A. C. Graesser (Eds.), *Metacognition in educational theory and practice* (pp. 193–219). Mahwah, NJ: Lawrence Erlbaum Associates.

García, O., & Baker, C. (Eds.). (1995). *Policy and practice in bilingual education: A reader extending the foundations.* Clevedon, UK: Multilingual Matters.

García, O., & Otheguy, R. (1994). The value of speaking a LOTE [Language Other Than English] in U.S. Business. *Annals of the American Academy of Political and Social Science, 532,* 99–122.

Gee, J. P. (1991). Socio-cultural approaches to literacy (literacies). *Annual Review of Applied Linguistics, 12,* 31–48.

Gee, J. P. (1997). Meanings in discourse: Coordinating and being coordinated. In S. Muspratt, A. Luck, & P. Freebody (Eds.), *Constructing critical literacies* (pp. 273–302). St. Leonards, Australia: Allen & Unwin.

Genesee, F. (1987). *Learning through two languages: Studies of immersion and bilingual education.* Rowley, MA: Newbury House.

Goldenberg, C. (1990). Beginning literacy instruction for Spanish-speaking children. *Language Arts, 67,* 590–598.

Goldenberg, C. (1994). Promoting early literacy development among Spanish-speaking children: Lessons from two studies. In B. H. Hiebert & B. M Taylor (Eds.), *Getting reading right from the start* (pp. 171–199). Boston: Allyn & Bacon.

Glesne, C., & Peshkin, A. (1992). *Becoming qualitative researchers.* White Plains, NY: Longman.

Goldenberg, C., & Gallimore, R. (1991). Local knowledge, research knowledge, and educational change: A case study of first-grade Spanish reading improvement. *Educational Researcher, 20,* 2–14.

González, J. M. (1975). Coming of age in bilingual/bicultural education: A historical perspective. *Inequality in Education, 19,* 5–17.

Grin, F. (1995). The economics of foreign language competence: A research project of the

Swiss National Science Foundation. *Journal of Multilingual and Multicultural Development, 16,* 227–231.

Gutiérrez, K. D., Baquedano-López, P., Álvarez, H. H., & Chiu, M. M. (1999). Building a culture of collaboration through hybrid language practices. *Theory into Practice, 38*(2), 87–93.

Gutiérrez, K. D., Baquedano-López, P., & Tejeda, C. (2000). Rethinking diversity: Hybridity and hybrid language practices in the third space. *Mind, Culture, and Activity, 6*(4), 286–303.

Hakuta, K. (1990). *Bilingualism and bilingual education: A research perspective, No. 1.* Washington, DC: National Clearinghouse for Bilingual Education.

Hargett, G. R., & Murray, S. L. (1999). *National longitudinal survey of schools interim case study report: Storm Elementary School.* Washington, DC: U.S. Department of Education, Planning and Evaluation Services.

Heath, S. B. (1983). *Ways with words.* Cambridge, England: Cambridge University Press.

Holobow, N., Genesee, F., & Lambert, W. (1987). *Summary of Kahnawake test results, Spring 1987.* Unpublished Report, McGill University, Montreal, Canada.

Hornberger, N. (1989). Continua of biliteracy. *Review of Educational Research, 59,* 271–296.

Hornberger, N. H. (1994). Continua of biliteracy. In B. M. Ferdman, R. M. Weber, & A. G. Ramírez (Eds.), *Literacy across languages and cultures* (pp. 103–139). Albany, NY: University of New York Press.

Hornberger, N. H. (1998). Language policy, language education, language rights. Indigenous, immigrant, and international perspectives. *Language in Society, 27,* 439–458.

Hornberger, N. H., & Skilton-Sylvester, E. (2000). Revisiting the continua of biliteracy: International and critical perspectives. *Language and Education: An International Journal, 14*(2), 196–122.

Houston Independent School District. (1996). *Bilingualism for all children: A dual language initiative.* Paper presented at the National Association for Bilingual Education Conference, Orlando, FL.

Howard, E., & Christian, D. (1997, March). *The development of bilingualism and biliteracy in two-way immersion students.* Paper presented at the annual meeting of the American Educational Research Association, Chicago.

Hudson, T. (1982). The effects of induced schemata on the "short circuit" in L2 reading: Non-decoding factors in L2 reading performance. *Language Learning, 32,* 1–31.

Hymes, D. (1972). On communicative competence. In J. B. Pride & J. Holmes (Eds.), *Sociolinguistics* (pp. 269–293). Middlesex, UK: Penguin.

Hymes, D. (1982). What is ethnography? In P. Gilmore & A. A. Glatthorn (Eds.), *Ethnography and education: Children in and out of school* (pp. 21–32). Washington, DC: Center for Applied Linguistics.

Jacobson, R. (1981). The implementation of a bilingual instruction model: The new concurrent approach. In T. B. Padilla (Ed.), *Ethnoperspectives in bilingual education research: Vol 3. Bilingual education technology* (pp. 14–29). Ypsilanti, MI: Eastern Michigan University.

Jiménez, R. T. (2000). Literacy and the identity development of Latina/o students. *American Educational Research Journal, 37*(4), 971–1000.

Jiménez, R. T., García, G. E., & Pearson, P. D. (1995). Three children, two languages, and strategic reading: Case studies in bilingual/monolingual reading. *American Educational Research Journal, 32,* 31–61.

Kalmar, T. M. (2001). *Illegal alphabets and adult biliteracy: Latino migrants crossing the linguistic border.* Mahwah, NJ: Lawrence Erlbaum Associates.

Krashen, S. (1982). *Principles and practice in second language acquisition.* Oxford, UK: Pergamon.

Krashen, S. D. (1999). *Condemned without a trial: Bogus arguments against bilingual education.* Portsmouth, NH: Heinemann.

Lachtman, O. D. (1995). *Pepita talks twice/Peipita habla dos veces.* New York: Atheneum.

Ladson-Billings, G. (1994). *The dreamkeepers.* San Francisco: Jossey-Bass.

Lambert, W. (1967). A social psychology of bilingualism. *Journal of Social Issues, 23,* 91–109.

Lambert, W. E. (1984). An overview of issues in immersion education. In J. Lundin & D. P. Dolson (Eds.), *Studies on immersion education* (pp. 8–30). Sacramento, CA: California State Department of Education.

Lambert, W. E., & Anisfeld, E. (1969). A note on the relation of bilingualism and intelligence. *Canadian Journal of Behavioral Science, 1,* 123–128.

Lambert, W. E., Genesee, F., Holobow, N., & Chartrand, L. (1993). Bilingual education for majority English-speaking children. *European Journal of Psychology of Education, 8,* 3–22.

Lambert, W. E., & Tucker, R. G. (1972). *Bilingual education of children. The St. Lambert Experiment.* Rowley, MA: Newbury House.

Landry, R. G. (1974). A comparison of second language learners and monolinguals on divergent thinking tasks at the elementary school level. *Modern Language Journal, 58,* 10–15.

Lang, K. (1993). Language and economists' theories of discrimination. *International Journal of the Sociology of Language, 103,* 165–183.

Langer, J. A., Bartoleme, L., Vasquez, O., & Lucas, T. (1990). Meaning construction in school literacy tasks: A study of bilingual students. *American Educational Research Journal, 27,* 427–471.

Legarreta-Marcaida, D. (1981). Effective use of the primary language in the classroom. In *Schooling and language minority students: A theoretical framework* (pp. 83–116). Los Angeles: California State University, National Evaluation, Dissemination, and Assessment Center.

Leibowitz, A. H. (1982). *Federal recognition of the rights of language minority groups.* Rosslyn, VA: National Clearinghouse on Bilingual Education & InterAmerica Research Associates.

Lindholm, K. (1992). Two-way bilingual/immersion education: Theory, conceptual issues, and pedagogical implications. In R. Padilla & A. Benavides (Eds.), *Critical Perspectives on Bilingual Education Research* (pp. 195–220). Tucson, AZ: Bilingual Review/Press.

Lindholm, K. (1994). Promoting positive cross-cultural attitudes and perceived competence in culturally and linguistically diverse classrooms. In R. A. DeVillar, C. J. Faltis, & J. P. Cummins (Eds.), *Cultural diversity in schools: From rhetoric to practice* (pp. 189–206). Albany, NY: State University of New York Press.

Lindholm, K. J., & Fairchild, H. H. (1990). Evaluation of an elementary school bilingual immersion program. In A. M. Padilla, H. H. Fairchild, & C. M. Valadez (Eds.), *Bilingual education: Issues and strategies* (pp. 126–136). Newbury Park, CA: Sage.

Lindholm-Leary, K. J. (2001). *Dual Language Education*. Clevedon, UK: Multilingual Matters.

Lipski, J., & Garcia, M. (2001). Siempre and todo el tiempo: Investigating semantic convergence in a bilingual dialect. *Hispania, 84*(2), 300–314.

Macedo, D. (1994). *Literacies of power*. Boulder, CO: Westview Press.

Macedo, D. (2000). The illiteracy of English-only literacy. *Educational Leadership, 57*(4), 62–67.

Manyak, P. (2000). Borderlands literacy in a primary-grade immersion class. In T. Shanahan & F. Rodriguez-Brown (Eds.), *Forty-ninth yearbook of the National Reading Conference* (pp. 91–108). Chicago: National Reading Conference.

McLaughlin, M. K., & Oberman, I. (Eds.). (1996). *Teacher learning: New policies, new practices. The series on school reform.* New York: Teachers College Press.

McLeod, B. (1994). *School reform and student diversity: Exemplary schooling for language minority students.* Washington, DC: National Clearinghouse for Bilingual Education.

McQuillan, J., & Tse, L. (1995). Child language brokering in linguistic minority communities: Effects on cultural interaction, cognition, and literacy. *Language and Education, 9*(3), 195–215.

Miles, M. B., & Huberman, A. M. (1984). *Qualitative data analysis.* Beverly Hills, CA: Sage.

Milk, R. D. (1982). Language use in bilingual classrooms: Two case studies. In M. Hines & W. Rutherford (Eds.), *On TESOL '81* (pp. 181–191). Washington, DC: Teachers of English to Speakers of Other Languages.

Molina, R. G. (1994). *Considerations for the successful implementation of a two-way bilingual immersion program.* San José, CA: River Glen Elementary School.

Moll, L. (1992). Literacy research in community and classrooms: A sociocultural approach. In R. Beach, J. L. Green, M. L. Kamil, & T. Shanahan (Eds.), *Multidisciplinary perspectives on literacy research* (pp. 211–244). Urbana, IL: National Council on Teachers of English.

Moll, L., & Dworin, J. (1996). Biliteracy development in classrooms: Social dynamics and cultural possibilities. In D. Hicks (Ed.), *Discourse, learning and schooling* (pp. 221–246). New York: Cambridge University Press.

Moll, L. C., & González, N. (1994). Lessons from research with language-minority children. *Journal of Reading Behavior, 26,* 439–456.

Mora, P. (1993). *Tomás and the library lady.* New York: Knopf.

Nagy, W. E., García, G. E., Durgunoğlu, A., & Hancin-Bhatt, B. (1993). Spanish-English bilingual children's use and recognition of cognates in English reading. *Journal of Reading Behavior, 25*(3), 241–259.

Náñez, J. E., Padilla, R. V., & Máez, B. L. (1992). Bilinguality, intelligence, and cognitive information processing. In R. V. Padilla & A. H. Benavides (Eds.), *Critical perspectives on bilingual education research* (pp. 42–69). Tempe, AZ: Bilingual Press/Editorial Bilingüe.

National Association for Bilingual Education. (1995). Bilingual education: Separating fact from fiction. *NABE Report, 18.*

National Center for Research on Cultural Diversity and Second Language Learning. (1994). *Two-way bilingual education programs in practice: A national and local perspective.* Santa Cruz, CA: Author.

Ochoa, S. H. (1998). Review of the Aprenda: La Prueba De Logros en Español. In J. C. Impara & B. S. Plake (Eds.), *The Thirteenth Mental Measurement Yearbook* (pp. 42–43). Lincoln, NE: Buros Institute of Mental Measurements.

Ochoa, S. H., & Pérez, R. (1995). Appraising curriculum and instruction practices of bilingual programs in elementary schools varying in effectiveness: A qualitative and quantitative comparison. *The Journal of Education Issues of Language Minority Students, 15,* 37–43.

Ovando, C. J., & Collier, V. P. (1985). *Bilingual and ESL classrooms.* New York: McGraw-Hill.

Palmer, P. J. (1998). *The courage to teach.* San Francisco: Jossey-Bass.

Peal, E., & Lambert, W. E. (1962). The relation of bilingualism to intelligence. *Psychological Monographs: General and Applied,* Vol. LXXVI, No. 27, 22–23.

Pérez, B., & Bustos Flores, B. (2002). Biliteracy Development in Two-way Immersion Classrooms: Analysis of Third Grade Spanish and English Reading. In J. V. Hoffman, D. L. Schallert, C. M. Fairbanks, J. Worthy, & B. Maloch (Eds.), *Fifty-first yearbook of the National Reading Conference* (pp. 357–367). Chicago: National Reading Conference.

Pérez, B., & Torres-Guzmán, M. E. (2002). *Learning in two worlds: An integrated Spanish/ English biliteracy approach* (3rd ed.). Boston: Allyn & Bacon.

Philips, S. U. (1983). *The invisible culture.* New York: Longman.

Purcell-Gates, V. (1995). *Other people's words.* Cambridge, MA: Harvard University Press.

Ramírez, J. D. (1992). Executive summary. *Bilingual Research Journal, 16,* 1–62.

Ramírez, J. D., Yuen, D. D., Ramey, D. R., & Pasta, D. (1991). *Final report: Longitudinal study of structured English immersion strategy, early exit and late-exit bilingual education programs for language minority children. Vol. 1* (Publication no. 300-87-0156). Washington, DC: U.S. Department of Education.

Rayner, K., & Pollatsek, A. (1989). *The Psychology of Reading.* Englewood Cliffs, NJ: Prentice-Hall.

Rosales, R. (2000). *The illusion of inclusion.* Austin, TX: University of Texas Press.

Saravia-Shore, M., & Arvizu, S. F. (1992). Implications for policy and practice. In M. Saravia-Shore & S. F. Arvizu (Eds.), *Cross-cultural literacy: Ethnographies of communication in multiethnic classrooms* (pp. 491–510). New York: Garland.

Secada, W. G., & Lightfoot, T. (1993). Symbols and the political context of bilingual education in the United States. In M. B. Arias & U. Casanova (Eds.), *Bilingual education: Politics, practice, and research* (pp. 36–64). Chicago: National Society for the Study of Education, University of Chicago Press.

Scollon, R., & Scollon, S. (1981). *Narrative literacy and face in inter-ethnic communication.* Norwood, NJ: Ablex.

Scribner, S., & Cole, M. (1981). *The psychology of literacy.* Cambridge, MA: Harvard University Press.

Skutnabb-Kangas, T. (2000). *Linguistic genocide in education—or worldwide diversity and human rights?* Mahwah, NJ: Lawrence Erlbaum Associates.

Soto, G. (1997). *Chato y su cena/Chato's kitchen.* New York: Putnam.

Spindler, G. D. (Ed.). (1963). *Education and culture: Anthropological approaches.* New York: Holt, Rinehart & Winston.

Strauss, A., & Corbin, J. (1990). *Basics of qualitative research: Grounded theory procedures and techniques.* Newbury Park, CA: Sage Publications.

Swain, M., & Lapkin, S. (1982). *Evaluating bilingual education: A Canadian case study.* Clevedon, UK: Multilingual Matters.

Tharp, T. G., & Gallimore, R. (1988). *Rousing minds of life.* Cambridge: Cambridge University Press.

Thomas, W. P., & Collier, V. P. (1997). *School Effectiveness for language minority students.* Washington, DC: National Clearinghouse for Bilingual Education.

Trujillo, A. L. (1992). Ethnoterritorial politics and the institutionalization of bilingual education at the grass-roots level. In R. V. Padilla & A. H. Benavides (Eds.), *Critical perspectives on bilingual education research* (pp. 162–192). Tempe, AZ: Bilingual Review/Press.

Tse, L. (1995). Language brokering among Latina adolescents: Prevalence, attitudes, and school performance. *Hispanic Journal of Behavioral Sciences, 17,* 180–193.

UNESCO. (2001). *World language report.* Paris: Author, Office of Statistics.

U.S. Census Bureau. (2000). *Census 2000 Redistricting Data* (P. L. 94-171). Washington, DC: U.S. Government Printing Office.

Valenzuela, A. (1999). *Subtractive schooling: U.S.-Mexican youth and the politics of caring.* Albany, NY: State University of New York.

Valdés, G. (1996). *Con Respeto: Bridging the distances between culturally diverse families and schools.* New York: Teachers College Press.

Valdés, G. (1997). Dual-language immersion programs: A cautionary note concerning the education of language-minority students. *Harvard Educational Review, 67,* 391–429.

Verhoeven, L. (1990). Acquisition of reading in a second langauge. *Reading Research Quarterly, 25*(2), 90–114.

Verhoeven, L. (1994). Linguistic diversity and literacy development. In L. Verhoeven (Ed.) *Functional literacy: Theoretical issues and educational implications* (pp. 199–220). Amsterdam: John Benjamins.

Willig, A. C. (1985). A meta-analysis of selected studies on the effectiveness of bilingual education. *Review of Educational Research, 55,* 269–317.

Wong Fillmore, L. (1991). Second-language learning in children: A model of language learning in social context. In E. Bialystok (Ed.), *Language processing in bilingual children* (pp. 49–69). Cambridge, England: Cambridge University Press.

Wong Fillmore, L. (1982). Instructional language as linguistic input. In L. C. Wilkinson (Ed.), *Communicating in the classroom* (pp. 143–156). New York: Academic Press.

Wong Fillmore, L., & Valadez, C. (1986). Teaching bilingual learners. In M. Wittrock (Ed.), *Handbook of research on teaching* (3rd ed., pp. 648–685). New York: Macmillan.

Vygotsky, L. S. (1978). *Mind and society.* Cambridge, MA: Harvard University Press.

Author Index

Subject Index